McGraw-Hill
Ryerson Limited

A Subsidiary of The McGraw·Hill Companies

ISBN: 0-07-090560-6

1234567890 TRI 098765432
Printed and bound in Canada.

National Library of Canada Cataloguing in Publication

Cavoukian, Ann, date
   The privacy payoff: how successful businesses build customer trust / Ann Cavoukian and Tyler J. Hamilton.

Includes bibliographical references and index.
ISBN 0-07-090560-6

1. Electronic commerce--Security measures. 2. Business enterprises--Computer networks--Security measures. 3. Privacy, Right of. I. Hamilton, Tyler J II. Title.

HF5548.32.C38 2002   658.4'78   C2002-902454-4

Publisher: **Julia Woods**
Editorial Co-ordinator: **Catherine Leek**
Production Co-ordinator: **Sandra Deak**
Editor: **Shaun Oakey**
Electronic Page Design and Composition: **Heidy Lawrance Associates**
Cover Design: **Silver Birch Graphics/Monica Koupter**
Cover Image: © **Ralph Mercer/Stone**

THE PRIVACY PAYOFF

How Successful Businesses Build Customer Trust

Anne Cavoukian, Ph.D.
& Tyler J. Hamilton

McGraw-Hill Ryerson

Toronto Montréal Boston Burr Ridge, IL Dubuque, IA Madison, WI
New York San Francisco St. Louis Bangkok Bogotá Caracas Kuala
Lumpur Lisbon London Madrid Mexico City Milan New Delhi
Santiago Seoul Singapore Sydney Taipei

THE PRIVACY PAYOFF

How Successful Businesses Build Customer Trust

To my amazing husband, George Tomko,
who makes all things possible,
and fills each day with joy and laughter.
Ann Cavoukian

To my mother, who gave me life,
and to my loving wife, Lyne,
who brought it happiness and meaning.
Tyler Hamilton

Table of Contents

Foreword

I echo the authors' sentiments that we are in the "defining decade" of privacy. And when we look back in 2010, I believe we will see September 11, 2001, as the defining moment.

The terrorist attacks of that day recast the public's attitude to the privacy issue. Before those horrific events, most citizens casually regarded privacy as a good idea that goes nicely hand in hand with a democratic society. Op-ed pieces ruminated on the threat to privacy posed by our increasingly networked society, but the debate focused less on George Orwell and more on corporate databases and greedy dot-coms. Less on Big Brother and more on little brother.

DoubleClick was the top target for privacy advocates for trying to mesh disparate databases and create better-targeted and more cost-effective online ads. But other companies made similarly clumsy moves, and almost all beat a hasty retreat when put under the media spotlight.

Malice was never a forethought in the private-sector privacy fiascos of the last four or five years. Companies didn't intend to have their networks breached, and certainly they didn't want to cause distress when compiling detailed customer databases. As for the latter, there was always a seemingly plausible rationale. Everyone benefits, a company apologist would argue, if an ad campaign for lawnmowers went only to homeowners and skipped apartment-block residents. This spared consumers the intrusion of irrelevant advertising, and companies benefited from more cost-effective ad campaigns.

When this is done with the consumer's authorization, great. It illustrates one of the best features of the digital era — enabling vendors to personalize services to huge numbers of consenting customers. By astutely exploiting information, merchants can improve the quality, appropriateness and customization of their products and services.

Yet rogue businesses repeatedly violate their customers' faith. They sell or rent the information they legitimately gather to third parties without our approval. The market for such information is insatiable. Companies want to know as much as possible about our past and current actions because it provides solid insight into our future behavior.

To further complicate the issue, each of us has a different (often inconsistent) sense of what constitutes privacy and permissible encroachments. While some demand the right to remain anonymous, others clamor, for example, to exchange every detail of their online behavior for free gift certificates or air miles. Of course, that's their choice. Privacy is all about the freedom to choose.

In the giddy dot-com run-up, companies liked to show off the power of their information and communications technologies. They were keen to announce new services made possible by creatively mining the mountains of data generated by the Internet. Amazon, for example, trumpeted how intimately it knew its customers, and how it could accurately recommend what other books a reader would enjoy based on the books she had already purchased. This is a great service.

But as the world's online bookselling pioneer, Amazon often sails in uncharted water. Even though it started business only in 1995, in short order it compiled the world's most detailed database of book buyers. As part of its campaign of constant innovation, in late 1999 the company revealed the book preferences of its customers based on the domain names of their email addresses. So we were told that customers from the @Microsoft.com domain were snapping up "The Microsoft File: The Secret Case Against Bill Gates" by Wendy Goldman Rohm. Amazon said the book "paints a harsh and unforgiving picture that's not at all flattering to Gates or the rest of Microsoft's top brass." Over at Intel.com one of the hot sellers was a book on Linux.

Amazon thought these insights illustrated the power of its technology and appealed to the public's curiosity. Instead, the public felt it was pointless information voyeurism. Customers were uncomfortable with the idea that their book purchases might reflect poorly on their employers or betray a corporate agenda, and didn't like feeling that someone was looking over their shoulder. The negative reaction forced the company to withdraw the service.

But the turmoil and changes unleashed by the Net in the past five years pales in comparison to what will happen in the next five. Mobile computing devices, broadband access, wireless networks and computing power embedded in everything from bicycles to factory tools are converging into a vast global network — a *Hypernet* — that will fuel exponential change in business model innovation. The Hypernet is to the Internet what the Internet was to early proprietary computer networks.

The gains achieved in digital technologies grow more astounding by the week. And for many technologies there is no end to the gains in sight. Transistors will continue shrinking, processor power will go on doubling and redoubling, chips will be embedded into every object, Internet bandwidth will soar, and humans will create more and more Web-based solutions to everyday problems.

Tomorrow's Hypernet will comprise a billion Net-connected mobile phones and billions of networked game consoles, handhelds, toys and information appliances. Devices are morphing into a bewildering variety and approaching throwaway prices. Technology adoption rates are blindingly fast, because happy consumers use the Internet to tell friends and family around the world about great new products or services. Computing is so ubiquitous that it recedes into the background.

As a result, to use privacy veteran Alan Westin's words, we now create an increasingly detailed digital shadow of ourselves as we go through life's routines. Almost everything we do is noted and recorded somewhere, such as when we make phone calls, enter secure buildings, buy groceries, fill drug prescriptions, surf the Web, exchange e-mail, rent videos, drive our GPS-equipped car, use our credit cards and on and on. If the various databases and monitoring devices are linked, an almost minute-by-minute record of anyone's activities can be generated in close to real time.

A year ago many citizens didn't really appreciate how extraordinarily detailed our digital shadows had become. But the post-September 11 privacy versus security debate has made the public keenly aware of the issues at stake.

A new security system for underground parking lots relies on motion detectors feeding signals to a computer. The computer understands that a person walking to her car usually follows a direct route. But a rapist or car thief doesn't behave that way. A rapist lurks in one area and a thief wanders the lot looking for the best car to steal. The computer senses these different movements and alerts security.

With September 11 in mind, some security and intelligence experts suggest the parking lot principle could apply to the entire population. If every bit of data generated by our day-to-day activities were fed into a computer, powerful software could detect a terrorist's unusual behavior.

Whether we want to put such a system in place is a profoundly important debate for our society to have. Even if it forestalled terrorist attacks, would we want to live in a society where every citizen's activity is monitored around the clock? The easy answer is no. But life in the real world is more complicated. Technology's temptations arise daily. It's so simple to open files and create databases, most of us forget the big picture and think it's the safest and smartest thing to do.

I believe we don't need to trade off privacy to have security. They are two sides of the same coin, and we need *both* for a just society. It is possible, for example, to create a building security system that requires a fingerprint or retinal scan before authorized personnel can enter. But it's not necessary for the system to maintain a minute-by-minute record in a central database of who is going in. Keeping track of who enters is a different issue than securing the building. We shouldn't confuse the two.

Ann Cavoukian and Tyler Hamilton understand how politically charged the public's attitude toward privacy and security has become. And this attitude has permeated the private sector and the way in which companies interact with customers. There are burning questions facing businesses regarding how they will treat the information of customers and others, and this book is an important contribution to the discussion. Privacy in the business world is not just an issue of ethics; it is a business issue. And the public tolerance for corporate error in this arena has evaporated.

I had the good fortune to write with Ann Cavoukian in 1995 the book *Who Knows: Safeguarding Your Privacy in a Networked World.* It was our effort to help raise the public's awareness of how privacy is threatened. Sadly, the past seven years didn't prove us wrong. The threat of networking technology grows. In this book, Cavoukian joins Hamilton to give corporations practical advice on how they can navigate and prosper in privacy's increasingly choppy waters. This book is a handbook for competitiveness. Every company needs to integrate privacy principles and action plans into its business and marketing strategies and operations.

Read and profit.

Don Tapscott

Don Tapscott is the author of nine books about information technology, competitiveness and society. In 1994 he co-founded Digital 4Sight, a think tank and business strategy company. He is also President of New Paradigm Learning Corp. and advises business and government leaders around the world.

Acknowledgements

So many people have assisted in the writing of this book — we are indebted to you all. We begin with Scott Charney, who painstakingly reviewed an early draft of our manuscript: thank you for giving so generously of your time and expertise. To Dr. Alan Westin, Dr. Larry Ponemon, and Thornton May, a heartfelt thanks for your assistance and words of encouragement.

We would also like to thank Professor Lawrence Smith for his contribution and Ann Brown for her valuable assistance and support. We owe a special thanks to Don Tapscott for agreeing without fail to write the Foreword to our book, as well as being incredibly supportive. We would also like to thank Dr. David Flaherty for his assistance and encouragement, as well as the many, many industry consultants, analysts, executives and colleagues who agreed to share their knowledge for this book. Appreciation goes out to IDC Canada, Forrester Research, KPMG, dataPrivacy Partners and a host of other research and consulting firms who were all valuable sources.

We owe a huge debt of gratitude to the Chief Privacy Officers who agreed to be interviewed and shared their expertise and personal experiences with us: to Peter Cullen, Kirk Herath, Oliver Johnson, Harriet Pearson, Jules Polonetsky, Zoe Strickland — many thanks for all your help and enthusiasm!

This book would not have become a reality without our publishing team at McGraw-Hill Ryerson, to whom we offer our sincere thanks: Julia Woods, Joan Homewood and Catherine Leek in the Toronto office, and Philip Ruppel and Lynda Luppino in the New York office. To our editor Shaun Oakey, thank you for making it all flow so well.

Another big thank you goes out to Andrew Bowins and the team at GCI Group in Canada who were most kind in offering their services to help market this book. Thanks also to Rachel Ross who lent a helpful hand developing our Web site at **www.privacypayoff.com.**

On a more personal note, the greatest appreciation goes to our family and friends: to our exceptional spouses, George Tomko and Lyne McMurchie, a heartfelt thanks for your unwavering support, enduring patience and tireless encouragement — we couldn't have done it without you! To brothers Onnig and Raffi Cavoukian, and, under the Hamilton clan, to Paul Hamilton, Joanne King, the Boriskas and the McMurchies — thank you for all your love and faith in us. To Tracey Tremayne-Lloyd, Veronica and Frank Maidman, Antoinette Schatz, Lawrence Surtees, Peter Hope-Tindall, Ken Kidd, Dick Loek and the folks at the *Toronto Star*, and the Beaches, Bramalea and University of Toronto crews — thank you for your unfailing support and friendship, your advice and for lending an ear.

We remain grateful to you all.

Chapter 1

At the Crossroads

"In an era where the Internet is increasingly
central to our lives at work, at home and at
school, it is more important than ever that
our industry give customers the assurance
that their information will remain secure,
respected and private."

Bill Gates, Microsoft Corp.
founder and chairman, 2000

Business is confronting one of the greatest challenges since the advent of
computerized information processing: consumer privacy. Organizations that
routinely make use of their customers' personal information should take note.
Similar to the way the environmental movement began to influence industrial manufacturing practices in the 1970s, concern for consumer privacy is
reframing the way organizations handle customer data. Consumer privacy is
not just a policy issue or a compliance issue — it is a business issue at the
heart of the new economy. For companies such as EarthLink, one of the largest
Internet service providers in North America, respecting customer privacy is
viewed as a competitive move with strategic advantages. In a six-city advertising
campaign in the fall of 2000, EarthLink handed out thousands of silver snack
bags in U.S. sandwich shops. Each bag contained three miniature chocolate
chip cookies and displayed a bright orange label that read: "Do you know

1

where your cookies come from?" The cookies represented Internet cookies, tiny files that Web sites routinely place on visitors' computers as a way of tracking their surfing habits, usually without the visitor's knowledge or consent. The purpose of the campaign was to explain to consumers just how Internet cookies could be used to invade their privacy. More important, EarthLink was keen to get the message out that when deciding between commercial interests and respecting its customers' privacy, it would choose the latter. "Our message — and a key point of differentiation — is that EarthLink is not in the business of exploiting its subscribers' personal data," Claudia Caplan, then vice-president of EarthLink's brand marketing, said when the campaign was launched. "Such practices fly directly in the face of the real Internet experience that is the cornerstone of our branding campaign."

EarthLink is among a growing number of companies, including IBM, Hewlett-Packard, RBC Financial Group and Expedia, that are taking a leadership role by treating consumer privacy as a business issue — and for good reason. Numerous studies over the years suggest that a majority of consumers are worried about when, and how, their personal information is being collected, how it is being used and whether it is being adequately protected. They want to know whether the information is being sold or shared, and if so, to whom and for what purpose. Above all else, they want to have some degree of control over their privacy in an age when increasingly sophisticated telecommunications, storage and software technologies have made monitoring a person's activities effortless. "The concern now is that we have gone too far in terms of the amount of processing going on, and the correlation of that information back to one's physical identity," says Dan Hunter, professor of legal studies at the Wharton School at the University of Pennsylvania. "Even more disturbing is that consumers don't know how the information is being used and so have no way of tracking it. One doesn't have to be a consumer-protection zealot to think there should be some controls on this."[1]

---

[1] "Up for Sale: Privacy on the Net," Knowledge@Wharton, CNET News.com. [online] March 25, 2001.

Indeed, there is a heightened feeling among industry groups that giving more control to consumers may begin to unlock the true potential of our electronic economy, where tension has been brewing between users of personal information and consumers who fear the loss of their privacy. Studies suggest that the loss of consumer confidence related to privacy fears has already hindered the growth of e-commerce by tens of billions of dollars.[2] The coverage of privacy issues in the media has jumped threefold since 1995, serving to feed those fears.[3] In the Internet travel industry alone, Forrester Research estimated a revenue shortfall of $2.8 billion in 2001 because of privacy concerns.[4] Governments throughout the world are taking notice, and in many jurisdictions there has been a concerted effort to restore confidence in e-commerce with data-protection legislation as a complement to industry self-regulation. Sweeping privacy laws are already in force in the European Union, Canada, Australia and Hong Kong, to name a few. As such, consumer privacy has become a business issue and a legal issue — increasingly difficult to ignore.

EarthLink sees gaining the trust of consumers by eliminating any concerns they may have over their privacy as a way of carving out a competitive advantage over its rivals. Since the Atlanta-based company was founded in 1994, it has gone out of its way to promote the benefits of anonymous Web surfing and an online world without junk e-mail, at the same time highlighting its own conservative and highly respectful use of customer information. In December 2000, the company became one of the first in the world to appoint a chief privacy officer to oversee its day-to-day privacy practices and consumer advocacy. It has launched multi-million-dollar advertising campaigns to draw attention to its

---

[2] A number of studies have tried to put a number on real or potential e-commerce losses resulting from privacy fears, including "Proactive Online Privacy: Scripting an Informed Dialogue to Allay Consumers' Fears," a report by Michele Slack, Alison Day and Evan Neufeld (Jupiter Communications, June 1999). Angus Reid and Forrester Research have both estimated losses in the billions of dollars.

[3] Jay Stanley, "Surviving the Privacy Revolution" (Forrester Research, February 2001).

[4] Betsey Stevenson and Alanna Denton, "Privacy Worries Cost Online Travel $2.8 Billion" (Forrester Research, December 3, 2001).

pro-privacy stance. It has also provided customers with ad-blocking software and anonymous surfing tools to further fortify their privacy on the Internet. The company's goal is simple and straightforward: use privacy to *win* and *keep* customers. And that goal is today's emerging business issue. This is the *privacy payoff* — the key message of this book. Michael Erdle, a privacy and Internet lawyer for Deeth Williams LLP in Toronto, told us, "Companies can use privacy as a marketing benefit. They will advertise the fact they have these privacy policies, because people would rather deal with them than somebody who doesn't. It's the same way people would rather buy products that are environmentally friendly. It's driven by the marketplaces."

One can draw parallels between environmentalism in the 1960s, '70s and '80s and today's early moves toward greater privacy protection. "Privacy in the information age is the analogue of environmentalism in the industrial age," Bill Lockyer, the attorney general of California, declared after the introduction of a state bill to protect the financial information of consumers. "These [are] issues we're going to have to deal with. The sooner we do it, in ways that are respectful of consumers' privacy, the better." The challenge — as it has been with environmentalism and will be with privacy — is to move the old guard in the direction of becoming new-economy thinkers. When protecting the environment emerged as a major issue in the 1970s, big business saw environmental rules and regulations as a threat. Compliance was considered too costly, particularly for companies bound by the short-term financial expectations of shareholders.

In the 1980s and 1990s, the tide began to turn, albeit slowly. Being green started to pay off. As consumers grew more aware of global warming, pollution and the depletion of the ozone layer, companies looking for an edge began marketing themselves and their products as environment friendly. Today, we have industries built around renewable resources, recycling, fuel-cell technologies, nontoxic and nonpolluting products, electric/hybrid vehicles and organic foods. Oil giant Shell predicts that renewable energy will produce half of the world's power by 2050 — a drastic change from 50 years ago, when renewable energy investments and projects were hardly on the radar screen. "We have to take the same attitude toward privacy as we did for the environment," says Stephanie Perrin, chief privacy officer for software firm Zero-Knowledge Systems. "If we can manage washing out cat food cans and recycling them, then we can handle cleaning up [consumer] data." Jay Stanley, an e-commerce analyst at Forrester Research, says the emergence of privacy issues serves as a countervailing force against the "information revolution" and what he calls its "radical effects" on data flow. Instead of going away, privacy concerns will only multiply and amplify if something isn't done. "Like a 1965 businessman who claimed that 'all this fuss over ecology is just a passing fad,' anyone today who thinks the privacy issue has peaked is greatly mistaken," wrote Stanley in a February 2001 report called "Surviving the Privacy Revolution."[5] The issue of consumer privacy is now only in its infancy.

Many companies chose early to embrace this message. RBC Financial Group, the largest financial institution in Canada, has had a privacy code in place since 1987 and in recent years has been studying the implications of privacy for its business. Peter Cullen, RBC's corporate privacy officer, says that internal studies suggest privacy accounts for 7 per cent of a customer's buying decision and therefore contributes 7 per cent to the overall economic value for the organization. "As privacy is recognized to be a more emotional issue, perhaps not surprising, the bank found it accounts for 14 per cent of the value of its RBC brand with respect to personal clients." For EarthLink, the payoff of a proactive privacy strategy was beginning to emerge in the summer of 2001. Surveys showed that the number of consumers who cited EarthLink when asked to name an Internet service provider had jumped by nearly 70 per cent in cities where the company focused its privacy-friendly marketing efforts. In a September 5, 2001, *New York Times* article, EarthLink's vice-president of branding said that she believed privacy was a "very, very large component" of those improvements.

[5] Stanley, "Surviving the Privacy Revolution."

Six days after that story was published, on a date now referred to as 9/11, the unimaginable occurred. In the space of two hours, the United States experienced the most destructive and horrific act of terrorism in world history. A nation in shock immediately focused its attention on the ineptitude of U.S. intelligence agencies and airport security. How could such a nefarious plot go undetected? How could a group of terrorists, some known to the authorities, manage to coordinate, communicate and execute such a plan without triggering the suspicions of any law enforcement authorities? The North American public — indeed, the whole world — suddenly felt completely vulnerable. Everyone wanted to feel more secure, even if that meant sacrificing civil liberties and personal freedoms, including privacy, and there followed a groundswell of support for invasive security technologies and increased public surveillance, particularly in the United States. Congress pushed through the U.S.A. Patriot Act, giving intelligence authorities new powers of investigation and surveillance that made it easier to intercept e-mail, tap phone calls and use satellite-tracking and video-monitoring techniques. Previously controversial covert technologies, such as the FBI's Carnivore e-mail sniffer (now called DCS1000) and keystroke-logging program Magic Lantern, were now considered less contentious tools of investigation. The rules had changed in this war against terror. Privacy took a back-seat — or so it seemed.

But in the months after 9/11, heightened fear and anxiety were gradually replaced by sober second thought. Questions began to be asked about the perceived conflict between privacy and security and the distinctive roles of government authorities and the private sector. Must privacy and security be viewed as mutually exclusive polar opposites? Or can security be achieved alongside privacy, making both complementary components in a smartly crafted program? Is it not possible for technologies of security to enhance privacy at the same time? (As you will read in **Chapter 11**, we challenge the idea that privacy and security must be viewed as polar opposites. In fact, we believe it is possible to shift to a win-win paradigm and to pursue the development of security technologies for enabling privacy, or STEPs, an acronym first coined by the Ontario Information and Privacy Commissioner.) And why are we so quick to blur the line between government objectives related to public safety and private-sector objectives related to consumer protection? Why should the FBI's use of covert technologies such as Carnivore and Magic Lantern have any bearing on private-sector business practices and the way that organizations handle customer information? The answer is that it should not — and it does not. It is one thing for a law-enforcement authority to install facial-recognition technology at an airport or to monitor, consistent with legal process, e-mail communications of suspicious members of the public; it is quite another when a business sells lifestyle information, medical data or financial information to another or monitors the Internet surfing of consumers without obtaining their consent or giving proper notice.

Evidence indicates that concerns about privacy have not abated since 9/11. Indeed, over time we may be in for a consumer and political backlash against overly intrusive security initiatives that fly in the face of liberty. As Benjamin Franklin wrote in his *Historical Review of Pennsylvania* in 1759, "They that can give up essential liberty to obtain a little temporary safety deserve neither liberty nor safety." For many in the business community who have been able to see through the emotional and political reaction to September 11, privacy is just as important today as it ever was. "September 11 has changed many things, but it hasn't changed our privacy strategy," Harriet Pearson, chief privacy officer of IBM, told us. "What has changed is the emphasis with which people were once talking about privacy. I spend a lot of time now discussing the need to balance privacy with security, and the need for privacy policies within business as a matter of maintaining trust." Pearson says fewer people are talking about privacy from what she calls a "purist, civil liberties" perspective, but she adds that this isn't necessarily a bad thing. "We've said all along that privacy is a matter of balance." Several chief privacy officers interviewed for this book were unanimous in their declaration that the government's battle against terrorism has not substantially changed their corporate privacy practices. The message was clear: We stand by our privacy policies unless forced to comply with the law. Building consumer trust continues to be a top priority.

Proof that consumer privacy gained newfound momentum after September 11, 2001, can be found in the headlines in the months that followed:

- "IBM Groups Will Target Privacy Protection" (November 12, 2001, *National Post*). Big Blue announced the creation of the IBM Privacy Management Council (a group of industry players assigned to review new privacy technologies) and the IBM Privacy Institute (a research body focused on long-term privacy and technology projects). Increasingly, large and influential companies such as IBM are taking leadership roles in the industry, and laying the foundation for privacy technology standards.

- "Tauzin Wants to Pass Privacy Bill Early Next Year" (December 4, 2001, Newsbytes). In North America, some lawmakers kept the consumer privacy torch burning even as a tornado of surveillance initiatives swept the continent. Billy Tauzin, chairman of the U.S. House Energy and Commerce Committee, said he would push for federal privacy legislation in early 2002. The Senate Commerce Committee later echoed this statement, proving that consumer privacy had not fallen through the cracks after September 11. Shortly after, the U.S. Federal Trade Commission launched an unprecedented crackdown on junk e-mailers, and more than 25 states proposed their own anti-spam legislation. Meanwhile in Canada, the Ontario government proposed a private-sector privacy bill that was considered the strictest in North America, to be introduced by the end of 2002.

- "Australia Introduces New Privacy Laws" (December 21, 2001, *Asia Pulse*). In the footsteps of the European Union and Canada, Australia began to enforce new private-sector privacy legislation in 2002. Malcolm Crompton, federal privacy commissioner of Australia, said 95 per cent of businesses that took part in a national public opinion poll revealed that the privacy of their customers' personal data was important to their organization. "Eighty per cent of business respondents said their business was dependent on their ability to protect and responsibly use their customers' personal information," Crompton emphasized.

- "Privacy Software Pre-Installed on HP PCs" (January 31, 2002, Newsbytes). For the first time in the computer industry, a major PC manufacturer — in this case Hewlett-Packard — pre-installed security and privacy software on one of its product lines. Zero-Knowledge Systems, the company supplying the cookie-blocking and ad-filtering software, said similar deals with other PC manufacturers were expected. HP's unprecedented move came as quite a surprise, and positioned the company as a clear trendsetter.

- "Comcast Backs Down over Privacy Concerns" (February 18, 2002, *Information Week*). Comcast, the third-largest cable operator in the United States, felt the heat after it was discovered that the company had begun recording the Web-browsing activities of its one million high-speed Internet users without their consent. Within days, and after intense media coverage, the company discontinued the practice. The attention this story received proved that the media, even with 9/11 and the war in Afghanistan featuring prominently in all newscasts, was not about to give up its role as the public's privacy watchdog.

- "Business Not a Beneficiary of Post 9/11 Trust Mood" (March 6, 2002, presentation by Dr. Alan Westin to the *Scientific American* Global Summit, New York City). In a post-9/11 consumer survey conducted by highly respected privacy expert and pioneer Dr. Alan Westin, it was found that "increased trust in government after 9/11 has not been paralleled by increased trust in businesses handling consumer information." Asked whether the terrorist activities of September 11 had affected their concerns about how online businesses collect and use personal information, the overwhelming majority indicated that their concerns remained high: 76 per cent said their views remained the same (i.e., no change after 9/11), while 22 per cent said that consumer privacy was more important post-9/11. Only 1 per cent said it was less important.

Perhaps the most significant sign that consumer privacy remains at the forefront of industry concern came on January 15, 2002, when Bill Gates sent a memo to Microsoft employees titled "Trustworthy Computing." In this memo, the founder and chairman of the world's largest software company elevated security and privacy to the "highest priority" for Microsoft's future Web strategy, known as .Net. The message came at a sensitive time for Microsoft, which had been facing one security or privacy controversy after another.

Code Red and Nimda, two of the world's most notorious Internet worms, thrived on vulnerabilities in Microsoft software, as did the majority of viruses before them. Privacy advocates accused Microsoft of using its Windows XP operating system and its Passport online authentication tool to force consumers into handing over their personal information as a requirement for taking part in the company's universe of Web services. Meanwhile, it seemed as if most of the company's software — from Internet Explorer to Windows XP to Passport — were discovered to have security weaknesses or had been exploited by a hacker. Even Microsoft's own corporate network had been the target of a successful hacker attack. Understandably, Microsoft customers were asking whether the company could be trusted to protect all this information.

Clearly, Bill Gates had seen the writing on the wall. In his memo, he wrote that pursuing the four key aspects of Trustworthy Computing — which he outlined as availability, security, privacy and trustworthiness — was seen as integral to the company's future success. "The data our software and services store on behalf of our customers should be protected from harm and used or modified only in appropriate ways." Gates added, "Users should be in control of how their data is used. Policies for information use should be clear to the user." Gates' memo continued:

> There are many changes Microsoft needs to make as a company to ensure and keep our customers' trust at every level — from the way we develop software, to our support efforts, to our operational and business practices. As software has become ever more complex, interdependent and interconnected, our reputation as a company has in turn become more vulnerable … If we discover a risk that a feature could compromise someone's privacy, that problem gets solved first. If there is any way we can better protect important data and minimize downtime, we should focus on this. These principles should apply at every stage of the development cycle of every kind of software we create, from operating systems and desktop applications to global Web services.

Microsoft's Trustworthy Computing initiative marks a major point in the company's history. To have privacy and security problems "solved first" is a shift of significant proportion for the company. "It's an incredibly important statement, and it reflects the growing concern among the industry, consumers and businesses about security and privacy," says Scott Charney, who was appointed Microsoft's chief security strategist soon after the Gates memo. Charney, formerly chief of the Computer Crime and Intellectual Property Section at the U.S. Department of Justice and co-leader of the Cybercrime Prevention and Response Practice at PricewaterhouseCoopers, told us that businesses need a balanced approach to handling consumer information. "Striking the right balance between sometimes harmonious but sometimes competing interests — such as privacy, security, public safety, national security and economic growth — is one of the great challenges we face." Although there are those who question whether Gates will be able to back up his words with action, the consensus in the industry is that the path has been laid for others to follow. And at no time has following this path become so crucial to the future health and commercial viability of the new economy.

Identity theft in North America is rampant. Hackers are keeping one step ahead of law enforcers. Junk mail is out of control and is likely to get far worse when wireless Internet and location-based technologies take hold. Internet viruses and worms are more harmful and persistent than ever, and their numbers continue to multiply. Cookies, Web bugs, spyware and other technologies of surveillance have become more sophisticated, easier to use and cheaper to deploy. Is it any wonder why consumers are worried about their privacy; about losing control over their own personal information? Such worries ultimately affect consumer confidence, and companies that can build back this confidence and establish trusting relationships with consumers stand to benefit the most.

Earning that trust means more than simply complying with the privacy laws and regulations that have emerged across North America, Europe and parts of

Asia, which all establish rules for collecting, using and sharing personally identifiable information. An increasing number of businesses, such as Earth-Link, realize that *trust* is a currency in the new economy, and profiting from this economy means proactively obtaining as much of this currency as possible. And this need not, as many organizations believe, impede the normal course of business — quite the contrary. As you will read in **Chapter 9**, marketing studies have shown that privacy and personalization are a winning combination. Consumers are more likely to hand over personal information in exchange for personalized content and services if they believe the information is properly used and safeguarded. And when services are personalized, consumers have a tendency to spend more.

In testimony to the U.S. Subcommittee on Commerce, Trade and Consumer Protection, Austin Hill, chief strategist at privacy software firm Zero-Knowledge Systems, said business objectives such as personalization, marketing and online transactions do not have to compromise consumer privacy. Building trust with consumers can be achieved, he said, by aligning business and privacy into a single, coherent strategy that combines effective policies with effective technologies. He pointed out that the business community is at a crossroads and has important decisions to make.

As both an entrepreneur and privacy advocate, I believe we are at a critical junction for privacy. We are currently experiencing the largest explosion of information in history. The new networks and devices being deployed will make personal information available anywhere, anytime. The overwhelming majority of this information being created and spread via a plethora of devices and networks will be personal information — and it will primarily reside with businesses and organizations, rather than with individuals themselves. The information and networking explosion affects every individual, organization and business. Whether the net effect will be positive for information privacy or negative will depend on the policies we adopt, and the availability of technologies to enforce those policies.[6]

[6] House Committee on Energy and Commerce, Subcommittee on Commerce, Trade and Consumer Protection. Prepared Witness Testimony, June 21, 2001.

But where does one start? A study by Michael Erbschloe, vice-president at technology research firm Computer Economics, found that only one in three U.S. companies had implemented a formal privacy plan as of spring 2001. "The majority said they do not know what to do or where to start, so they have not done anything," said Erbschloe. We suggest this book as a good place to start. There are ten reasons why we believe companies should care about consumer privacy. You should read this book if all or most of the following ten statements apply to you:

1. You want to avoid damage to your company's reputation, particularly negative articles appearing in the press.
2. You want to avoid being penalized by any existing or future laws that set rules for how consumer information should be collected, used and stored.
3. You want to avoid civil and class-action lawsuits that may result from unintentional — if not intentional — abuses of personal data or what may appear to be unfair and deceptive information practices.
4. You want to monitor the activities of your employees but not intrude upon their work lives to the point where staff morale, and in turn productivity, suffer.
5. You want to make sure your company measures up to the privacy standards adopted by strategic partners so as not to jeopardize valuable business relationships.
6. You want to do business and collect consumer information in other countries that have their own privacy laws and customs.
7. You want to gain the trust and confidence of your customers so they won't be tempted to feed you false data, rendering the information in your database that you depend on for marketing, advertising, personalization and customer service useless.
8. You would expect the same treatment of your own personal or corporate information.
9. You want to convince both new and seasoned Web users that shopping on the Internet is secure and that their information is protected, thereby

encouraging them to become more active participants in the Internet economy, which will ultimately grow to the benefit of all.

10. You want to gain an edge over competitors who have failed to embrace privacy best practices that consumers look for when deciding where to spend their online dollars. By following best practices, you also want to gain advantages over rivals who are interested in complying only with the minimum standards of law or regulation.

In reading this book, you will see that there are immense benefits to protecting the privacy of customers and potential customers, hence the title, *The Privacy Payoff*. You will see that it simply makes good business sense. Failure to proactively embrace sound privacy practices is risky at best. First and foremost, customers expect the protection of their personal information, and when those expectations are not met, they will take their business elsewhere. Second, governments expect organizations to meet certain privacy standards, and when those standards are not met, regulators will take action. Third, the courts expect organizations to comply with relevant laws and follow their stated policies, and when compliance with those laws and policies is not met, legal battles ensue, media scrutiny begins and corporate brands get tarnished. There is a reason why some publicly traded companies, such as interactive television upstart TiVo, have gone so far as to highlight these privacy risks in their financial reports to shareholders.

On the flip side, customers who feel their privacy expectations are met will reward organizations with their loyalty — their business stays with you. Meeting customer expectations also reduces exposure to private and class-action lawsuits, the wrath of regulatory agencies and the unpredictable costs that are associated. This, in turn, minimizes exposure to bad publicity, which can harm your company's brand and over time have a negative effect on company performance. "People want their privacy," Peter Hope-Tindall, chief privacy architect for dataPrivacy Partners, told us. "People expect their privacy will be respected. People will patronize companies that protect their privacy and sometimes will even pay more for the privilege. On the other hand, people will complain about, boycott, litigate against and sell the shares of any company that treats their personal information as if it were just another corporate asset."

The privacy payoff that we speak of is even further reaching. Not only do businesses benefit, but the payoff of privacy reaches consumers, investors, the Internet, the economy — our global society as a whole. It reaches into the heart of democracy, to values such as choice and personal security. "Privacy is not measured solely with a financial yardstick," wrote privacy policy consultant Robert Gellman. "Privacy is relevant to many aspects of our daily lives."[7]

This book will walk you through the history, rules, trends, statistics, technologies and events that, in our view, have turned consumer privacy into the defining business issue of this decade. We have included our recommendations for how your company can modify its business practices to benefit most from protecting consumer privacy.

Chapter 2 examines the unfulfilled expectations of e-commerce and attributes part of the problem to a lack of attention to consumer privacy in the business community. We look at several studies, including industry-leading research from Dr. Alan Westin. The chapter also explores further the concept of "trust" as currency in the information economy, its importance in both business-to-consumer and business-to-business commerce, and what it will take to refuel the e-commerce engine that we are all relying on to propel our economy forward, particularly as we move from a wired to wireless world.

Chapter 3 explores the meaning of privacy — both historical definitions and those more applicable to today — and begins an examination of the privacy principles that have emerged over the decades. We take a detailed look at "fair information practices," which underpin most laws and self-regulatory initiatives that revolve around individual privacy, such as the OECD's universally recognized principles, Canada's CSA Model Code and the U.S. Federal Trade Commission's "Big Four" privacy principles. We also describe the distinction between privacy and security — two related but different concepts. Although the

---

[7] Robert Gellman, "Privacy, Consumers, and Costs" (March 2002, **www.epic.org/reports/dmfprivacy.html**).

words are often used interchangeably, achieving one objective does not necessarily achieve the other.

Chapter 4 surveys the global regulatory environment with a focus on the evolution and current status of privacy legislation in the United States, Canada and Europe. The chapter details the European Union Directive on Data Protection, Canada's Personal Information Protection and Electronic Documents Act, the U.S.-E.U. "Safe Harbor" agreement, and a number of sector-specific laws in the United States that deal with personal health information and financial information as well as the collection of personal information from children. We inspect the pros and cons of privacy laws and attempt to forecast where privacy regulations may be heading.

In **Chapter 5** we tell you how a well-executed privacy plan can give your company a competitive advantage, and offer up a persuasive cost-benefit analysis that concludes that privacy is both good business and good *for* business. Included in this chapter are a variety of means by which to diagnose the state of your organization's information practices. We highlight the importance of privacy impact and risk assessments, policies, audits, and statements and symbols. We explain why a comprehensive approach, supported from executive ranks and followed through by proper employee training, is necessary to create a privacy culture within an organization. We explain the role of outside privacy architects and consultants and the valuable guidance they can provide.

Chapter 6 deals with the new "O" — the emerging executive position of chief privacy officer, or CPO. We explain why a company may wish to appoint a CPO and what qualities make a person suitable for such a position. Highlighting this chapter are job profiles of six CPOs who have pioneered this role; each offers an insightful "day in the life" story. We also list a number of online resources that CPOs — or anyone assigned to address privacy issues — can turn to for the latest news and information.

Chapter 7 zeros in on the issue of security as it relates to privacy. Without proper security policies, procedures and technologies in place, an organization risks exposing its customers' personal information to identity thieves, hackers and rogue employees. Companies must safeguard customer data from both internal and external threats if they wish to keep the trust of their customers. Corporate and wireless networks, Web sites, desktop computers, laptops, databases and the physical structure of an office must be properly fortified without unduly restricting operations. We describe how this might be done. Equally important, we discuss the importance of employee training as a way to avoid and respond to security mishaps.

Chapter 8 takes a close look at the reasons why people are hesitant about, and at times fearful of, conducting business online or through other electronic means. It tackles a list of intrusive or potentially intrusive technologies that make consumers feel they are being watched. The chapter concludes with a detailed look at the problem of identity theft — how rapidly it is spreading and what can be done to slow it down. It illustrates the dangers of having so much personal information collected through Web sites, circulating through the Internet and stored in databases, all without proper attention to privacy policies and procedures.

Chapter 9 tackles the needlessly controversial relationship between privacy and marketing. We start with what marketers think about the issue of privacy. Then we chronicle how their views are evolving. We look at the debate between opt-in and opt-out marketing, as well as the benefits of permission-based marketing, and the relationship between personalized services, customer trust and consumer spending. All of this extends into a discussion about the emerging world of mobile and location-based services, and the resulting marketing opportunities. We conclude by drawing attention to the problem of false data (both inaccurate and fabricated), its negative influence on marketing initiatives, and what can be done to build databases that are more accurate and reliable.

In **Chapter 10** we narrow our focus to privacy in the workplace. How can a proper balance be struck between an employer's needs (e.g., for security and productivity) and an employee's need for privacy? We recognize that the right to privacy in the workplace is not equal to that outside of the workplace. But nor is it nonexistent. We draw a distinction between targeted surveillance and blanket surveillance and look at the various methods and technologies used to monitor the activities of employees. We examine how this surveillance applies to employees' health information, genetic data and work records. Finally, we review some of the legal implications of workplace monitoring and offer tips on the best approach to take.

Chapters 11 digs deep into the world of privacy-enhancing and privacy-enabling technologies — affectionately called PETs — that businesses can use as part of a comprehensive privacy plan. We describe a number of PETs geared toward businesses and consumers, including encryption, privacy-management software, anonymizers, P3P-enabled Web sites and browsers, and a variety of safeguarding technologies. We also profile a handful of companies that are dedicated to designing, supplying and promoting PETs. We also take a look at STEPs — or Security Technologies Enabling Privacy — which represent a new paradigm for achieving security without compromising privacy. For both PETs and STEPs, we stress the importance of a "build it in" approach — where possible, make sure that privacy is considered at the design stage, not a Band-Aid pressed on at a later date. We demonstrate why "Privacy by Design" will become an integral part of data protection in the years to come.

Chapter 12 presents a concrete action plan for business. We outline 25 tips that will guide your organization toward better privacy and prepare you and your company for the road ahead. Included is a list of Web resources to help you in your journey.

In the **Epilogue**, we attempt to predict what the future holds. What's clear is that the actions we take today will have a profound impact on the information economy of tomorrow. We must get it right.

We *will* get it right.

Chapter 2

In E-commerce We (Must) Trust

> "What was once seen as a threat to civil
> society is now a clear and present danger
> to the economic health of the country. Unless
> privacy is protected soon, the revolutionary
> potential of the Internet may never be
> realized . . . The invasion of privacy may turn
> out to be the greatest menace to
> the New Economy."
>
> *Business Week,* March 1998

Unfulfilled Expectations

Claudio Rodrigues and his industry peers were eager to avoid the privacy trap that had caught many of their digital economy predecessors by surprise. It was the fall of 2000, a time when the North American e-commerce engine — revved to the maximum only a year earlier — was beginning to sputter along like a rusty lawn mower running out of fuel. Dot-com upstarts, once shiny examples of the new economy, began losing their luster as quickly as they ran out of cash. An industry once rich with opportunity was growing desperate. To make matters worse, it was also a year when some of the highest profile names in the Internet and computing industry had been lambasted by consumer rights groups — and hung up to dry by the media — for allegedly misusing the personal information of customers with little regard for their privacy. Not only had the much-touted Internet economy lost its momentum but, perhaps not coincidentally, consumer confidence in e-commerce, never strong to begin with, was waning. The disappointing performance of e-commerce was, in part, a product of unreasonably high expectations and hype, but it was also a reaction to the lack of attention given to privacy concerns.

Web advertising firm DoubleClick became the most visible target of this criticism. The company, a leader in its category, admitted it was planning to launch a service that would track the Internet-surfing habits of consumers and simultaneously match this data to personally identifiable information such as names and e-mail addresses. The story was quickly picked up by the media: "Privacy Advocates Fault New DoubleClick Service," reported a February 15, 2000, story in the *New York Times*. A March 1, 2000, headline in the *Wall Street Journal* read "Alta Vista, Kozmo Distance Themselves from DoubleClick over Privacy Worries." Those headlines showed how scrutiny directed at one company was raising red flags for the entire online industry. But DoubleClick wasn't alone in underestimating the furor that would arise. Since 1999, similar reports have caused havoc for some of the biggest players in high-tech and e-commerce, among them Intel, Amazon.com, RealNetworks, GeoCities and Toysmart (see sidebar).

Naturally, this focus on privacy concerned an executive like Rodrigues, who at the time was vice-president of marketing at Cell-Loc, a Canadian startup from Calgary that specializes in providing wireless technologies that track mobile phones — as well as the people who use them. In December 2000, Cell-Loc and more than a dozen other location-technology firms laid the foundation for what became the Wireless Location Industry Association, or WLIA. The group, based in Washington, D.C., is now a united voice for the nascent wireless location industry, which is expected to play a major and somewhat controversial role in the next wave of electronic commerce — also known as mobile commerce or, more specifically, location commerce. Most of us have already heard about this not-so-distant future, when it will be common for consumers to purchase products, use services, be notified by businesses and receive

THREE HEADLINES, THREE HEADACHES

"Privacy Groups Object to New Intel Chip, Ask Investors to Sell Stock" was the headline of a March 1, 1999, article in the *Wall Street Journal*. In the early months of that year, consumer and privacy groups began promoting a boycott of Intel products — and shares — after it was discovered that the chipmaker's new Pentium III processors contained a personal serial number (PSN) that made it easy to track a person's surfing habits. Most experts eventually argued that the privacy risks were overblown, but the damage had already been done in the court of public opinion — Intel eventually switched the PSN default to "off." In April 2000, the company decided to phase out the feature entirely, dousing a year-long public relations firestorm.

"User Claims Amazon Collected Private Information" was the title of a Bloomberg News report on January 7, 2000, that told the story of Joel D. Newby and his lawsuit against Amazon.com. Newby had been a regular user of online software provided by Alexa Internet that monitored the movement of Net users as they roamed the Internet and provided links that were relevant to the Web sites being visited. Amazon bought Alexa in April 1999, after which Newby noticed that the online retail giant began recommending video titles to him that were loosely related to his previous book and movie purchases. Newby alleged that Amazon, through its Alexa purchase, broke the law by collecting personal data about his online interests without informing him. Newby launched what eventually became a class-action lawsuit, forcing a settlement from Amazon of up to $40 for each person affected by its collection practices. The U.S. Federal Trade Commission later accused Amazon of "deceptive" privacy practices, but the regulator decided not to pursue an investigation when Amazon adjusted its privacy policies.

"RealNetworks Changes Privacy Policy Under Scrutiny" was a November 1, 1999, story on CNET's News.com that reported how quickly the maker of online music players changed its privacy policy and apologized to consumers after it was caught monitoring their listening habits. An identification number assigned to each downloaded version of its music player software, RealJukebox, made the tracking possible. The program used an Internet connection to automatically report data, such as song titles, back to RealNetworks. The company then matched the data with user ID and on-file registration information. RealNetworks says it merely wanted to use the information to understand its customers better, thus allowing it to target advertising and provide more "personalized services." The controversy was that RealNetworks never disclosed the practice in its privacy policy, which had been certified by a Web privacy seal program run by TRUSTe (see **Chapter 5**). Though the company was quick to change its policy, the lawsuits still flowed in.

advertising messages that are "geo-coded" for the Internet and delivered through a wireless device wherever a person is. What are the directions to five bank machines nearest to where you're standing? What's the status of traffic within a ten-mile radius of your car? Geo-coded mobile Internet services make it easy to find the answers, and wireless location experts such as Cell-Loc, Cambridge Positioning Systems and SignalSoft create the tracking technologies that make it possible to find and record the precise whereabouts of these mobile Netizens.

Wireless location or geo-coded services will be discussed in more detail later in this chapter. But it goes without saying that the privacy implications of such a powerful technology run deep, and the members of the WLIA know it. Part of the reason WLIA was created was to develop a ground-level action plan that could help the wireless location industry avoid the privacy pitfalls that their earlier high-tech peers were unable to avoid. "Privacy is at the forefront of this industry's radar," Rodrigues told us, speaking as the first chairman of WLIA just weeks after the association was founded. "So many others got punished for it, and rightly so. This group said it's going to be proactive and get principles in place before we get into the game. Privacy is the first advocacy issue we plan to tackle."

WLIA wasn't the only wireless group to take this approach. Organizations with a much broader mandate, such as the Cellular Telecommunications & Internet Association, have developed a similar mindset. "One of the pitfalls of Internet privacy has been the fact that the Internet has always been reactive to privacy issues," said one CTIA spokeswoman. "We've turned 180 degrees in the other direction and said, let's look at people's concerns, and let's take a proactive stance on this."[1] In other words, build privacy into your e-commerce plan — make it privacy by design, not privacy as afterthought. Create an environment of consumer confidence as early as possible so barriers to commerce, such as the perceived threat to privacy, are kept low, or even eliminated, over time. As you continue reading this book, you will get a better understanding of how your business can foster respect for consumer privacy and reap the rewards —

[1] Heather Fleming Phillips, "Wireless Industry Treads Carefully on Privacy," San Jose *Mercury News*, February 7, 2001.

the *payoff* — of customer trust. We believe that this can be done without adversely obstructing the free and necessary flow of information, which is the bedrock of the new economy.

Squandered Trust

Scott McNealy, the outspoken chief executive officer of Sun Microsystems, once said that consumers should just "get over" the reality that they have no privacy in the information age. Many viewed his statement as insensitive to the valuable position privacy holds in a free market economy. Since then, McNealy, one of the biggest critics of the privacy movement, has modified his stance. In a column he wrote in May 2001 for the *Washington Post*, he admitted — as privacy advocates and consumer watchdogs have long argued — that it simply makes good business sense to respect and protect the personal data of consumers, particularly if it means gaining and maintaining their trust. "Most people would gladly reveal their personal preferences, as long as they feel certain the information won't be misused," wrote McNealy, admitting that it took some prodding by watchdogs in the media for the industry to wake up to the issue. He added that trust is the "real currency" of the Internet. "Squander what you have and you'll find out how hard it can be to get more."[2]

As DoubleClick found, trust is difficult to get back. In early 2000, the Web advertising network announced its plan to match consumer data it collected over the Internet with huge amounts of personally identifiable information held by recently acquired Abacus Direct, a compiler of mail-order catalogue buyer data. The strategy, which would have allowed DoubleClick to much more accurately target its advertisements to the 100 million or so Web surfers it had anonymously profiled, also called into question whether DoubleClick was violating its own privacy policy. The U.S. Federal Trade Commission, the privacy watchdog that investigates unfair and deceptive information practices, decided to take a closer look.

[2] Scott McNealy, "The Case Against Absolute Privacy," *Washington Post*, May 29, 2001.

The next ten months for the company were marked by public outrage, lawsuits and the FTC investigation — and the controversy contributed to a 90 per cent decline in the value of the company's stock. It would be misleading to claim that DoubleClick's woes during this time could be blamed entirely on the privacy issue, since a weakened advertising market was dragging down its revenues. On the other hand, the unwanted publicity and scrutiny of its information practices had thrown a wrench into its business plan.

On January 21, 2001, the FTC closed its investigation of DoubleClick, largely because the company had backtracked on its Abacus plans soon after the controversy erupted.[3] But the damage had already been done, and a handful of class-action lawsuits and consumer watchdogs continued to keep the company under a spotlight. In March 2002, DoubleClick settled all state and federal class-action lawsuits related to its information practices. The company agreed to pay up to $1.8 million (U.S.) in legal costs and launch a privacy-education advertising campaign on the Web. As part of the settlement, DoubleClick also promised to purge old customer data from its computer systems and do a better job of disclosing how it uses the personal information of consumers. The ghost of privacy past still haunts DoubleClick as a team of internal privacy officers and external consultants fight to recapture that online currency called trust.[4]

Listening to Consumers

May 2000 could be considered a key turning point for the U.S. e-commerce industry. The FTC, which had previously viewed self-regulation as the best way

---

[3] At the end of 2001, DoubleClick discontinued its "intelligent targeting" service, which at the time represented a tiny percentage of the company's business. The premium service let marketers target their advertisements based on the browsing patterns of Internet users. DoubleClick said the service was cancelled because clients found it too costly, but some analysts said the service was unpopular partly because of privacy concerns.

[4] In October 2001, DoubleClick partnered with the Privacy Council, a privacy consultancy based in Richardson, Texas. DoubleClick's intention was to extend its own privacy policy and data-collection practices to its clients and partners, many of whom may not be compliant with its new privacy standards.

of addressing the privacy concerns of online consumers, proclaimed that self-regulation, while commendable, wasn't working as well as expected. In an unprecedented move, the FTC altered its position, arguing that legislation was needed on top of self-regulation to create an environment of certainty in the online world. This new position was based on an FTC survey that found only 20 per cent of the busiest U.S. Web sites complied with the four minimum-standard privacy principles: *notice* (telling consumers how their information is collected and used, what information is collected and who is using it), *choice* (letting consumers choose how their information is to be used), *access* (letting consumers review and correct electronic records containing information about them) and *security* (protecting consumer data from abuse, loss or theft).

Robert Pitofsky, FTC chairman at the time, said that online businesses were getting a failing grade on privacy during a critical time in the development of the Internet marketplace. He pointed out that a majority of the commissioners were in favor of legislation. "Without such protections, electronic commerce will not reach its full potential," he prophesized. Six months later, the situation didn't appear to be any better. "There's still a significant portion of companies not getting the message," FTC commissioner Mozelle Thompson told an industry conference on privacy. "There are too many holes in the Swiss cheese."

The benefits and shortfalls of self-regulation will be discussed in **Chapter** 4. What's important here is to recognize that inconsistent adoption of privacy principles through self-regulation (the "holes in the Swiss cheese") have influenced how consumers worldwide behave online, what they fear, what they perceive as risky and, perhaps most important, how they spend their money. According to the U.S. Department of Commerce Census Bureau, the total value of online sales in the United States was only 1 per cent ($32.6 billion (U.S.)) of all retail sales in 2001. In Canada, the percentage has been generally lower. Statistics Canada found that the total value of customer orders taken over the Internet was only $10.4 billion (Cdn) in all of 2001, representing just 0.5 per cent of overall private-sector sales. In both countries, online retail sales still represent a tiny fraction of overall retail sales, clearly indicating that the hype associated with e-commerce during the late 1990s has failed to match reality.

Consumers have not embraced the online world as originally hoped. In our view, the evidence indicates that much of this failure has to do with the disregard for consumer privacy and the absence of online protections for customer data, particularly during the early days of e-commerce. To this day, the majority of online consumers remain concerned and cautious. Consider the following research:

- In the United Kingdom, independent research conducted in 2000 for the Information Commission found that three-quarters of those surveyed were "very or quite concerned" about the quantity of information that organizations store about them. In the first quarter of 2001, the commission received 8,875 data-protection complaints, compared to 1,747 a decade earlier.[5]
- International Data Corp., in its "Online Consumer Internet Privacy Survey, 2000," found that four out of five U.S. respondents left Web sites more than once during a six-month period because of privacy concerns. About one in five left more than six times. Worse still, two out of three Web shoppers said they deliberately chose, more than once, to not buy goods from an e-tailer over the same six-month period. "For sites vying for new customers, the impact can be considerable," wrote IDC analyst Jonathan Gaw.[6]
- A survey conducted in 1999 by Jupiter Communications concluded: "Privacy issues could potentially put an $18-billion dent in the $40-billion (U.S.) e-commerce revenue projected by 2002."[7]
- An April 2000 survey of Canadians conducted by Angus Reid Group found that 84 per cent were "very concerned" or "somewhat concerned" about giving out personal information. Of those who have never shopped online, 74 per cent said they were concerned about the security of giving their credit card number over the Internet; and 52 per cent said it was because they didn't

[5] Sarah Left, "Complaints Over Data Privacy Soar" Guardian Unlimited [online], July 12, 2001, **www.guardian.co.uk.**

[6] Jonathan Gaw, "Online Personalization in an Era of Privacy Enforcement" (report for International Data Corp., October 2000).

[7] Michele Slack, Alison Day and Evan Neufeld, "Proactive Online Privacy: Scripting an Informed Dialogue to Allay Consumers' Fears" (Jupiter Communications, June 1999).

like giving out their personal information. Angus Reid predicted that privacy and security fears were probably robbing online retailers of "billions of dollars."[8]

Many factors influence consumer attitudes toward privacy and the Web. New Internet users tend to fear the unknown and feel it is too risky to make online transactions, largely because they believe their information will be used fraudulently or their personal data will accidentally spill onto the Web, for purposes unknown. Credit card numbers are a case in point. "New users are almost twice as likely as veteran Internet users to report high levels of concern over online credit card theft, and they are only half as likely as Internet veterans to have purchased something online," writes researcher John Horrigan, in his 2000 report on new Internet users and what they mean to the future of e-commerce.[9] Indeed, the concerns of novice users are naturally heightened every time the media report yet another Web site security breach that has exposed thousands, if not hundreds of thousands, of credit card numbers on the Internet. This perception of risk creates what many have called a transaction gap or divide. Novice Web users will hesitate to cross this chasm unless they are reassured about the security of their personal data and given greater control over how it is used.

As more seasoned users become increasingly aware of the value of their personal data in the digital economy, privacy revolves around the issue of personal control. There are also those who have a deep-seated distrust of large organizations — such as governments and corporations — that translates directly into an overly cautious and critical approach to e-commerce and online business. Many simply refuse to participate. Surveys and studies from North America, South America, Europe, Japan and Australia support these views. Of course, no survey tells the whole story. Some consider survey results quite conservative. "If you're really

[8] Angus Reid Group, "Security and Privacy Issues Keeping Millions from Shopping Online" (survey, April 27, 2000).
[9] John B. Horrigan, "New Internet Users: What They Do Online, What They Don't, and Implications for the 'Net's Future" (Pew Internet and American Life Project, 2000).

concerned about privacy, you don't respond to surveys," points out Tim Dixon, chairman of the Australian Privacy Foundation.[10]

Mr. Privacy

Some of the most respected research on the public's attitudes toward privacy has been done by Dr. Alan Westin, professor emeritus at Columbia University and president of Privacy and American Business, a non-profit think-tank that studies business-privacy issues. As a consultant, his list of clients ranges from IBM and Intel to Equifax and VISA. Westin has also been the academic adviser to more than 45 national privacy surveys between 1979 and 2001, throughout which privacy and related concerns have grown steadily important in the minds of U.S. consumers. What's unique about Westin's surveys is how he segments the public into three major groups: *privacy fundamentalists, privacy pragmatists* and *privacy unconcerned*. (See **Figure 2.1**).

Privacy fundamentalists are very distrusting of public- and private-sector organizations, support pro-privacy legislation, feel technology will be used in an abusive way to intrude upon their lives and are generally adamant about protecting their personal information. Privacy is sacred for this group. Refusing to trade personal data in exchange for special deals, gifts or rewards points is a matter of principle.

On the opposite end of the spectrum are the privacy unconcerned, people who believe that privacy advocates are fanatics who are drawing attention to a problem that doesn't exist. Unconcerned consumers ask, "What's the big deal?" They will gladly fill out personal surveys if it means getting a free magazine subscription or 5 per cent off a book purchase at an online retailer. Many among this group don't realize how unauthorized use of their personal information can come back to haunt them. They perceive no risk.

---

[10] Tim Dixon, "Public Attitudes to Privacy: A Global Overview" (presentation in Cambridge, Massachusetts, March 8-9, 2001).

Figure 2.1

How the Public Divides on Privacy

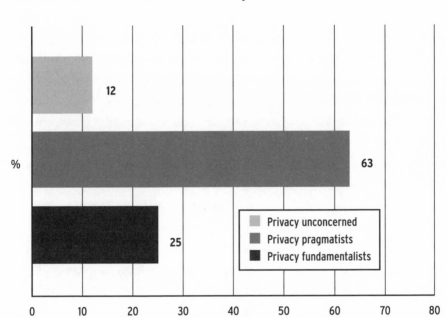

Source: U.S. House Committee on Energy and Commerce, Subcommittee on Commerce, Trade and Consumer Protection, Prepared Witness Testimony, Dr. Alan Westin, May 8, 2001.

In the middle of this great divide are the privacy pragmatists, a group that is likely to allow their personal information to be used in exchange for more personalized service and customer perks, such as discounts and special offers, but only if they are satisfied that the organizations collecting their data engage in fair information practices. (We will discuss these practices in great detail in **Chapter** 3.) For privacy pragmatists, the willingness to release their information, visit a particular Web site, or shop at that site, is based on the perception of risk, standards of trust, and the belief that organizations are genuine in their attempts to safeguard the personal data being collected.

According to survey results released by Westin in early 2001, 25 per cent of American adults are privacy fundamentalists, a figure that is consistent with surveys from the 1990s. Meanwhile, the portion of people who are privacy unconcerned has dropped to 12 per cent, from about 20 per cent in the 1990s. (See **Figure 2.1**.) What happened? Westin suggests that those unconcerned consumers who are now growing more concerned may be reacting to media reports, aggressive telemarketing, direct mail and spam (unwanted e-mail promotions) that simply didn't exist to the extent that they do today. Consumers may also be more aware of how computing, networking, storage and surveillance technologies are increasingly being used to create detailed personal profiles, often without their knowledge or consent, and without any opportunity for them to correct erroneous data.

These rising concerns have resulted in a larger group of privacy pragmatists, who now represent 63 per cent of American adults, up from 55 per cent in the 1990s. "The change in the numbers that we got this year [2000] makes even clearer than before that the battle for business is for the hearts and minds of the privacy pragmatists, now almost two-thirds of the public," Westin reports. "If you win them, you win the battle; if you lose them, you lose the battle."[11] In his May 8, 2001, testimony to the U.S. Subcommittee on Commerce, Trade and Consumer Protection, Westin sent a clear message to both legislators and businesses that consumers expect more if more is expected from them:

A decade of extensive survey research, much of it solid and credible, documents a steadily rising rational and justified public demand to set new privacy-protecting rules for collection and use of consumer personal information by business. The work of this decade, among survey researchers and Congresspersons alike, is to discover what will persuade the 125 million American Privacy Pragmatists that we have the right blend of business initiatives and legal oversight for good consumer information relationships with business.

If we expand Westin's findings beyond the United States and estimate conservatively that at least half of all adults in Europe, Japan, Canada and Australia are

---

[11] Consumer Bankers Association, "New Survey Findings Reveal Shift Toward 'Privacy Pragmatism,'" *CBA Reports*, February 1, 2001.

privacy pragmatists, then the number of potential Internet consumers who can be "won over" by good privacy practices runs into the hundreds of millions. Without gaining consumer trust, and thereby securing the active participation of this huge global audience, the true potential of e-commerce may never truly be realized.[12]

From B2C to B2B

Privacy is not merely a business-to-consumer (B2C) issue. It is also a business-to-business (B2B) concern, relating to the confidentiality and security of a company's customer information during interactions with strategic partners, suppliers, distributors, resellers, contract workers, public relations agencies, outsourcers and other players. As more companies restructure processes and adopt new technologies to function internally as e-businesses, interaction in a supply chain will increasingly take place electronically. This change can create significant efficiencies for organizations, but it can also open them up to more risk. For this reason, it makes greater sense to put measures in place that protect the personally identifiable information of customers. Keeping such information secure not only protects the customer but it also safeguards an important business asset, and puts in place the underlying security infrastructure that can protect other proprietary information and intellectual property. The goal is to prevent this data from falling into the wrong hands, including competitors that could use your customer information to their own advantage.

There are trickle-down benefits to making sure your business partners have passed inspection when it comes to your customers' privacy. Companies such as Microsoft and DoubleClick have begun to enforce not only their own privacy

---

[12] In a survey of 1,500 Americans conducted between November 5 and 22, 2001, the number of privacy fundamentalists increased substantially to 34 per cent, while privacy unconcerneds dropped to 8 per cent and privacy pragmatists fell to 58 per cent. Conducted shortly after 9/11, the results indicate that the terrorist events and goverment reaction may have directly sparked greater concern for privacy issues. The 2001 survey, entitled "Privacy On and Off the Internet: What Consumers Want," was conducted by Harris Interactive for Privacy and American Business and was released in February 2002.

policies but also the information practices of their closest partners. In some cases, privacy auditors such as PricewaterhouseCoopers are hired to make sure that members to an e-marketplace or within a corporate family have policies and codes of conduct that meet the same standards. "You're seeing businesses taking aggressive steps to police each other," says Jules Polonetsky, chief privacy officer for DoubleClick, which is eager to prevent a repeat of the past. "We're working on reviewing [partner] sites to make sure they're living up to the language we've put in their contracts." In 2001, more than 50 DoubleClick clients and partners were dropped because they breached their privacy agreements with the online ad network. Such enforcement contributes to the consumer-trust factor we discussed earlier. An added benefit is that it protects a company against lawsuits and bad press that could otherwise tarnish all participants in a business relationship.

Refueling the E-commerce Engine

As we have shown, there is growing consensus among pollsters, researchers, academics, politicians and businesses that adherence to privacy principles when engaging in commerce on the Internet isn't simply a matter of self-regulation or statutory compliance; it's a demonstration of good business sense. And as we'll see in the following chapters, in today's world, businesses will be more successful and will provide better customer service if they incorporate fair information practices into their business strategies.

There is much at stake. According to U.S. technology research firm Forrester Research, global Internet commerce — both business-to-business and business-to-consumer — is expected to be worth a staggering $6.8 trillion in 2004, representing nearly 9 per cent of all commerce worldwide.[13] Could this dollar value be made even higher if the barriers of fear and perceptions of risk are lowered? We believe that it could. What is more certain, however, is that this figure could fall short of expectations if businesses continue to monitor the surfing habits

[13] Forrester Research, "Worldwide eCommerce Growth," 2000-2004, **www.forrester.com.**

of consumers without their permission, if companies break their promises to not sell the data they have collected and if organizations fail to safeguard customer data to prevent it from being easy prey for hackers.

Still not convinced? An August 2000 survey from the Pew Internet and American Life Project found that 94 per cent of Internet users want privacy violators to be punished, particularly when consumers have been misled about a company's information practices; 11 per cent of Web surfers believe a company's owners should be put in prison if the business violates its own privacy policy. In the same situation, 27 per cent said owners should face fines, 26 per cent said the site's plug should be pulled, and 30 per cent said the Web sites should be publicly blacklisted — all remedies that would have a profound impact on the performance of the Internet economy.[14] Talk about a tough crowd!

And it's a crowd that is likely to get even tougher as new Internet and e-commerce products are introduced to the market. We've already mentioned wireless location technologies and geo-coded services, which could significantly turbo-boost the growth of e-commerce. It has been estimated that by 2006 one in four people on the planet will own a wireless phone. In North America, there could be 137 million wireless data users by 2005. And an estimated 90 per cent of all wireless subscribers will have access to location-based e-commerce services on their handsets by as early as 2004. This bodes well for companies such as Cell-Loc, which initially developed its location-based technology to take advantage of a U.S. Federal Communications Commission requirement that all U.S. mobile phone carriers be capable of tracking 911 callers.

Whether tracking technology is land-based or satellite-based (using the U.S. military's Global Positioning System), it is incredibly accurate and constantly improving. The data — that is, a person's location — is captured, passed along to a marketer or service provider and then tied together with other databases of personally identifiable information to help deliver location-specific advertising and products over the mobile Web.

---

[14] Susannah Fox, "Trust and Privacy Online: Why Americans Want to Rewrite the Rules" (Pew Internet and American Life Project, August 20, 2000).

Find yourself lost? Press the "Locate Me" button on your mobile phone. Running out of gas in a foreign city? Just use a service that finds the 10 gas stations closest to your car. Geo-locator technology can even be used to enhance dating services, by ringing the phones of two "compatible profiles" that pass within 50 feet of each other in public. Once they meet, this newly united couple can use a location service to get directions to the five closest Italian restaurants. Pet-tracking and child-find services are also a useful function of this technology, not to mention location-based billing. Of course, those are just the consumer applications. Businesses are already using location technology to keep track of trucks, rental cars, trains, taxis and even city snow plows. Automatic vehicle-location services can help recover stolen vehicles, and other assets, by tracking their precise whereabouts and notifying the proper authorities. There has even been talk about location-based pay-as-you-go car insurance policies that charge you based on when and where you drive your vehicle. If you avoid driving into a busy downtown core, for example, an insurance provider may offer you a discount. If your car sits idle in a garage while you're on vacation, then your policy will automatically be suspended until you begin driving again. Rental car companies such as Acme Rent-A-Car are already using GPS technology to track when and where customers drive over the speed limit. As you will see in **Chapter 8**, such practices have become highly controversial. Are consumers prepared to put their faith and trust in businesses that want to monitor where and when — or how fast — they drive?

As for advertising, marketers will be able to use location-based technology to deliver walk-by and drive-by ads that are more personalized and targeted than anything ever envisioned in the early days of e-commerce. Digital or electronic coupons, delivered to your mobile phone or your in-car navigation system as you approach a store, restaurant, gas station or coffee shop will also be commonplace — and for many, an annoyance — as location technologies and services mature.

In February 2000, Forrester Research released one of the first surveys that looked at how consumers would react, from a privacy perspective, to the barrage of location-based services to be introduced over the coming decade. Not surprisingly, the results revealed strong concern. Of more than 1,500 North

Americans who took part in the survey, 61 per cent believed it was "extremely" or "very" likely that data about a person's precise location would fall into the wrong hands if a business had access to it. Wrote Forrester analyst Jay Stanley, "Wireless technologies extend the step-by-step tracking practices of the Internet to the monitoring of individuals' movements in the physical world. This will amplify fears of Big Brother and strengthen the privacy advocates."[15]

Will mobile consumers have the option to turn off the location-based feature of their handsets? Will Cell-Loc, which is capable of tracking any cell phone user today without their knowledge, be disciplined enough to turn off the services itself? Will consumers be given the choice to opt in, or at the very least opt out of receiving location-specific advertising over a mobile device? Since the screens on most of these devices are very small, will it be realistic to expect that privacy policies will be read? If not, what's the alternative?

To get an early start on answering these questions, and calming early fears, the Wireless Location Industry Association (WLIA) drafted privacy policy standards meant to guide its members as they implemented their business strategies. The draft outlines many of the principles to be discussed in **Chapter 3**, among them choice, consent, purpose, openness and security. WLIA members are expected to consistently adopt the principles in the document and display them in the form of an easily accessible and understandable privacy policy. "Adoption of these guidelines serves clear notice that WLIA and its members support protection of consumer privacy," the outline states. "This enables companies in the [wireless signal location] industry to develop technologies and provide high-quality service to consumers, resulting in long-term and mutually beneficial relationships that achieve the added value implicit in the technology without penalty to individual privacy."

It is a commendable initiative, but it is also just the start. Protecting privacy, particularly in the online world, is very much in its infancy. This will be the defining decade.

---

[15] Jay Stanley, "Surviving the Privacy Revolution" (Forrester Research, February 2001).

The Bottom Line

The growth of the digital economy will be intimately linked to how effective organizations can be in dispelling consumers' privacy fears and establishing a level of trust and consumer confidence that is mutually beneficial to both sides. This is not a black-and-white issue.

Following fair information practices does not preclude collecting customer data. Protecting consumer privacy does not mean severing relationships with those very consumers. On the contrary — following the principles underlying fair information practices, to be discussed in the next chapter, will help put consumers at ease and will open up a world of valuable, not to mention accurate, information that could give you the advantages you need in this competitive environment.

There's no question that mistakes will be made along the way as companies modify their policies, procedures, technologies and business cultures to address the pressing issue at hand. But the payoff will make it exceedingly well worth the while. The alternative, from a business perspective, is untenable. Companies ignore privacy at their own peril.

Chapter 3

Privacy Roots, Privacy Routes

"Civilization is the progress toward a
society of privacy. Privacy is the process
of setting man free from men."

Ayn Rand, *The Fountainhead*

The Meaning of Privacy

Answering the question "What is privacy?" isn't as simple as you might think.
We all have a sense of what privacy is, we enjoy privacy every day, and we miss
it when it is taken away. And yet, when we try to define it, we find that privacy,
while easy to recognize, is difficult to describe.

Here are a few noteworthy definitions of privacy:

- "The claim of individuals, groups or institutions to determine for themselves
  when, how and to what extent information about them is communicated to
  others."[1]
- "The extent to which we are known to others, the extent to which others have
  physical access to us, and the extent to which we are the subject of others'
  attention."[2]

[1] Alan Westin, *Privacy and Freedom* (New York: Antheneum, 1967), p. x.
[2] Ruth Gavison, quoted in Ferdinand D. Schoeman, ed., *Philosophical Dimensions of Privacy: An Anthology* (Cambridge: Cambridge University Press, 1984), p. 379.

- "A degree of inaccessibility of persons, of their mental states and of information about them to the sense and surveillance devices of others."[3]

For many, privacy is key to ensuring human dignity and respect, as well as the preservation of personal autonomy. For others it means placing physical restrictions — doors, fences, locks and guard dogs — on outside access to one's private world. This is known as territorial privacy. Anybody who has grown up in close quarters with brothers or sisters knows all about territorial privacy.

Privacy of the person, or bodily privacy, is associated with intrusions of an individual's body, including such actions as forced sterilization and immunization, unauthorized blood transfusions and compulsory body searches. In January 2001, employees at Burlington Northern Santa Fe Railroad of Forth Worth, Texas, were allegedly threatened with job termination unless they agreed to provide a blood sample after filing an injury claim. It turns out that the company, without notifying employees, was using the samples to conduct genetic tests to predict predisposition to carpal tunnel syndrome. A lawsuit followed, but a $2.2-million settlement was quickly reached and the company agreed to stop the testing.

Information Privacy

Often, categories of privacy overlap. The Burlington Northern case, for example, could just as easily fall under workplace privacy (the topic of **Chapter 10**), genetic privacy or medical privacy, which in turn could overlap with communications privacy or, the one we're most concerned with here, *information privacy*. Essentially, information privacy relates to an individual's ability to control the use and disclosure of information about him- or herself, and to determine who is permitted access to this information and who is not. In essence, it functions as

---

[3] Anita Allen, quoted in Sheri Alpert, "Smart Cards, Smarter Policy: Medical Records, Privacy and Health Care Reform," *Hastings Center Report*, vol. 23, no. 6 (1993), p. 19.

a contract between two parties who agree, "I will give you this personal information to be used solely for this purpose, and you will restrict your use of the information to that purpose, in exchange for my business." The central premise of this book is that it is in your best business interests to protect information privacy and, where possible, offer "privacy contracts" to your customers. Information privacy, as an umbrella term for other categories of privacy involving the uses of personal information, is the primary focus of this book.

Another category of privacy relates to personal behavior and efforts to keep sensitive personal matters such as religious activities, sexual orientation and political preferences out of the public sphere. In Afghanistan, women who worked outside the home, drove or attended school after the age of eight were severely punished by the ruling Taliban militia. In parts of Northern Ireland, being Catholic or Protestant may get you hurt depending on what part of town you are in or what street you walk down. In some parts of the world, being exposed as gay or lesbian is the equivalent of a death sentence. Meanwhile, in North America, doctors who perform abortions can be subject to harassment and physical harm if their identities are publicly revealed. One need only look back to the days of Hitler, Nazi Germany and the Gestapo "thought police" to witness the atrocities that can occur when personal privacy and freedom of thought are violated. As David Flaherty, former information and privacy commissioner in British Columbia, has noted: "Privacy is like freedom: we do not recognize its importance until it is taken away." And once it is taken away, it is virtually impossible to get back.

What is equally troubling is when those encroaching on someone's privacy inadvertently gather the wrong information or draw incorrect conclusions about that person. This is typically the result of using data that is inaccurate or incomplete. Being judged out of context can have serious consequences. Whether you're a politician who is the victim of a smear campaign or a young professional having problems getting a loan, the results can be emotionally frustrating and often financially damaging. Jeffrey Rosen, associate professor at the George Washington University Law School, writes "There are many fearful consequences to the loss of privacy, but none perhaps more disquieting than this: privacy protects us from being misdefined and judged out of context."[4] Rosen says the protection of privacy is more important than ever in today's world of "short attention spans," where information can be easily confused with knowledge.

To Be Let Alone, or at Least in Control

In its most basic form, U.S. Supreme Court Justice Louis Brandeis defined privacy in 1890 as "the right to be let alone." But Justice Brandeis went much further in writing that the Constitution's framers "sought to protect Americans in their beliefs, their thoughts, their emotions and their sensations. They conferred, as against the government, the right to be let alone — the most comprehensive of rights and the right most valued by civilized men." Behind such a broad notion of privacy is the concept of "negative liberty," or "freedom from" the intrusion of the government, whether that intrusion be kicking in the front door of people's houses in the middle of the night, secretly peering into their bedroom windows or monitoring where they go and what they buy while surfing the Web. The U.S. Supreme Court reinforced this right to "freedom from" intrusion in June 2001, when it ruled that the secret use of thermal-imaging technology to detect heat-emitting equipment for growing marijuana was a constitutionally illegal search of a personal residence. In *Kyllo v. United States*, the court said that a "firm line" must be drawn at the entrance to a home, unless law-enforcement authorities can produce a warrant. "That line, we think, must be not only firm but also bright."

Of course, Thomas Hobbes, Jeremy Bentham and John Stuart Mill — three philosophers most associated with the concept of negative liberty — weren't around long enough to experience the Internet or high-tech infrared surveillance technology. And clearly, in this age of electronic commerce, James Bond gadgets, high-speed networking, powerful computing and precision surveillance, the notion

---

[4] Jeffrey Rosen, "The Eroded Self" *New York Times Magazine*, April 30, 2000, p. 46. (Article was adapted from Rosen's book *The Unwanted Gaze: The Destruction of Privacy in America*.)

of privacy associated with this original concept of liberalism has been significantly watered down.

Perhaps someone who lives in complete isolation with virtually no contact with the outside world could make the claim that privacy is absolute, but we cannot. It is generally accepted that people in a modern society — a digital society — function day to day with regular intrusions into their lives, most of them seemingly harmless. In this sense, privacy is far from absolute. From the moment your alarm clock goes off to the moment you crawl under the bed covers and turn off the lights, your life is in many respects an open book to the outside world, whether you're aware of it or not. The parking lots and toll highways you use throughout the day record your times of entry and departure. The buildings you enter and exit take your picture and then monitor your movements with video cameras. Older cell phones can be intercepted by anybody with a cheap scanner from Radio Shack, though such an act is illegal. Bank machines record and time-stamp your financial transactions while video cameras focus in on your face — or perhaps your fingerprint or retina.

If you send a postcard in the mail it can be read by hundreds of people along the way. If you send e-mail, it can be forwarded to thousands, even millions, of people around the globe within seconds. If you purchase an item at a store on credit, the time, place and nature of the transaction is recorded and analyzed by your credit card company. A video store clerk knows your movie preferences by accessing your file on the company database. The receptionist in your doctor's office has your complete medical chart at her fingertips. And the teenage cashier at the local pharmacy can know what medication you use and whether you're taking birth control pills or are a regular purchaser of lubricated, extra-ribbed condoms. The list goes on and on — and that's only in a single 24-hour period. The above doesn't include workplace monitoring, the use of loyalty cards or the information that is regularly and often covertly collected about consumers whenever they venture onto the Internet.

While absolute privacy may be unrealistic and undesirable, insufficient privacy protection is neither desirable nor healthy for free market societies. "If a dossier society makes an individual think twice before using a frequent shopper card to buy a tube of Preparation H in a supermarket, we pay a price," says privacy policy consultant Robert Gellman.[5] Clearly, there is a need for balance. But in a society of many competing values — individual versus collective; rights versus duties; self-determination versus public welfare; confidentiality versus public safety — it may be more appropriate to use the term "balancing act," since tilting too far in one direction can have grave personal, political or economic consequences. As well, people from different cultures, political persuasions or economic backgrounds will all have their own views on where the line of balance should be drawn. As corporate executives and industry professionals, your opinions will filter through the business world, where they will be further balanced against corporate interests and the overarching need to maximize shareholder value.

But set aside your business persona for a moment and think about your own life. Does it matter that you are able to maintain a private life, separate and apart from your public or work life? Are there some things that you would share only with those closest to you, or with no one at all? Think of transcripts containing your child's failing grades, a record relating to a relative's suicide attempt or history of drug or alcohol abuse, notes written down by a psychiatrist about your interest in leaving your spouse, your response to a personals ad, or details of an abortion, a personal bankruptcy or a severe depression. On June 27, 2001, drug maker Eli Lilly e-mailed a group of customers reminding them to take their Prozac. Because of a programming error, the message listed the e-mail addresses of more than 600 people with bulimia, obsessive-compulsive disorder and depression. Would you want your personal e-mail address to appear on that list? The American Civil Liberties Union filed a complaint to the U.S. Federal Trade Commission, which charged Eli Lilly for violating a promise of confidentiality in its online privacy policy. Half a year later, and after much media attention, the drug maker reached a settlement with the FTC requiring it to improve its online security and employee training.

[5] Robert Gellman, "Privacy, Consumers, and Costs" (March 2002, **www.epic.org/reports/dmfprivacy.html**).

Without your express consent, do you want your friends and neighbors to know how much money you make, or that you never paid off your student loan? What about past brushes with the law, or the fact that you may be seeing a psychotherapist or have had a sexually transmitted disease? Having problems getting an erection? Are you on Viagra as a result? Or perhaps you're taking anti-depressants to overcome the depression of wearing a prosthetic breast, the result of a difficult struggle with breast cancer?

Of course, you may choose to release such sensitive information to certain individuals: your mother, your doctor, your lawyer, your fiancée or even a complete stranger. You may even decide to hand that information over to an online business that caters to your specific needs. Exercising that choice — entering into that contract — would be far more preferable than having that information collected and shared without your knowledge. As a business, offering that choice to your customers is the first step to boosting their confidence and gaining their trust.

In 1958, it was English academic and philosopher Isaiah Berlin who introduced the concept of positive liberty. Whereas negative liberty is "freedom from" outside intrusions and obstructions, positive liberty can be viewed as "freedom to" pursue a course of action. "This positive sense of the word 'liberty' derives from the wish on the part of the individual to be his own master," wrote Berlin in "The Two Concepts of Liberty." "I wish, above all, to be conscious of myself as a thinking, willing, active being, bearing responsibility for my choices." In essence, positive liberty empowers the individual, an idea that is often lost in the traditional debate about privacy, which tends to portray people as helpless victims of big government and big business.

Indeed, notions of empowerment, control, choice and self-determination are the very essence of information privacy — that is, giving individuals the ability to determine under what conditions their personal information is collected, who can access it and how it will ultimately be used. As Berlin might have said, information privacy makes people "masters" of the data that identifies them as individuals, citizens, workers, consumers, patients, students, tourists, investors.

This personally identifying information may be a name or an identifying number such as a social security number or social insurance number. It may include an address, telephone number, age, sex, medical records, psychiatric history, blood type, genetic history, prescription profile, fingerprints, criminal record, credit rating, race, religion, ethnic origin, sexual orientation, marital status, education, place of work, employment history, personal interests, favorite movies, lifestyle preferences and much more. A great deal of this information, when correct, can help businesses get to know their customers better (with their consent), allowing for greater personalization of service and targeted marketing. It can also enable businesses to allocate scarce resources more efficiently, in turn making them stronger players in an increasingly competitive marketplace.

But the personal and often sensitive information of consumers *must* be handled fairly and with care. As custodians of this information, businesses are entrusted with its safekeeping and proper use.

Fair Information Practices

In Germany, the ability to determine the fate of one's personal information is considered so important that in 1983 the Constitutional Court ruled that all citizens had the right to what is called informational self-determination. Individuals, not the government, are the ones who determine the fate of their personal information. Spiros Simitis, former data protection commissioner of the German state of Hesse and one of the world's leading authorities on privacy, states, "Since this ruling ... it has been an established fact in this country that the constitution gives the individual the right to decide when and under what circumstances his personal data may be processed."[6]

---

[6] Spiros Simitis, quoted by David H. Flaherty, *Protecting Privacy in Surveillance Societies* (Chapel Hill: University of North Carolina Press, 1989), p. 377.

Three years earlier, the Organization for Economic Cooperation and Development, or OECD, developed a set of practices to ensure the fair treatment and handling of personal information collected by all organizations. These principles are commonly referred to as the Code of Fair Information Practices, or FIPs, and they are the basis of virtually all privacy legislation worldwide.[7]

The essence of fair information practices, in plain language, is not difficult:

- Only the information that is truly needed should be collected.
- Where possible, it should be collected directly from the individual to whom it pertains (the data subject).
- The data subject should be told why the information is needed.
- The information should be used only for the purpose identified at the time the data is collected.
- The information should not be used for other (secondary) purposes without the data subject's consent.
- The information used should be accurate and kept reasonably secure.
- Data subjects should be given the opportunity to see their personal information and correct it if it is incorrect.
- There should be a general policy of openness and transparency about an organization's information practices.
- An organization should appoint someone accountable for following the above principles.

FIPs are directed at and impose certain responsibilities on any data user (in this case, businesses) wishing to obtain the personal information of individuals (in this case, consumers). They also have the effect of empowering consumers, which, as discussed, is important for gaining consumer trust and customer loyalty.

---

[7] The complete text of the OECD Guidelines may be found in OECD, *Guidelines Governing the Protection of Privacy and Transborder Flows of Personal Data*, 1981, I.L.M. 422, OECD Doc. No. C(80)58 final; **www.oecd.org/EN/document/0,,EN-document-43-1-NO-24-10255-43,00.html.**

Collection and Use Limitation

Perhaps the most important FIPs have to do with placing limitations on how much customer personal information can be collected and how it can be used. The use-limitation principle is the bedrock of privacy practices because it restricts the use of the collected information to that specified at the time of collection. This is the "primary" purpose of the collection — the main reason for collecting it — as distinct from any subsequent "secondary" uses. The importance of this restriction cannot be overemphasized. It requires that the data user collect and use the information solely for the specified purpose, and it prohibits the disclosure of this information — including selling, exchanging or renting — to third parties for additional secondary purposes. If a business wants to sell the information to third parties, it has to get the customers' consent.

In some privacy legislation, the primary purpose may be extended to include "compatible" or "consistent" purposes, often based on a "reasonable person" test: Would a reasonable person consider the additional purpose to be consistent with the primary purpose? For example, a company that sends e-mail marketing information on automobiles could acceptably also send information on automobile products such as tires and mufflers. However, e-mail marketing related to life insurance would be considered a secondary purpose requiring additional consent.

Openness and Transparency

Another FIP deals with openness of the data users' information practices: consumers should be given the opportunity to know how their information is being used. The conditions under which their personal information is held should be "transparent," meaning that consumers should be made aware of how their information is being stored, managed and put to use for the primary purpose that was expressed at the time of collection.

Two other FIPs require that consumer information be protected with reasonable security safeguards and that only information that is accurate and up-to-date should be used. Again, openness and transparency come into play here. An organization must be open about its policies and practices in order for consumers to know that accuracy and confidentiality are assured.

Data Quality and Security

The requirement that personal data be accurate, relevant to the purposes for which it is used and up-to-date becomes even more important in this day of powerful computers, advanced networking, high-speed communications and extensive data mining. If accurate information about consumers is stored, errors will be self-perpetuating as the incorrect data spreads electronically across the Internet and into countless numbers of other databases. As we all know, the Internet is just as quick at spreading lies, viruses, corrupt data and skewed information as it is at spreading truths. Once bad data is set free, both the consumer and the business have lost all control of that information. "The Internet gives untruth a head start it surely never needed," reports Carl M. Cannon in the *American Journalism Review.* "And what a head start: If an e-mailer sends a message to 10 people and each person who receives it passes it on to 10 more, by the ninth transmission, this missive could reach a billion people. This is the real computer virus: misinformation."[8]

Protecting data quality entails strong security safeguards that prevent unauthorized access to the information, unauthorized destruction or modification and unauthorized disclosure to third parties for secondary purposes. As hackers get more sophisticated, networks become more complex and glitches become more widespread, technical safeguards in the form of firewalls and strong encryption will take on a much greater role.

Individual Participation and Accountability

Giving consumers the right to access information about them is a fundamental premise of privacy protection. Otherwise, their ability to maintain control over such information and ensure its accuracy would not be

---

[8] Carl M. Cannon, "The Real Computer Virus (Misinformation on the Internet)," *American Journalism Review*, vol. 23, no. 3 (April 2001).

possible. Consumers would not know what information about them was being held in various databases by various organizations. They would not be able to verify the use of this information or check its accuracy. Without this access, consumers might choose to withhold personal information, perhaps giving it out to a company's competitor.

For these reasons, consumers should be permitted access to the information about them, within a reasonable amount of time and in an intelligible form. They should also be allowed to correct erroneous data about themselves. Having accurate data is obviously in a company's best interest. If a company chooses to deny a person access to his or her file, it should give the person a reason for the denial and the opportunity to appeal the decision to a person accountable for privacy within the company.

Accountability is, in fact, the final principle of the OECD's fair information practices. Someone within an organization should be responsible for making sure that fair information practices are being followed regularly and consistently. This person — such as a data controller, a chief privacy officer or a corporate privacy officer — is held accountable should there be a problem with or a challenge to a company's FIPs. The best policies in the world are of no value if they are ignored; FIPs should be taken seriously and implemented in their entirety if they are to be effective. Assigning accountability to a high-ranking individual, such as a member of an executive team who reports directly to the board of directors, the chief executive officer or the chair, will make consumers take notice and likely result in a more successful implementation of fair information practices within your company.

Here are the eight principles contained in the OECD's Code of Fair Information Practices, the *OECD Guidelines Governing the Protection of Privacy and Transborder Flows of Personal Data*.

Collection Limitation

Limited to the collection of personal data; data should be obtained by lawful and fair means and, where appropriate, with the knowledge or consent of the data subject.

Data Quality

Personal data should be relevant to the purposes for which it is to be used and, to the extent necessary for those purposes, should be accurate, complete and kept up-to-date.

Purpose Specification

The purposes for which personal data are collected should be specified not later than at the time of data collection, and the subsequent use limited to the fulfillment of those purposes or such others as are not incompatible with those purposes and as are specified on each occasion of change of purpose.

Use Limitation

Personal data should not be disclosed, made available or otherwise used for purposes other than those specified (purpose specification) except: a) with the consent of the data subject, or b) by the authority of law.

Security Safeguards

Personal data should be protected with reasonable security safeguards against such risks as loss of unauthorized access, destruction, use, modification or disclosure of data.

Openness

There should be a general policy of openness about developments, practices and policies with respect to personal data. Means should be readily available of establishing the existence and nature of personal data, and the main purpose of their use, as well as the identity and usual residence of the data controller.

Individual Participation

An individual should have the right:

(a) To obtain from a data controller, or otherwise, confirmation of whether or not the data controller has the data relating to him;

(b) To have communicated to him, data relating to him: i) within a reasonable time; ii) at a charge, if any, that is not excessive; iii) in a form that is readily intelligible to him;

(c) To be given reasons if a request made under subparagraphs (a) and (b) is denied, and to be able to challenge denial; and

(d) To challenge data relating to him and, if the challenge is successful, to have data erased, rectified, completed or amended.

Accountability

A data controller should be accountable for complying with measures which give effect to the principles stated above.

The CSA Model Code

The same year that the OECD's fair information practices were published, 1980, the Council of Europe passed Convention 108, which committed member states to introduce data-protection legislation based on commonly shared principles. During the 1990s, with the private-sector privacy debate heating up and the European Union preparing a Directive on Data Protection, Canada felt the need to develop its own privacy standards for the private sector. The Canadian Standards Association (CSA) spent two years drafting a generic privacy code with the help of representatives from the federal government, leading corporations and businesses, privacy advocates and consumer groups. The code was intended to be used as a model for private-sector organizations. "The standard was conceived as a voluntary instrument to guide business and other organizations in the management of personal information, and in respecting the rights of the individuals with whom they deal," wrote Canadian privacy experts Stephanie Perrin, Heather Black, David Flaherty and Murray Rankin.[9]

The 1996 CSA privacy code, like most, is modeled on the OECD guidelines, except that it strengthens two components: "consent," by having it stand alone, and "challenging compliance," which strengthens a person's right to challenge an organization's compliance with any of the principles, not simply refusals of access or the accuracy of the collected data. As well, accountability is held to be so fundamental that it is placed first in the list of 10 principles. The CSA code formed the basis of Canada's Personal Information Protection and Electronic Documents Act, private-sector privacy legislation that came into force on January 1, 2001.

---

[9] Stephanie Perrin, Heather Black, David Flaherty and T. Murray Rankin, *The Personal Information Protection and Electronic Documents Act* (Toronto: Irwin Law, 2001), p. 13.

Here is a summary of the CSA Model Code for the Protection of Personal Information.

1. **Accountability** — An organization is responsible for personal information under its control and shall designate a person who is accountable for the organization's compliance with the following principles.

2. **Identifying Purposes** — The purposes for which personal information is collected shall be identified by the organization at or before the time the information is collected.

3. **Consent** — The knowledge and consent of the individual are required for the collection, use or disclosure of personal information except where inappropriate.

4. **Limiting Collection** — The collection of personal information shall be limited to that which is necessary for the purposes identified by the organization. Information shall be collected by fair and lawful means.

5. **Limiting Use, Disclosure and Retention** — Personal information shall not be used or disclosed for purposes other than those for which it was collected, except with the consent of the individual or as required by law. Personal information shall be retained only as long as necessary for the fulfillment of those purposes.

6. **Accuracy** — Personal information shall be as accurate, complete and up-to-date as is necessary for the purposes for which it is to be used.

7. **Safeguards** — Personal information shall be protected with security safeguards appropriate to the sensitivity of the information.

8. **Openness** — An organization shall make readily available to individuals specific information about its policies and practices relating to its handling of personal information.

9. **Individual Access** — Upon request, an individual shall be informed of the existence, use and disclosure of personal information about the individual and shall be given access to that information. An individual shall be able to challenge the accuracy and completeness of the information and have it amended as appropriate.

10. **Challenging Compliance** — An individual shall be able to challenge compliance with the above principles with the person who is accountable within the organization.

The FTC's "Big Four"

The U.S. Federal Trade Commission has been involved in the privacy debate since the mid-1990s. It has initiated hundreds of actions against companies engaged in unfair data-collection practices, making it one of the most active government consumer-protection agencies in the world with respect to privacy. In the beginning, the agency favored self-regulation as a way of balancing the needs of industry versus the rights of consumers. But in 2000, after taking a serious look at the progress, or lack thereof, made through self-regulation, the FTC decided it was time for Congress to implement legislation that would work hand in hand with self-regulation.[10] It proposed that such legislation, aimed at consumer-oriented commercial Web sites, be based on the following four principles, which are themselves based narrowly on the OECD's Code of Fair Information Practices:

1. **Notice** — Web sites would be required to provide consumers clear and conspicuous notice of their information practices, including what information they collect, how they collect it (e.g., directly or through unobvious means such a cookies), how they use it, how they provide choice, access and security to consumers, whether they disclose the information collected to other entities and whether other entities are collecting information through the site.
2. **Choice** — Web sites would be required to offer consumers choices as to how their personal identifying information is used beyond the use for which the information was provided (e.g., to consummate a transaction).

---

[10] Under FTC chairman Timothy Muris, the commission subsequently backed away from the call for legislation. See Chapter 4.

Such choice would encompass both internal secondary uses (such as marketing back to consumers) and external secondary uses (such as disclosing data to other entities).

3. **Access** — Web sites would be required to offer consumers reasonable access to the information a Web site has collected about them, including a reasonable opportunity to review and to correct inaccuracies or delete information.

4. **Security** — Web sites would be required to take reasonable steps to protect the security of the information they collect from consumers.

Security Does Not Equal Privacy

The terms "security" and "privacy" are often used interchangeably, but they are not one and the same. Security is an important ingredient of privacy, but it is not the only ingredient; it is where you begin, not where you end. Privacy subsumes a much broader spectrum of protections that places restrictions on the collection, use and disclosure of personal information and establishes the right of access and correction for data subjects, which in this case are consumers. If we zoom in on the specific issue of security, we find yet another subset, or suite, of protections.

The Security Suite

To have strong security in an online world, five areas must be addressed: authentication, data integrity, confidentiality, authorized access, and non-repudiation.

- **Authentication** — When dealing with remote, faceless transactions, as is the case when doing business online, authenticating the identity of the parties involved is important, especially as the sensitivity of the information being communicated increases. When transmitting highly sensitive information — for example, financial or medical data — public key encryption involving the use of private keys to sign documents may be used. Authentication presumes that the earlier stage of enrollment of identity has taken place, where the identification of the parties has first been established. Authenticating that an online user is who he or she claims to be is a very important step, but not an easy one. Digital signatures, biometrics, public key infrastructures and certi-fication authorities are but a few of the responses to this daunting challenge.

- **Data integrity** — Ensuring the integrity or quality of the data is vital, espe-cially when the information is highly sensitive, such as health data. Someone intercepting medical test results and altering a key finding could have devastating consequences for an individual. Ensuring that the infor-mation hasn't been changed or tampered with goes well beyond the issue of accuracy or inaccuracy.

- **Confidentiality and authorized access** — Once the information has been transmitted and has safely reached the intended recipient, it is the organi-zation's responsibility to safeguard the data by ensuring that only those authorized to access it are permitted to do so. To authorized users, infor-mation must be easily accessible. But the opposite must be true for those who are not authorized. Implementing protocols that restrict access to author-ized parties alone is an essential step, along with including audit trails that can track times and places of entry. Securing the information from prying eyes and ensuring that it can be accessed only under proper authority, with procedural controls in place, are key elements of confidentiality.

- **Non-repudiation** — The sleeper of the security suite involves proving that the information was actually sent or received by a user. A system of data management must be able to prevent someone from reneging on a transac-tion or a communication. Take, for example, someone who submits a "buy" order one morning to his online broker for 100 shares of a stock trading at $10 a share. Later that afternoon, much to his dismay, the buyer learns that his stock has dropped to $5 a share. His broker has to have some assurance that his client can't renege on the order by arguing, "No, that wasn't me, I didn't place that order." While non-repudiation is a laudable goal, achieving it is a formidable task.

To summarize, while security is a fundamental and essential ingredient of privacy, it is not the only ingredient. The term "privacy" covers a broad spectrum of protections involving personal control over the uses of one's personal information, as well as the data user's responsibility for protecting the information in its custody and control, ideally through the use of fair information practices.

The Bottom Line

In this chapter we have outlined various definitions of privacy, as well as the principles of fair information practices that underpin codes of business conduct in the United States, Canada and Europe. Privacy, in its most basic sense, may be the right to be let alone. But in the Internet economy, where consumer data is the lifeblood of many businesses, information privacy is more about giving consumers the ability to choose where their information goes, to know how it will be used and to correct what is incomplete or false. It is also about securing the information so that it goes to the right places, is used for the expected primary purposes and is accessed by authorized eyes only. It is about giving consumers control, so that in return, they can give you their trust and the business relationship that comes with it.

Chapter 4

The Global Regulatory Environment

"[Without] federal legislation that sets
standards to be followed by everyone, it is
unlikely that consumers' privacy can be
adequately protected from identity theft,
commercial harassment and hucksterism."

Sheila Anthony,
U.S. Federal Trade Commissioner

Setting the Stage: An Historical Perspective

In North America, early privacy laws were directed at government actions only.
This was a function of the historical distrust of government, and such laws
served to rein in the immense power that government wields. The business
community was exempt, but as abuses from the private sector began to emerge,
so too did the political response. Today, the private sector is a dominant focus
of privacy regulation and legislation. In the global economy, businesses need to
know which countries have what types of privacy laws, as well as how to
comply with the laws in their jurisdiction. This chapter will take an historical
look at the development of privacy laws, how the legislative environment has
evolved over more than three decades to affect the larger business community,
and what the legal landscape looks like in North America, Europe and other

major commerce zones today. We will also take a look at the pros and cons of private-sector privacy legislation and the basic requirements for compliance.

When the issue of individual privacy first appeared on political radar screens, the major concern was with government and government-regulated organizations. The ability of the public sector to collect and centralize massive amounts of personal information about citizens has always been viewed as a potential threat to liberty and democracy. Without proper legislative restrictions in place, the fear is that government, to entrench its power and block its political adversaries, could use the personal information of the people against the people. Left unchecked, such activities can cast an oppressive chill over a society, leaving people to wonder when, if and how their personal information might one day be used against them. It was precisely against this type of governmental intrusion that Justice Brandeis first made his claim regarding "the right to be let alone." The growing use of computer technology amplified this concern. Paper-based documents, previously locked away in filing cabinets in scattered government buildings, were gradually being replaced by centrally stored electronic files, easily accessible from remote computer terminals. Wide-area and local-area computer networks made it possible to move these files easily from department to department and from computer to computer.

Unauthorized access to citizens' personal information was of course a concern in the pre-computer era, but the barriers of distance, the decentralization of data and the high cost of manually correlating paper-based data served at least to deter or minimize abuse. Pulling together data on an individual during this era wasn't an easy task, according to the U.S. Information Infrastructure Task Force:

> [I]n order to build a profile of an individual who had lived in various states, one would have to travel from state to state and search public records for information about the individual. This process would have required filling out forms, paying fees and waiting in line for record searches at local, state and federal agencies, such as the departments of motor vehicles, deed record offices, electoral commissions and county record offices. Although one could manually compile a personal profile in

this manner, it would be a time-consuming and costly exercise, one that would not be undertaken unless the offsetting rewards were considerable.[1]

Today, of course, such dossiers could be built almost instantaneously with little effort and cost. Hardware, software and communications networks continue to become more powerful and economical, allowing information to be used in ways that were previously impossible or prohibitively expensive. What were once pockets of databases are now linked together as parts of massive data pools. Distance is increasingly irrelevant as data networks become faster and less expensive to operate. Storage is virtually unlimited. Data collection is in many ways automated, and the information gathered is more detailed and better organized than ever possibly imagined. Meanwhile, the processing power of computers continues to increase, making the detection of trends, anomalies and patterns of behavior as easy as the push of a button.

The Evolution of Regulation

United States

In the United States, concern for privacy protection started in the late 1960s. In 1970, the Fair Credit Reporting Act, although not designed to be a privacy law, gave consumers the opportunity to examine their credit files and correct errors. It also placed restrictions on the use of information in credit records. For example, credit-reporting agencies are not permitted to release financial information about individuals except for "legitimate" business needs, such as to establish their credit-worthiness. Legitimate business needs, however, can be interpreted very broadly. In addition, although credit-reporting agencies are permitted to share credit information only with employers, insurance companies and government

[1] U.S. Information Infrastructure Task Force, Privacy Working Group, *Privacy and the National Information Infrastructure: Principles for Providing and Using Personal Information*, June 6, 1995.

— and only for "a business transaction involving the consumer" — violations are reportedly common.

A number of congressional study groups in the late 1960s examined the growing ease with which automated personal information could be gathered and matched with other information. One such group was an advisory committee of the Department of Health, Education and Welfare, which in 1973 drafted its own code of fair information practices, setting out the following principles:

- There must be no personal data record-keeping systems whose very existence is secret.
- There must be a way for an individual to find out what information about him or her is in a record and how it is used.
- There must be a way for an individual to prevent information about him or her obtained for one purpose from being used or made available for other purposes without consent.
- There must be a way for an individual to correct or amend a record of identifiable information about him or her.
- Any organization using records identifiable to a person must ensure reliability of the data for their intended use and must take reasonable precautions to prevent misuse of the data.[2]

This code evolved into the 1974 Privacy Act, which applied only to federal agency records. The Act established the Privacy Protection Study Commission, but it was a temporary body with a limited advisory role. A comprehensive report from this commission, *Personal Privacy in an Information Society*, released in 1977, contained some 160 recommendations for improving information practices in both the public and private sectors. The report was far-reaching in its scope, tackling such areas as consumer credit records, mailing lists, bank

---

[2] Summarized from U.S. Department of Health, Education, and Welfare, *Records, Computers and the Rights of Citizens, Report of the Secretary's Advisory Committee on Automated Personal Data Systems* (Washington, D.C., 1973).

records, insurance records, employment files, medical records and school records. But there has been little follow-up.

A major weakness of the Privacy Act is that no independent oversight agency — such as a privacy commissioner or data protection board — was created. A provision providing for the creation of a Federal Privacy Board with the sole responsibility of overseeing the act was deleted in negotiations before the Act was passed. Oversight was given to the Office of Management and Budget (OMB), an already overextended body that had little interest in leading the privacy crusade.

The United States still has no independent oversight body — no watchdog to make sure that the Privacy Act is being followed, although attempts have been made in that direction. In 1994, for example, Senator Paul Simon introduced a bill that would have replaced the OMB with a five-member Data Protection Board. The board would mainly take on an advisory role, helping to guide the private sector in developing its own privacy codes. The bill was never passed.

Other forms of privacy protection exist in various federal and state laws, but most are narrow in scope and have been adopted haphazardly. The result is a piecemeal approach to privacy legislation, in which sector-specific laws are passed to address specific problems as they arise. For organizations, keeping track of these rules can be a daunting task. In the mid-1980s, Judge Robert Bork was being considered as a nominee for the U.S. Supreme Court. A video rental store that he frequented disclosed a list of the judge's video rentals to a newspaper. Although nothing embarrassing was revealed, congressional outrage (and fears of one's own video-viewing patterns being exposed) led to quick passage of the Video Privacy Protection Act. Law professor Joel Reidenberg, an authority on privacy regulations, explains that such a "mosaic approach" to U.S. privacy legislation results from the "American fear of government intervention in private activities and the reluctance to broadly regulate the industry. The result of the mosaic is a rather haphazard and unsatisfactory response to each of the privacy concerns."[3]

[3] Joel R. Reidenberg, "Privacy in the Information Economy: A Fortress or Frontier for Individual Rights?" *Federal Communications Law Journal*, vol. 44, no. 2 (1993), p. 209.

A number of other industry-specific laws in the United States, while not intended to protect privacy in themselves, do contain some privacy-protective features: the Fair Credit Reporting Act of 1974, the Fair Debt Collection Act of 1977, the Electronic Funds Transfer Act of 1978, the Communications Act of 1984, the Cable Communications Policy Act of 1984, the Telephone Consumer Protection Act of 1991 and many others. Over the past few years, the volume of privacy-related bills under debate in Congress or state legislatures has exploded, largely as a result of the Internet economy and the threats that new data-collection and surveillance technologies are posing to individual privacy. Dozens of bills are being considered at a state and federal level, dealing with everything from workplace privacy to safeguarding genetic data to restrictions on wireless location-tracking technologies. In the first half of 2001 alone, lawmakers introduced more than 50 bills, proving that the "mosaic approach" continues to thrive. In fact, three significant federal statutes have gone into effect in recent years, dealing respectively with financial, health and children's privacy. These laws will be discussed later in this chapter.

Canada

In Canada, a privacy commissioner was established under the Canadian Human Rights Act in 1977. In 1982, the appointment of a privacy commissioner was part of the federal Privacy Act. Canada signed the OECD guidelines in 1984 (as had the United States in 1980), committing itself to adhere to those principles. Most provinces and territories have since passed their own privacy laws, which, like the Privacy Act, apply strictly to government records: Quebec in 1982, Ontario in 1988, Saskatchewan in 1992, British Columbia in 1993, Nova Scotia in 1994, Alberta in 1995, Yukon in 1996, the Northwest Territories in 1997, Manitoba in 1998, Nunavut in 1999, New Brunswick in 2001, Prince Edward Island in 2001 and Newfoundland in 2002. Unlike the United States, each of these regions has appointed independent information and privacy commissioners, or the equivalent ombudsman, responsible for ensuring compliance. Again, both provincial and federal legislation — until recently — applied only to government departments or regulated organizations. The private sector, except in Quebec, did not have to deal with broad privacy legislation.

Quebec has been a world leader with respect to privacy legislation for both the public and private sectors. Section 5 of the Quebec Charter of Human Rights and Freedoms, established in 1975, includes the "right to respect for private life." In 1994, Quebec passed Bill 68, or the Act Respecting the Protection of Personal Information in the Private Sector, giving the province one of the highest standards of data protection in the world. Passage of the legislation also gave Quebec a four-year head start on the European Union's Directive on Data Protection.

Canada, like the United States, also has a number of sector-specific laws that, although not designed specifically to protect privacy, do contain privacy rules that offer some limited protection of personal information held by various organizations. Federal laws that apply to financial institutions include the Bank Act, the Insurance Companies Act and the Trust and Loan Companies Act. The Telecommunications Act is a federal law overseen by the Canadian Radio-television and Telecommunications Commission, which acts as regulator to the telephone and cable industries. As well, some provinces have their respective counterparts, such as, in Ontario, the Insurance Act, the Loan and Trust Corporations Act and the Consumer Reporting Act.

Enacting specific laws to deal with specific problems has been common in both the United States and Canada, but this ad hoc, piecemeal approach has failed to provide the full range of protections contained in the Code of Fair Information Practices set out by the OECD. It was only in 2000 that Canada passed federal privacy legislation, aimed specifically at the private sector, that builds on the OECD guidelines. The Personal Information Protection and Electronic Documents Act will be discussed in greater detail later in this chapter.

Europe

European privacy protection began in 1968 with work initiated by the Council of Europe, which felt it necessary to study the threats and effects of technology on human rights. It was recognized at the time that new computer technologies could link and transmit data in ways not widely available before, and that this capability posed a threat to individual privacy. The council recommended that an instrument be developed to protect personal data held by both the private and public sectors. This instrument ultimately took the form of a resolution — known as Convention 108 — to protect individual freedoms by placing limits on the collection, storage and transmission of personal information. Convention 108, also known as the Convention for the Protection of Individuals with Regard to Automatic Processing of Personal Data, was introduced in 1981.

In 1969, just a year after the Council of Europe took up the privacy cause, the OECD began to examine the implications of "trans-border data flow" on personal data. The resulting Code of Fair Information Practices has been used as the basis of privacy legislation in Europe, the most proactive region in the world with respect to data protection, with laws applying equally to the public and private sectors.

One of the first privacy laws ever enacted in Europe was the Swedish Data Act, in 1973, followed by the West German Data Protection Act in 1977 and the French Law on Informatics, Data Banks and Freedoms in 1978. Each of these countries chose a different method of implementing its laws: the Swedes adopted a licensing system, the Germans established a data protection commissioner, and the French created the National Commission on Informatics and Liberties. Despite the differences of each system, they share one vital component: each law includes some means of ensuring that principles contained in the legislation are implemented and followed. In other words, they each had a method of oversight and enforcement. Of the 30 countries that are members of the OECD, more than half have either passed some form of privacy legislation, are in the process of doing so or are studying the issue.

The Pros and Cons of Privacy Laws

Opponents of privacy legislation generally argue that rules and regulations will restrict domestic and global commerce by tying the hands of organizations that rely heavily on the information they collect. They believe that the cost of complying with privacy laws would place an unfair financial burden on the global business community. After all, the biggest question companies ask is, "How much is all this going to cost?" It's a legitimate concern, both for large and small organizations. Staff may need to be hired to properly study legislation and implement compliance programs; some companies may choose to hire outside experts to audit their data management systems, study their processes and craft privacy policies; new information technologies may need to be purchased to aid in compliance, while existing systems may have to be upgraded; there is also a fear of increased legal costs, since legislation is presumed to expose companies to a greater number of civil lawsuits and watchdog investigations. For small companies and startups, with their limited resources, these are particularly legitimate concerns.

There is no question that compliance with privacy legislation comes with a price, and we will attempt a rough assessment of the costs in **Chapter 5**. But as consumers become more aware of privacy issues and increasingly protective of their personal information, companies can expect to pay a much higher price for not following the fair information practices that embody most privacy laws. Supporters of privacy legislation generally cite the "consumer confidence" argument. As we discussed in **Chapter 2**, the growth of electronic commerce has been hampered by consumers' concerns over their loss of personal privacy, concerns that have translated into distrust, causing many online consumers to abandon e-commerce sites that don't appear to take seriously the issue of privacy and data protection. The argument that consumers would be more likely to spend money online if they truly felt their privacy was being respected and if they could exercise some control over how their personal information is used, is supported by numerous consumer polls. The increased economic activity that would result, particularly for companies that have won the trust of consumers, would, we believe, more than offset the upfront and continuing costs associated with regulatory compliance.

Self-regulation was an attempt to bolster consumer confidence, but as the U.S. Federal Trade Commission and numerous studies have pointed out, it has largely failed. The problem with self-regulation is that there are no mechanisms of enforcement, and no penalties can be imposed on those who stray. Without the ability to enforce consistent rules, widespread consumer trust is an elusive goal. This is why support for legislation is growing among consumers, politicians and, gradually, within the business community itself.

The costs of basic compliance will vary from one organization to the other. Small organizations won't have to spend as much as large organizations, since their information-processing systems are much simpler and their activities are more focused. New organizations will have fewer challenges than older organizations, since building privacy into a business plan from the ground up tends to be easier than retrofitting an organization that may be set in its ways. There are also numerous tools — ranging from free to affordable to expensive — that any company can use to design privacy policies or perform self-audits. (These will be discussed in later chapters.)

It is also worth noting that the leap from self-regulation to legislation might not be as large as many believe. A number of the principles in the OECD guidelines are already followed by industries that practice self-regulation. For those organizations that are genuinely committed to self-regulation, the transition to an environment of legislation could be a much smoother ride than expected. But all this may be moot. The reality is that broad-based legislation is already here or is being developed in many jurisdictions outside the United States. Within the United States, it is only a matter of time before a similar regulatory environment emerges. As the Meta Group, a U.S. technology research firm that follows privacy issues, explains, "Any company that believes it can continue to collect information surreptitiously as part of its business plan will provide its investors with major disappointments over the next two years."[4] In the early 2000s, data-gathering organizations will face an environment where sector-specific self-regulation is likely to be complemented by broad-based legislation. Those who act quickly to adapt to this environment will be the ones who benefit the most through early gains. Those who resist will risk falling behind or being penalized.

[4] Meta Group, "Privacy Requires Standards," special commentary for CNET News.com [online], March 5, 2001.

In the United States, the business community is slowly beginning to warm up to the idea of broad-based federal privacy legislation. In January 2001, the American Electronics Association, the oldest high-tech trade association in North America, declared that it would support federal legislation that would pre-empt state laws. Louis Gerstner, chair of IBM, and Carly Fiorina, CEO of Hewlett-Packard, are among a growing number of executives who have cited the need for privacy legislation. Too much confusion has resulted from the state-by-state, sector-by-sector "mosaic" approach. Meanwhile, the voluntary nature of self-regulation has created an uneven playing field, with no scoreboard, no referees and participation from only half the team. Now more than ever, businesses are looking for the certainty that can be gained from a consistent application of the law. The Cellular Telecommunications and Internet Association, for example, has petitioned the Federal Communications Commission for rules aimed at safeguarding personal privacy with mobile phones. The group is particularly concerned with new location-tracking technologies and wants a formal set of rules with which all mobile phone companies in the United States would have to comply. One need only look to Europe or Quebec to see that privacy legislation targeted at the business community does not spell economic doom. Several years after the introduction of Quebec's private-sector data-protection law, predictions that the economic skies would fall have not come true. It's business as usual.

The New Economy: Private-Sector Legislation

The legislative landscape for privacy continues to change in tandem with an emerging and maturing information economy, where trade is global, commerce is increasingly electronic and knowledge — gained through collecting and analyzing information — is king. Big Government, Big Business, Big Brother. With the click of a mouse, a consumer in New York can purchase goods from the other side of the world, gamble on a Web site operated out of a "server farm" in Antigua and participate in an online flower auction run out of the Netherlands. Likewise, businesses can accept orders from anybody with a computer and a credit card, regardless of where they live or work. Throughout such transactions, personal data is effortlessly collected, stored, shared and moved around. The birth and phenomenal growth of the Internet, which has become the heart and soul of the new economy, has forced us all to take a deeper look into the issue of information privacy and the need for data-protection legislation, on both the domestic and international levels.

Some regions, such as Europe, are pushing the envelope more than others when it comes to data protection. Others, such as the United States, are holding back as businesses, politicians and consumer groups weigh the need for broad legislation against a sector-specific approach, self-regulation, market forces and technological solutions. A global standard has yet to emerge, but it is becoming clear that regional differences in the application of privacy laws could erect barriers for trade and commerce. This decade will be a telling one — we think it will be the defining decade for privacy.

Let's take a look at privacy legislation around the world that is aimed specifically at the private sector and has been designed to protect consumer data in the information age.

EU Directive on Data Protection

Throughout the 1970s and 1980s, many countries in Europe passed broad-based data-protection laws aimed at both the public and private sectors, with Germany and France among the most progressive. However, by the end of the 1980s, some countries, such as Spain and Italy, were noticeably lagging, despite the introduction of Convention 108 by the Council of Europe in 1981. It was near the end of the 1980s that the European Community — which eventually became the European Union — began to assess the legislative landscape that resulted from Convention 108 and measure it against the continuing drive to harmonize national laws in Europe, particularly those with a potential impact on trade and commerce.

The result of this assessment was the European Union's Directive on Data Protection, one of the more recent steps in a four-decade attempt to create a unified internal or "common" market in Europe. (The full text of the E.U. Data

Protection Directive is at **aspe.os.dhhs.gov/datacncl/eudirect.htm**.) A directive, in this context, is a legal instrument that is binding on the 15 member states of the European Union. Each member, within a specified time, must apply the standards of the directive to its own national legislation, or else the directive takes precedence. The aim is a single European standard for data protection to replace the mixed bag of strict, weak and nonexistent national laws. In effect, obstacles to the free movement of personal data throughout the EU would be removed and the protection of data would be consistently applied.

The European Union issued its directive in 1995, giving its member countries — Austria, Belgium, Denmark, Finland, France, Germany, Greece, Ireland, Italy, Luxembourg, the Netherlands, Portugal, Spain, Sweden and the United Kingdom — until October 1998 to bring their national legislation in line with the regional standard. Many other European countries outside the EU have also chosen to comply with the directive, either for practical reasons or because of pre-existing treaties. Switzerland, Norway, the Czech Republic, Hungary and Poland have already passed compliant legislation or are considering doing so. It should be pointed out that the EU directive generally raises privacy standards for most countries but lowers them for others. In Germany, for example, the government is updating its 1997 teleservices data protection law, one of the strictest in the region, to make it easier for businesses to obtain consumer consent.

Since the aim of this book is to serve as a business primer on information privacy issues, we will not go into the details of the directive, which is a lengthy and complex read. What we will look at are a few definitions under the law and the underlying principles as they apply to the EU private sector. These principles are largely based on the OECD principles for fair information practices.

Article 2 of the directive contains some important definitions that are worth noting if your business is a multinational or engages in global trade. *Personal data* is "any information relating to an identified or identifiable natural person," or "data subject." An *identifiable person* is "one who can be identified, directly or indirectly, in particular reference to an identification number or one or more factors specific to his physical, psychological, mental, economic, cultural or social identity." *Processing* means "any operation or set of operations which is performed upon personal data, whether or not by automatic means, such as collection, recording, organization, storage, adaptation or alteration, retrieval, consultation, use, disclosure by transmission, dissemination or otherwise making available, alignment or combination, blocking, erasure or destruction." A *controller* is a "natural or legal person, public authority, agency or any other body which alone or jointly with others determines the purposes and means of the processing of personal data," and a *processor* is a "natural or legal person, public authority, agency or any other body which processes personal data on behalf of the controller." The use of the term "natural person" means an individual does not need to be a citizen or permanent legal resident of a European Union country to be subject to the directive.

Article 6 deals with data quality and uses. The processing of personal data must be conducted "fairly and lawfully." Such information can be collected only for "specific, explicit and legitimate purposes." Data controllers cannot stray from those purposes when processing this data, and the information itself must be "adequate, relevant and not excessive" with respect to the purposes for which it is collected. As well, the data must be "accurate and, where necessary, kept up to date." If data is inaccurate or out of date, every reasonable step must be taken to have it "erased or rectified." Article 6 also deals with the principle of retention, stating that personally identifiable data should not be stored any longer than required to fulfill the purpose for which it was collected. If it is to be stored longer, efforts should be made to anonymize and safeguard the data.

Article 7 outlines the criteria for making data processing legitimate. In essence, a controller can process personal data only if the data subject has "unambiguously" given consent, the processing is necessary to carry out a contract, the processing is necessary to protect the "vital interests" of the data subject (e.g., a medical emergency) or the processing is necessary for the performance of a task carried out for the public interest.

Articles 10, 11 and 12 address disclosure and consumer access to one's own data. Article 10 stipulates that a controller, when attempting to obtain personal information directly from a data subject, must identify itself, its purpose for processing the data, as well as the categories of data being processed and information on how consumers can access their data and correct inaccuracies. Article 11 is almost a repeat of article 10, except that it applies to personal information that has not been obtained directly from the data subject. In this case, controllers must follow the same rules of disclosure at the time personal data is recorded or when this data is about to be shared with a third party. Under Article 12, data controllers must, "at reasonable intervals and without excessive delay or expense," provide the data subject with confirmation, in an "intelligible form," of whether the data relating to him or her is being processed, the purpose of the processing, the categories of data being processed and the recipients of this data. The data subject is also given the right to correct inaccuracies and add to incomplete information. Article 14 gives data subjects the right to rectify and erase data and to block processing of data that is being used unlawfully.

Finally, articles 16 and 17 deal with confidentiality and security. Article 16 states that no one other than those with authority and who are under the instruction of the controller can process the data, unless required to do so by law. Article 17 states that a controller must implement "appropriate technical and organizational measures to protect personal data against accidental or unlawful destruction or accidental loss, alteration, unauthorized disclosure or access," particularly when such data is being transmitted over a network.

The processing of certain types of data is generally prohibited. Under Article 8, sensitive data that reveals racial or ethnic origin, political opinions, religious or philosophical beliefs, trade union membership or health or sex life cannot be processed. There are exceptions, however. In special circumstances, "explicit" consent would achieve exemption. As well, such information can be processed if providing such data is an obligation under employment law, is of vital interest to the data subject, is required for health-care purposes, is required in a criminal investigation or is a matter of public record.

One of the most controversial parts of the directive is Article 25, dealing with the transfer of personal data to countries that are not part of the European Union. The transfer of personal data outside of the EU is permitted only if the "country in question ensures an adequate level of protection." The determination of what constitutes an "adequate level of protection" depends on the circumstances surrounding the data transfer operation, the nature of the data (sensitive or nonsensitive), the purpose and duration of the processing operation, the country of origin and the country of destination. It also depends on "the rules of law, both general and sectoral, in force in the third country in question and the professional rules and security measures which are complied with in that country."

There are some exceptions to the "adequate protection" requirement, but article 25 nonetheless makes the European Union a disruptive force on the world stage when it comes to privacy legislation, since non-EU countries wanting to do business in the region may find themselves shut out if they fail to pass the "adequacy" test.[5] "The EU Directive represents a dramatic increase in the reach and importance of data protection laws," write Peter Swire and Robert Litan in *None of Your Business*.[6] In essence, the EU's outward-reaching regional law is imposing privacy standards on the international community at large, or at least any country wishing to do business with members of the EU. And who wouldn't want to do business there? With nearly 400 million people within its borders, the EU is one of the most important trading and commerce zones in the world. Between the U.S. and the EU alone, data transfers were valued at about $120 billion in 1999.[7] The directive will affect most countries in the world in some way, considering the global nature of data flow, trade and commerce.

The EU Directive on Data Protection has stirred up considerable concern in North America, to the extent that Canada, in an effort to meet the "adequacy"

---

[5] Exceptions to article 25 are contained in article 26. The transfer of personal information to a country that lacks its own adequate protection is permitted if the data subject has given "consent unambiguously;" the transfer of data is required to carry out a contract; the transfer is necessary or legally required in the public interest and the transfer is meant to protect the vital interest of the data subject.

[6] Peter Swire and Robert Litan, *None of Your Business*, (Washington, D.C.: Brookings Institution, 1998), p. 24.

[7] Mary Mosquera, "Global Web Privacy Presents Cultural Challenges," TechWeb News [online], September 13, 2000.

test, has developed its own national privacy legislation and the United States, at least for the time being, has negotiated a "Safe Harbor" agreement that will help to overcome the two regions' very different approaches to privacy protection.

Canada and PIPEDA

In April 2000, the Canadian Parliament passed Bill C-6, creating what is now called the Personal Information Protection and Electronic Documents Act, or PIPEDA. Like the EU directive, PIPEDA is an attempt to give consumers greater control over how the private sector handles their personal data. Another similarity is that the legislation imposes a national standard on all Canadian provinces and territories. If a province does not have its own substantially similar private-sector privacy legislation in place by January 1, 2004, the federal statute will apply to provincial businesses.

PIPEDA is based on the privacy principles identified by the Canadian Standards Association in its 1996 Model Code for the Protection of Personal Information, which itself is based on the OECD guidelines for fair information practices. (For the full text of PIPEDA and the CSA code, visit **www.privcom.gc. ca/legislation/index_e.asp**.) The CSA Code was largely a response to the EU Directive on Data Protection, which threatened Canada-EU data flow. Not surprisingly, the Canadian business community was at first resistant to legislation, arguing that self-regulation would be sufficient to protect consumer privacy rights. But that argument began to change in 1995, when John Gustavson, president of the Canadian Direct Marketing Association, or CDMA (now the Canadian Marketing Association), decided that baseline legislation based on the CSA code would be a better approach. Gustavson, speaking on behalf of the CDMA's 780 members, put out a press release on October 3 of that year to explain the association's position:

> Fundamental changes in our society are taking place in an era of information technology ... More and more we are seeing the inter-relation of databases and growth in the accumulation of transactional data. All Canadians have the right to know about and consent to the collection of personal information about them. And the CDMA

believes legislation is the most effective means of ensuring all private-sector organizations adhere to the same basic rules in handling this information.[8]

Gustavson's reasoning was simple: opting for relatively soft legislation today was better than waiting for "a bunch of horror stories that might lead to more draconian legislation tomorrow."[9] Support for legislation also came from Bruce Phillips, the federal privacy commissioner at the time, who began to realize that self-regulation wasn't living up to expectations. Meanwhile, the Information Highway Advisory Council, a group set up by the minister of industry, recommended to the federal government in 1995 that it use the CSA code as the basis for national privacy legislation. The result was PIPEDA, which came into force on January 1, 2001. The EU Commission ruled that PIPEDA provided "adequate protection" of personal information under EU standards, which means companies in the European Union will be able to exchange personal information with Canada when PIPEDA's third and final phase commences on January 1, 2004. The CSA code is appended to PIPEDA.

PIPEDA is being introduced in three phases. Phase 1 immediately applied to federally regulated businesses that collect, use, share or disclose personal data, including employee data, in the course of commercial activity. These businesses include banks, airports, airlines, telephone and cable companies, broadcasters and nuclear facilities. Personal health information is exempt from this phase of implementation. Individuals, artists, journalists, writers and researchers are permanently exempt if the data is collected for specific projects or individual use. Phase 1 also applies to any transmission of information across provincial or national borders for the purpose of a commercial transaction. This may affect organizations such as credit reporting agencies or those that lease, sell or exchange mailing lists. Foreign companies with Canadian subsidiaries, headquarters or offices are equally affected. Finally, phase 1 applies to *all* commercial activity in the Canadian territories — Yukon, the Northwest Territories and Nunavut.

---

[8] CDMA, "Direct Marketers Call for National Privacy Legislation" (press release, October 3, 1995).
[9] Tyler Hamilton, "Privacy Mishaps Can Sink Firms" Toronto *Star*, January 8, 2001.

Phase 2, which took effect on January 1, 2002, extends to commercial activity relating to personal health information — that is, any information about an individual's mental or physical health, including information about received medical services, such as tests and examinations. Phase 3 is scheduled to take force on January 1, 2004, when any commercial activity in the country that involves the collection, use or disclosure of personal information will be subject to the act. As mentioned, organizations may be exempt from PIPEDA if the activity in question is covered by substantially similar provincial legislation, which is the case in Quebec. It is expected that a number of provinces will have their own legislation by 2004, while smaller provinces with fewer resources will likely opt to be covered by the federal statute.

Under PIPEDA, all organizations handling personal data will eventually have to:

1. Show *accountability* for privacy abuses and breaches by developing internal polices and practices that protect personal data and by appointing a point-person, such as a chief privacy officer, who is responsible for compliance.
2. Demonstrate and communicate a *purpose* for the data being collected that a "reasonable person" would consider appropriate under the given circumstances.
3. Obtain direct and timely *consent* to gather, share and use data, and obtain additional consent when new purposes for the information are identified.
4. *Limit* the collection of data to a demonstrated purpose, without deceiving or misleading the data subjects.
5. *Limit* the use, disclosure and retention of data to a demonstrated purpose, making sure to destroy, erase or render anonymous information that is no longer required for that purpose.
6. Maintain *accuracy* of information being collected and used by keeping it up-to-date, complete and correct.
7. Assure *safeguards* to keep that information in the right hands and prevent accidental disclosure.
8. Be more *open* with information collection practices by informing customers, clients and employees of any policies and practices in place to manage their

personal information and by making these polices and practices understandable and easily available.

9. Provide individuals *access* to information about them and the ability to correct
or amend personal information that is found to be inaccurate or incomplete.

10. Give consumers an opportunity for *recourse* by developing simple and easily
accessible complaint procedures, by informing consumers of these procedures
and by investigating any complaints that are received.

Under PIPEDA, the privacy commissioner of Canada is given the power to
launch investigations in response to complaints or to audit the personal-
information management practices of organizations that are believed to be
contravening the law. The commissioner can subpoena witnesses and get search
warrants to aid in an investigation. If a breach of the law is determined, the
commissioner can attempt to mediate the dispute. If an organization persists
with practices deemed to contravene the law, the commissioner can publish
reports that may, when picked up by the press, damage an organization's
reputation in the court of public opinion. Organizations can also be taken to
federal court, where they may be fined as much as $100,000 (Cdn).

George Radwanski, who assumed the role of federal privacy commissioner
in September 2000, is the first federal privacy watchdog to oversee legislative
compliance in both the private and public sectors in Canada. Canadians can
now lodge complaints to the privacy commissioner if a public or private organization denies them access to data about them; collects such data without their
consent; uses or discloses personal data beyond the scope of original consent;
refuses to correct inaccurate or incomplete information; or does not adequately
safeguard the data.

One of the interesting features of PIPEDA is its "whistle-blowing" clause. Any
person or employee who believes an organization is violating privacy legislation
can notify the privacy commissioner and be assured that his or her identity will
be protected. It is also an offence for any organization to retaliate against an
employee it suspects or knows has complained to the commissioner.

"There is a careful balance in the act between what is needed to protect individual privacy without killing the growth of e-commerce," Gustavson of the CMA told us in an interview. "It's a delicate compromise. When we started I would have bet a fair amount of my own money that a compromise would never be reached." Jules Polonetsky, chief privacy officer of DoubleClick, said PIPEDA is representative of a new wave of privacy legislation that adheres to OECD guidelines and targets the private sector. "If your goal is to operate in lots and lots of different countries, you can pretty much do it consistently around the world if you follow the baselines of the OECD guidelines, which is the underpinnings of Bill C-6 [PIPEDA]."

Just as the EU directive affects U.S. companies doing business in Europe, PIPEDA will affect U.S. companies that rely on the transfer of personal data across the 49th parallel. But as Polonetsky pointed out, any company that adheres to the OECD guidelines is well on its way to compliance. And it might be worth the effort. After all, Canada continues to be the United States' largest trading partner. With Canada and the EU now on a similar legislative trajectory, and other countries around the world making similar moves, there's even more reason for U.S. companies to take note. Just as inconsistent national regimes can be the death knell of international commerce, international harmonization can facilitate commerce and reduce the costs associated with global trading.

U.S.-EU "Safe Harbor"

In the United States, the EU Directive on Data Protection is more than just European privacy legislation. It is viewed by many as an attempt by the European Union to create a de facto global privacy standard, one that imposes the will of Europe on the United States. U.S. firms that are in the habit of collecting, using and sharing consumer data in the absence of any domestic legislation now find themselves threatened with foreign prosecution if their data-collection practices cross into Europe.

To bridge the various privacy approaches adopted in the United States and Europe, the U.S. Department of Commerce and the European Commission agreed in 2000 to a voluntary "safe harbor" framework: a self-regulatory scheme that allows U.S. companies to meet the "adequacy" test under article 25 of the EU directive. U.S. companies participating in this safe harbor arrangement can continue to collect data from citizens of the European Union and at the same time avoid prosecution under the directive. There is, of course, a proviso: participating companies must be certified to be compliant with the safe harbor. As the U.S. Department of Commerce explains:

> To be assured of safe harbor benefits, an organization needs to self-certify annually to the Department of Commerce in writing that it agrees to adhere to the safe harbor's requirements, which include elements such as notice, choice, access and enforcement. It must also state in its published privacy policy statement that it adheres to safe harbor. The Department of Commerce will maintain a list of all organizations that file self-certification letters and make both the list and the self-certification letters publicly available. To qualify for the safe harbor, an organization can (1) join a self-regulatory privacy program that adheres to the safe harbor's requirements; or (2) develop its own self-regulatory privacy policy that conforms to the safe harbor.[10]

At the time of writing, more than 200 companies had signed the safe harbor agreement, including big-name players such as Intel, Hewlett-Packard, Dun & Bradstreet, Microsoft, and DoubleClick. "This is an important way for us to make sure we have a set of baseline standards that we can follow," said Polonetsky of DoubleClick.[11] Intel lawyer David Hoffman said, "We do not believe that something completely [based] on voluntary compliance would be an appropriate system."[12] With such major players on board, the expectation is that more companies will see value in participating in the program.

---

[10] "Safe Harbor Overview," available at the U.S. Department of Commerce Web site, **www.export.gov/safeharbor/sh_overview.html.** This Web site contains detailed information for any company interested in learning more about the EU-US Safe Harbor agreement.
[11] Brian Krebs, "DoubleClick Joins US-EU Safe Harbor Program" Newsbytes [online], August 22, 2001.
[12] "Intel to Abide by EU Privacy Rules," Reuters, July 2, 2001.

Some companies have decided not to participate, at least so far, because they view compliance with safe harbor to be a costly exercise. However, any company practicing self-regulation by following the OECD's fair information practices has already taken most of the required steps, thereby minimizing any additional costs. Other companies simply don't like the inflexibility of entering such a broad and far-reaching agreement. They know that as soon as they commit in writing to a specified set of principles, they become bound by a public promise. But as Jacques Francoeur, director of trust practices with NetFront Communications, says, companies make binding promises every day simply by posting a privacy policy on their Web sites. "When a company posts a privacy policy or makes public a set of management assertions, the potential or implicit risk [of non-compliance] shifts to an explicit risk. This is because the organization can now be benchmarked against its own policy or stated assertion. If found not in compliance, or to be conducting practices not disclosed or in contradiction to its policy, it can be prosecuted and fined for misrepresentation."[13]

In our view, companies that choose to participate in the safe harbor clearly have certain benefits over those that do not. For one, all 15 members of the European Union must recognize that a safe harbor company meets the "adequacy" test of the directive. The need for a safe harbor company to seek approval from a European Union country before transferring data will be waived or permission automatically granted. The result is a much more streamlined process, since a firm not participating in the safe harbor arrangement may be asked to sign a standardized, potentially stricter pro-privacy business contract with each EU company it conducts data transfers with. "The safe harbor framework offers a simpler and cheaper means of complying with the adequacy requirements of the directive, which should particularly benefit small and medium enterprises," according to the U.S. Department of Commerce.[14]

---

[13] Jacques Francoeur, "Online Trust: The Five Principles" (executive white paper, NetFront Communications, Sunnyvale, Calif., March 1, 2000).
[14] U.S. Department of Commerce, "Safe Harbor Overview."

Essentially, U.S. companies participating in the safe harbor agreement must, in writing, declare that they agree and will comply with the following seven privacy principles, which, again, are based on the OECD guidelines:

- **Notice** — Organizations must notify individuals about the purposes for which they collect and use personal information and the types of third parties this information will be disclosed to. They must also provide contact information so individuals can make inquiries, lodge complaints or attempt to limit the use or disclosure of their information.

- **Choice** — Organizations must give individuals the opportunity to opt out of situations where personal information about them will be disclosed to a third party or used for purposes beyond those originally expressed. For sensitive information (i.e., medical), consent must be explicit, such that individuals must opt in before data is disclosed to third parties or used for additional purposes.

- **Onward Transfer** — To disclose information to a third party, an organization must apply the notice and choice principles. It must also make sure that the third party is a participant in the safe harbor agreement and therefore complies with the EU directive "adequacy" finding. Otherwise, the two organizations must enter into a written agreement that requires the third party to apply the safe harbor principles.

- Access — Individuals must have access to their personal information and must be given the opportunity to correct, amend or delete that information when it is found to be inaccurate. In the case of nonsensitive information or data that poses little threat to privacy, a company may choose to deny access if the cost of providing it outweighs the privacy risk.

- **Security** — Organizations must take reasonable precautions to protect personal information from loss, misuse and unauthorized access, disclosure, alteration and destruction.

- **Data Integrity** — Personal information must be relevant for the purposes for which it is to be used. Steps should be taken to make sure the data is accurate, complete and current for its intended use.

- **Enforcement** — To ensure compliance with safe harbor principles, "independent recourse mechanisms" must be readily available and affordable so individuals have a way to lodge complaints and dispute the data-collection practices of a company. Such mechanisms must provide for ways to investigate complaints, resolve disputes and award damages where applicable laws or rules apply. Procedures for verifying compliance and ensuring remedies for non-compliance must also be in place.

The Department of Commerce outlines two ways of achieving the enforcement principle. The first option is for a company to join a private-sector privacy seal program that itself complies with safe harbor. The second option is to submit to "government supervisory authorities," such as the Federal Trade Commission, or by making a commitment to cooperate with relevant authorities in Europe. It appears that the FTC will play a major role in enforcement. "Where a company relies in whole or in part on self-regulation in complying with the safe harbor principles, its failure to comply with such self-regulation must be actionable under federal or state law prohibiting unfair and deceptive acts, or it is not eligible to join safe harbor," states the Department of Commerce. The FTC can seek administrative orders and civil penalties of up to $12,000 a day. Of course, this doesn't include the very damaging bad publicity that can arise when investigations are launched or penalties are handed out.

Finally, an organization that repeatedly violates safe harbor principles will be removed from the list, after which it will be unable to take advantage of the streamlined process provided through the agreement. This, in effect, could blacklist a company, since European organizations that are legally bound by the EU directive will be hesitant to enter into one-on-one contracts with known violators. Also, U.S. companies that have operations in Europe but are not part of safe harbor open themselves up to legal action from data-protection authorities in Europe. David Aaron, former undersecretary for international trade at the Department of Commerce, said it is only a matter of time before European officials begin flexing their muscles by launching high-profile privacy suits against U.S. companies. He said the highly competitive nature of some industries could see rivals snitching on each other to European privacy authorities.[15]

Other U.S. Developments

But the tide she is a-turning. We have a Congress that is getting the word from constituents; a judiciary that remembers Justice Brandeis and his "right to be let alone;" a press beginning to assign privacy as a beat; and a man in the White House who may not be averse to being thought of as the privacy president.

William Safire, "The Privacy President?" NYTimes.com, April 19, 2001.

As the global reach of the EU Directive on Data Protection puts pressure on U.S. organizations, several sector-specific laws and a slew of proposed privacy bills are beginning to apply pressure on the domestic level. Privacy has become a highly politicized issue in the United States, perhaps as a result of the FTC's May 2000 request for federal privacy legislation. (As you will read later, the FTC has since backed away from this position.) During the 2000 presidential campaign that followed, many congressmen and senators ran on a privacy platform, something unheard of in the 1990s. But after the election of the Bush administration, the mood quickly changed in 2001. Nearly 50 privacy-related bills were introduced in the 107th Congress, but Republicans and Democrats remained divided on key details, such as the types of data that should be covered and whether opt-in or opt-out consent should be favored.

Republicans generally consider privacy a low priority, with many viewing data protection legislation as a potential threat to economic growth. There is a movement within Congress to establish a commission responsible for studying and reporting on the need for legislation. This commission would be given 18 months to gather its findings, a timeline that critics consider a Republican

---

[15] Kathleen Melymuka, "Premier 100: Data Privacy Key to Global Business, Panel Says," **www.computerworld.com,** May 21, 2001.

stalling tactic. However, early in his term, President George W. Bush was surprisingly pro-privacy in his views, although the jury is still out on his actions. (These pro-privacy views were expressed before the terrorist attacks on September 11, 2001. Since then, President Bush's focus has understandably been on national security.) As well, the Democrats' control of the Senate has added some momentum to the privacy debate.

Opinions on how things will turn out are divided, and the outcome is even more uncertain in light of September 11. Some believe that broad-reaching federal privacy legislation could still be years away as long as Republicans and Democrats quibble over details, and because post-9/11 priorities in the United States — and indeed, around the world — have hastily shifted to public security at the expense of civil liberties. Others, recognizing that private-sector business practices and law-enforcement efforts against terrorism are two separate causes, say bipartisan support for federal legislation could come sooner as the private sector and politicians on both sides of the debate look for common ground in an attempt to pre-empt a potentially stricter or more complicated patchwork of state laws. John McCarthy, director of Forrester Research's Internet policy group, said the ultimate legislative catalyst is likely to come from a "privacy Chernobyl" — or, as one senator called it, an "Exxon Valdez" of privacy — that spurs politicians into action.

The privacy bills under consideration address a wide range of issues: genetic data, wireless tracking services, workplace surveillance, "opt in" versus "opt out," identity theft, consumer profiling, e-mail spam, social security numbers and law-enforcement technologies, to name just a few. Still, some action has already been taken. Specifically, privacy-friendly federal laws exist today that protect financial and medical data, as well as limit the online collection of personal information from children. Also, privacy amendments to existing laws strengthen data protection in the United States. Consider the following:

Children's Online Privacy Protection Act (COPPA)

This legislation, which came into force in 2000, stipulates what a Web site must state in its privacy policy if it caters to children under the age of 13. It also outlines when and how a site operator must get "verifiable" consent from a parent, as well as any responsibilities the operator has to further protect child privacy online. Verifiable consent must in some cases come through the phone, mail or fax if the child's identifiable personal information is to be publicly posted or shared with others. If the data is used for internal marketing, then consent through e-mail is acceptable until 2005, after which more verifiable confirmation will be required. Generally, a privacy policy must be clearly posted and must explain the kinds of children's information being collected, whether it is collected directly through the child or passively through cookies, how the information is used, whether it is disclosed to other parties, and what options the parent has in providing consent. The Children's Advertising Review Unit of the Council of Better Business Bureaus, the Entertainment Software Rating Board and TRUSTe (an online privacy-seal program) have all been approved by the FTC as "safe harbors" for COPPA, meaning Web sites that participate in one of these self-regulatory programs are deemed compliant with the law. COPPA has so far been successful in changing the way Web sites do business with children — though many operators continue to be fined. In April 2001, the FTC required the operators of three Web sites — Girlslife.com, Bigmailbox.com and Insidetheweb.com — to pay $100,000 in penalties and to dispose of certain data that had been collected. Exactly a year later, the Ohio Art Company, maker of the popular Etch-A-Sketch toy, was fined $35,000, and another 50 Internet operators were sent terse warnings about their collection of children's information.

On a related note, a U.S. education reform bill signed into law in January 2002 contains a clause that limits the collection of student information by private-sector organizations. Companies often give schools much-needed computer equipment, Internet services and other products in exchange for the right to monitor students' Web habits and e-commerce purchases. Under the law, parents can exclude their children from such data-collection arrangements by notifying the school.

For more information on COPPA, go to **www.ftc.gov/bcp/conline/pubs/ buspubs/coppa.htm**.

Gramm-Leach-Bliley Act (GLBA)

The privacy provisions of this 2000 financial reform law require that financial institutions wishing to disclose the personal information of customers to nonaffiliated companies must provide their customers with notice of their data-sharing practices. They must also give customers an opportunity to opt out of certain disclosures. Companies are subject to the privacy provisions of GLBA if they offer financial products and services to customers, such as banking, tax return preparation, financial planning, credit cards, mortgages and insurance plans. The act of notice must be continued each year, and it must detail the types of non-public personal information being collected and disclosed, the parties to whom this information may be disclosed, how to opt out of such disclosure and what measures have been taken to safeguard the data and assure confidentiality. GLBA provides disclosure requirements that do not exist in the Fair Credit Reporting Act of 1970. There is considerable debate about what constitutes a financial institution under the law, since many online and offline ventures are not considered financial institutions in the traditional sense but nonetheless provide financial services and products to their customers. Yahoo and America Online are examples of two Internet companies that have taken measures to comply with GLBA. Some lawyers suggest that any large company engaged in financial services activity might want to follow the rules of GLBA — as a precaution. The FTC and a number of other regulatory bodies are responsible for setting more detailed rules for safeguarding financial data. Under proposed rules from the FTC, each financial institution would have to appoint someone to coordinate safeguard programs — such as more thorough background checks on partners and employees — and assess security risks in the various operations of a company. The FTC stated, "To ensure flexibility the proposed rule provides that each information security program should be appropriate to the size and complexity of the financial institution, the nature and scope of its activities, and the sensitivity of the customer information at issue." The FTC has the power to penalize violators with administrative orders, fines, license revocation, or license denial.

For the privacy provision text of the Gramm-Leach-Bliley Act, go to **www.ftc.gov/ privacy/glbact/index/html**.

Health Insurance Portability and Accountability Act (HIPAA)

When Congress enacted HIPAA in 1996, it mandated the creation of privacy standards for personally identifiable health and medical information. The privacy rule came into effect in 2001. The aim is to set a federal floor for safeguarding the electronic movement of this information, since there are many holes in the old "mosaic" of federal and state laws. In many instances, there was nothing to stop a health plan from passing along a person's medical information to a bank or an employer. Based on this information, a bank might decide to refuse a mortgage or credit card, or an employer might decide against hiring someone because of a certain health condition. The privacy provisions set a minimum federal standard, yet more stringent state laws will continue to apply over and above HIPAA. In general, the HIPAA privacy rule gives patients greater control over their health information and sets boundaries for the use and sharing of health records, the movement of which has become much more fluid in the age of the Internet and high-speed networking. The privacy rule also outlines what safeguards must be implemented to protect personal health information and what penalties — fines or sanctions — can be imposed on those who violate patients' privacy rights. HIPAA lets patients find out how their information may be used and what disclosures of their information have been made. It requires that information being released be kept to the minimum needed for the purpose of the disclosure. Finally, it gives patients the right to access, examine and obtain a copy of their own health and medical records, as well as the option to request corrections. All "covered entities" under the law must develop clear privacy procedures, assign a person who is responsible for overseeing and implementing these procedures, and train employees to know and respect such procedures. These organizations must also communicate or provide information to patients about what privacy rights they have under the law and how their information can be used. The regulatory body overseeing HIPAA is the federal Department of Health and Human Services, which is open to modifying the HIPAA privacy rule to correct any unintended negative effects on the delivery of health care. The rule continues to be contested by the health-care community.

For more information on HIPAA and its privacy rules, visit **aspe.os.dhhs.gov/ admnsimp**.

Bankruptcy Law Reform

When bankrupt online toy seller Toysmart.com announced in 2000 that it planned to sell its database of customer information, a huge controversy erupted. At a time when dot-com companies were dropping like flies, what was there to stop these desperate ventures from breaking their privacy policies in an effort to sell the massive amounts of consumer data they had collected? After the Toysmart announcement, consumer and privacy groups, as well as TRUSTe, pleaded with federal regulators to step up to the plate. The result was a privacy bill, part of broader bankruptcy legislation reform, that prohibits the sale of customer databases if such a transaction contravenes a previously stated privacy policy. However, a court can permit the sale if, after due consideration of the facts, circumstances and conditions of the sale, there appears to be no major impact on privacy.

The FTC says it is more committed than ever to enforcing privacy laws in the United States. FTC chairman Robert Pitofsky was replaced in June 2001 by Timothy Muris, a law professor at George Mason University in Virginia and a former director of the FTC's Bureau of Competition and the Bureau of Consumer Protection. When Muris was appointed to the chairman's position, there were doubts that he would be as active as Pitofsky on privacy. But as Muris settled into his new position, he said that he takes the issue of privacy very seriously. "I've spent more time on privacy than any other issue — a lot more," Muris said in one media report.

In October 2001, Muris announced that he was increasing the size of his privacy enforcement staff by nearly 50 per cent to combat problems with online fraud, spam, deceptive telemarketing, identity theft and companies that do not live up to their privacy policies. And although he backed away from the FTC's request (under Pitofsky) for federal privacy legislation, calling such a move too premature, two of the FTC's five commissioners, as well as privacy groups and key politicians, insisted that baseline legislative standards, in addition to self-regulation, are still the only way to get all companies playing by the same rules. However, Muris did not completely rule out future legislation. He hinted that the FTC could change its position if privacy-protection initiatives by the private sector, and the existing patchwork of U.S. legislation, continue to fall short of expectations.

Of course, legislators need not seek permission from the FTC to push for a federal privacy law. A week after Muris's decision, a bipartisan group of U.S. lawmakers — apparently disagreeing with the FTC's change of heart — pushed forward with a private-sector federal privacy bill. Even against a backdrop of terrorism and fear, those in power continue to recognize the importance of consumer privacy protection in the United States.

Asia/Pacific Rim

Other parts of the world have passed or are considering privacy legislation that will impose new rules of conduct on the private sector. Some of these laws are in direct response to the EU directive. Hong Kong and New Zealand both have private-sector legislation predating the EU directive, and Australia recently passed legislation to put it more in line with the European Union. Thailand finished drafting its first data-protection law in 2001. The draft is based on the EU directive and legislation in New Zealand and Hong Kong. Meanwhile, the Japanese cabinet approved a data-protection bill in 2001; it is expected to come into force in 2003. Government agencies in Japan would be empowered to issue directives covering the use of personal data and to punish offenders, either through a hefty fine or a prison sentence of up to six months.

The Bottom Line

Privacy legislation will be a fact of life in the new economy. Most, if not all, businesses will have to take the global legislative environment into account when they are handling consumer information and developing business plans that require the regular collection, use and sharing of customer data. Despite the rules that privacy laws impose, any company already following the OECD's Code of Fair Information Practices has an advantage over those that do not.

Legislation creates a level playing field where all organizations and competitors must play by the same rules. In such an environment, consumers will become more trusting of online businesses and more willing to hand over their personal information. Businesses, meanwhile, will come to incorporate fair information practices into their operations, to the point where respect for consumer privacy becomes second nature in any commercial transaction.

Legislation, however, tends only to create baseline minimum standards for conduct. Companies that embrace best practices, and generally treat privacy as a business issue, will gain significant advantages over rivals that are focused on legal compliance alone.

Chapter 5

Privacy: The Next Business Imperative

"Anyone today who thinks the privacy issue
has peaked is greatly mistaken ...
We are in the early stages of a
sweeping change in attitudes that will
fuel political battles and put once-routine
business practices under the microscope."

Forrester Research, 2001

A Competitive Edge

Privacy has many faces: it is a human rights issue, a legal issue, a technological issue and a consumer issue. But privacy is also a business issue — a competitive issue. It is also a customer service issue. Ignore self-regulation and legislation for a moment and focus on your company's goals of building trusting, long-term relationships with existing customers; of converting browsing consumers into buying customers; of securing a competitive advantage over industry rivals; and of building a widely respected online and offline brand. Now, imagine you are an executive at a different company that, five or ten years into the future, has made no effort to introduce fair information practices into its business operations. At such a company, do you believe it would have been more difficult to achieve the above-mentioned goals? We have no doubt that it would.

As awareness of privacy builds, any company that doesn't treat privacy as a core business issue will find itself at a disadvantage in the Internet marketplace. Its customers will have more reason to abandon their loyalties and will be less likely to buy its products. These same customers will be more inclined to seek out competitors who can give them the control they desire and increasingly demand over their personal information. Ignoring privacy reflects negatively on a company's brand, which, in a society of networked consumers who are increasingly savvy about privacy issues, can fall out of favor literally overnight. "This is an issue that, if you're on the wrong side of it, you can't possibly win," says Michael Power, a legal expert on privacy matters and a partner with Canadian law firm Gowling, Lafleur, Henderson.

In this chapter we will discuss what it takes, and costs, to be on the right side of the privacy issue. We will take a look at the question of ownership of the personal information relating to consumers. Does it belong to the individual to whom it relates? Does it belong to the company that collects, organizes and ascribes value to it? Or is it a partnership between the two? We will then explore how to conduct a cost-benefit analysis of becoming privacy compliant. After that, you will learn about privacy diagnostics, privacy impact assessments, the difference between a privacy consultant and a privacy architect, and the importance of privacy policies, seals, symbols, audits and in-depth training. We will end the chapter with two pieces of advice that should help your business avoid the potential pitfalls of implementing a privacy program.

Whose Information Is It, Anyway?

Our names and addresses and personal transactions are valuable information assets worthy of recognition that we have property rights in them. Unless we assert these rights, we will lose them. If such information has economic value, we should receive something of value in return for its use by others.

Anne Wells Branscomb, *Who Owns Information?*

The above statement may be cause for alarm and a source of contention for many in the business community, who most likely consider the customer information they collect and add value to as their own property. This is understandable, since the lifeblood of many organizations is the information that pumps through their operations. On the other hand, there is a growing belief among consumer groups and consumers themselves that personal information is the personal property of the individual it came from. This notion of personal information as property (by which we mean information that could form the basis of a contract) has been gathering momentum as consumers become increasingly aware of the commercial value of their personal data in a digital economy. Who's right?

The consumers' argument, which you may or may not agree with, certainly has merit to consumers. Therefore, organizations should at least attempt to consider it, thereby gaining a better understanding of customer concerns. For many people, there is not much difference between the collection and use of their personal information and the shooting of a photographic portrait to be published in a magazine. Both are representations of the individual. If someone takes a picture of you and wants to reproduce it in a book, the normal practice is for the photographer to obtain your consent. You might then be in a position to collect royalties from its use. But if someone gathers information about you — where you live, what you do, your habits and your lifestyle — and then reproduces it electronically in a list that is sold over and over again to a variety of organizations, chances are you won't even know it is happening. That is, not until you begin to receive such annoyances as junk mail, telemarketing calls, spam e-mail and pop-up Web ads. These daily intrusions are not only a nuisance but to some an outrage, because personal information is being used as an entry point into their lives — a door through which visitors come in, whether they're invited or not. Some people may view this as electronic trespassing. It is for this reason that people wish to have greater control over the "door," so they can let in those whom they trust and value and keep out those who are not welcome — identity thieves, scammers, overly aggressive marketers and anybody else they deem to be a threat or major annoyance. (See **Chapter 8** for a closer look at consumer worries.)

Lawrence Hunter and James Rule, in a research paper presented to the Ontario Information and Privacy Commissioner in 1993, suggested that every person should own the rights to the commercial exploitation of his or her personal information, and these rights could in turn be retained or sold, much like mineral rights or movie rights.[1] The only caveat, of course, is that this would apply only to commercial transactions. In the context of the rights of citizens in relation to the state, however, privacy should not be a matter of negotiation: legislated protections will always be necessary to safeguard the fundamental human rights of individuals in the context of government.

In response to Hunter and Rule, many businesses might argue that the customer information they possess lacks value until it has been organized, updated and analyzed, similar to the way raw metals are simply rock until they are mined and processed and turned into gold rings, cutlery and car fenders. Since costs are incurred to inject value into raw data, many businesses argue that they own the personal information of their customers, just like any other property or company asset. Besides, business might also argue that consumers are in many cases already compensated for their information in the form of greater convenience, personalization, loyalty points, discounts, electronic coupons, special promotions and at times even free merchandise.

So we are left with this dilemma: consumers and businesses at opposite ends, in a seemingly endless tug-of-war. How can these two opposing views be harmonized? How can both consumers and businesses claim ownership over the same information, the same property?

Why not consider a partnership? In any partnership, each owner has a responsibility to the other yet they share common goals. Both want to benefit from or be rewarded for the information collected. Both want the information

---

[1] Ann Cavoukian and Don Tapscott, *Who Knows: Safeguarding Your Privacy in a Networked World* (New York: McGraw-Hill, 1997), p. 91.

to be useful, purposeful, accurate and up-to-date. Both want to prevent data from falling into the wrong hands. At the same time, decisions as to how this information will be used cannot be made unilaterally. Consumers must be given a seat at the table, as well as greater control over the destiny of their personal data; they need to be able to enter into contracts relating to the uses of their personal information. By providing their customers with adequate notice, choice and access, businesses will send the message to customers that they are being treated as equal partners. By seeking customer consent when plans for how information will be used are introduced or changed, businesses will also be providing better customer service. Failure to do so will result in a breakdown of the partnership and a loss of trust that will be hard to recapture. "Businesses can no longer take their customers for granted," wrote Ann Cavoukian and Don Tapscott in *Who Knows: Safeguarding Your Privacy in a Networked World*. "The consumers of today have great expectations, and if you fail to meet them, they will move on to companies that can."[2] Satisfying consumer expectations is a major component of good customer service.

From our perspective, it may be useful to go one step further by *choosing* to treat the personal information of your customers as their personal property, as a courtesy. Taking this approach engenders a unique respect for what one can and cannot do with someone else's information. If consumers feel they have ownership over their personal information — and therefore personal control over how it is used — they are more likely to entrust that information to you. Organizations that choose this path may be pleasantly surprised by the results. Businesses may fear that customers will have exaggerated expectations of what their information is worth, but we believe the marketplace, as with every single information product and service, can manage this effectively. Ultimately, we believe the marketplace will be the best at determining the value of a name, address or other type of demographic data.

---

[2] *Ibid.*, p. 167.

A Cost-Benefit Analysis

Throughout this book, we have discussed that the main benefit to having good privacy practices is that it nurtures a trusting environment in which commerce can better flourish. Consumers who trust the companies they deal with and who have confidence that their privacy is being respected will feel more comfortable engaging in online transactions and entering into long-term business relationships. Though it may be difficult to put a monetary value on these benefits, some studies suggest that businesses are missing out on billions of e-commerce dollars because of consumers' privacy fears. Any company that acts to ease those fears can potentially reap the rewards that others will miss out on.

Still, there remains considerable concern in the business community that the cost of privacy compliance will be prohibitively high, particularly for smaller companies that lack the financial resources to implement privacy regimes. Much debate over the cost issue was triggered in 2001 after Robert Hahn, director of the Joint Center for Regulatory Studies of the American Enterprise Institute and the Brookings Institution, introduced a study that suggested new rules for privacy could cost U.S. businesses between $9 billion and $36 billion.[3]

The study, underwritten by the Association for Competitive Technology, reached what we feel are biased and unrealistically high conclusions based on information gathered from 17 Internet consulting firms. These firms were each asked to estimate how much they would charge to modify a Web site to comply with any of the access and enforcement provisions of proposed online privacy legislation. Estimates ranged from $46,000 to $670,000. Hahn took those figures, determined that the average cost would be $100,000, and then multiplied this amount by the number of sites he estimated would be affected by new Internet privacy rules. Out of 3.6 million U.S. Web sites thought to collect personal information, Hahn figured that anywhere between 2.61 per cent (or

[3] Robert W. Hahn, "An Assessment of the Costs of Proposed Online Privacy Legislation" (May 7, 2001; **www.actonline.com**).

94,000) and 10 per cent (or 360,000) would choose to make the $100,000 investment, placing the cost range at between $9 billion and $36 billion.

"If correct, that means more struggling tech companies would be driven to bankruptcy," wrote Declan McCullagh, Washington bureau chief for Wired News, in one of his online reports. Hahn's study quickly made its way to McCullagh's Politech Web site at **www.politechbot.com**, where debate erupted over the reliability of its findings. Perhaps the most thorough and cutting criticism of the study came from author, law professor and privacy expert Peter Swire, who wrote on the Web site that there were "serious analytic flaws" in Hahn's conclusions. "The assumptions in the study drive toward substantially overstated costs," wrote Swire, adding later that "the Hahn study quantifies only the costs of privacy protection, with no estimate of the benefits."

According to Swire, Hahn did not adequately address a number of key issues:

- Many companies, through self-regulation, have already addressed many privacy concerns in recent years, meaning the additional cost of complying with legislation would presumably be less than starting from scratch. "It's as if one reports the cost of building a house without subtracting out the cost of a foundation and a couple of walls that are already in place."
- There was a failure to distinguish between small and large Web sites. Obviously, simpler sites would not have to spend as much as complex ones, but the $100,000 average cost cited by Hahn is based on building a large, complex site.
- Hahn used higher than required standards for building a privacy-compliant data-management system, even though different Web sites have different needs and it is unlikely that any legislation based on fair information practices would call for such measures. Swire said it is not surprising that the consultants surveyed for the study produced such a high price tag. "The $100,000 average estimated cost is a reflection of an unreasonably strict set of criteria, rather than of the likely cost of actual compliance with legislation."

- Finally, Hahn assumes that all consulting work on a privacy-compliant system would be a custom job, requiring, each time, that new software be designed from the ground up. Instead, Swire believes a likely scenario is that less expensive, off-the-shelf software packages will be moderately tailored to suit a company's needs. Over time, like any product, the costs will drop substantially. There are already signs that this is happening. (See "How to Diagnose Privacy" later in this Chapter.)

Swire added that the incremental cost of compliance could be further reduced "because privacy compliance will likely be undertaken as part of a broader upgrading of a site, of the sort that is often done in the rapidly changing Internet environment." In fact, efforts to become compliant with fair information practices are likely to produce many unforeseen benefits. The year 2000, or Y2K, bug, for example, forced thousands of companies to take stock of their information systems and, where necessary, upgrade technologies. In doing so, organizations were also given the opportunity to streamline processes, create efficiencies and eliminate obsolete or redundant information systems. Similarly, getting a solid and comprehensive handle on data flow and infor-mation management will help an organization identify inefficiencies, discover misplaced or inaccurate data, flush away useless data and detect potential problems — well beyond privacy — that could lead to a better run, more profitable business. "Privacy saves money," wrote privacy policy consultant Robert Gellman in his report "Privacy, Consumers, and Costs." "If privacy rules force record keepers to keep fewer records or to maintain records for a shorter period, the costs of record maintenance will be reduced."[4] Simply put, it's a great opportunity to clean house.

Pierrot Peladeau, a long-standing privacy advocate, lawyer and business consultant, has helped many companies in Quebec introduce privacy polices

---

[4] Robert Gellman, "Privacy, Consumers, and Costs" (March 2002, **www.epic.org/reports/ dmfprivacy.html**).

into their organizations. Peladeau reported that a number of companies he worked with saved hundreds of thousands of dollars by introducing privacy-protective measures that overhauled their information practices. In one company, the time required to read outdated information in customers' files amounted to a few thousand hours a year. Thousands of hours had been wasted annually collecting, compiling and storing information that was unneeded and never used. In another example, a nineteen-page form was reduced to one page, saving considerable financial and human resources. For this reason, Peladeau considers data protection to be a cost-reduction tool that saves money. He found that a manager could easily waste up to the equivalent of a month per year in poor information-management practices.[5]

Keep in mind that privacy has been regulated in European Union countries for many years in both the public and private sectors. The economy there has not been adversely affected. The cost of protecting privacy has not driven companies to bankruptcy.

Privacy Infringement as an Externality[6]

Violations of information privacy can be viewed as an external cost, or externality, in the same way that environmental protection was originally — and to a great extent, still is — considered an external burden. Nobel laureate Ronald Coase introduced the concept of external cost, which is essentially a cost produced by one entity but borne by another. For example, a manufacturing process may cause pollution. If the manufacturer is not required to clean up the pollution, it creates a negative externality in the form of environmental deterioration and health problems for those living in the neighboring communities. Coase observed that externalities relate to unpriced consequences that can have an effect on the parties involved. For example, if a manufacturing plant pollutes

---

[5] *Supra*, note 1, at pp. 191-92.

[6] Special thanks to Dr. George Tomko and Professor Larry Smith for their invaluable assistance with this section.

the environment, it harms those who are exposed. Conversely, shutting down the plant or requiring that pollution controls be added increases costs, which in turn harms those who buy and sell its manufactured products. In a similar vein, businesses that indiscriminately misuse consumer information often create an external cost in the form of privacy infringement, and that cost is borne by the individual whose private life has been exposed, whose safety is perhaps compromised or whose mortgage or job applications have been unfairly rejected. However, placing the onus on companies to remedy or prevent privacy violations would increase their costs and these costs, in turn, would eventually be passed on to customers. In both cases, the externality exists, regardless of who bears the costs.

To resolve this conflict, Coase argues that the burden should be placed where the cost is the least, to maximize society's welfare. In the case of privacy, this would require businesses to remedy the externality. In our view, it would be far more costly and extremely difficult for individuals to prevent or avoid the burden associated with the misuses of their personal information (simply locating and tracking the databases involved would be an enormous challenge); business could handle such costs with relative ease. Notwithstanding that the "lowest cost" strategy may not always lead to the most ethical choice of who should bear the cost, in the case of privacy we will argue that it does — businesses, not consumers, create these "privacy externalities" by their misuses of their customers' personal information. A similar case was made for placing the burden on manufacturers to install smokestack scrubbers versus allowing countless individuals to inhale dirty air.

The question that then arises is how these costs should be handled. Should they be dealt with in a proactive manner, where privacy practices are built in up front, or in a reactive, liability regime that compensates a person or group of people for damages caused by the unauthorized or improper use of their personal information? Coase and subsequent researchers have demonstrated that it is socially desirable for an externality to be eliminated when the expense of doing so is less than the damage it causes. That said, what is the least costly way of eliminating the externality? We believe that the cost of proactively implementing privacy practices designed to prevent the externalities from developing would be far less expensive than the cost of privacy infringement that would result from a liability regime — litigation, regulatory penalties, loss of consumer confidence and trust, damaged reputation, lost business, loss of market share, and inaccurate, poor-quality information. "The cost of a privacy 'PR blowout' can range from tens of thousands to millions of dollars, depending on the company's size and the visibility of its brand, and this doesn't include lost business and damage to reputation," states Forrester Research.[7]

Some organizations may choose to take their chances, in the same way that homeowners or business owners may choose not to take out property insurance: they weigh the likelihood and estimated cost of fire, flood or theft against the cost of the insurance policy and decide to assume the risk themselves. They favor an *ex post* model, preferring to deal with the consequences after they occur, rather than protecting themselves beforehand. We believe that this is a very risky strategy for privacy, and it is doomed to backfire. First, individuals, consumer groups, attorneys general and politicians have become much more active on the issue of privacy, resulting in increased enforcement and litigation. Second, it is impossible to predict the costs of dealing with consequences later (in an *ex post* regime), creating an undesirable level of uncertainty that both markets and shareholders typically shun. Third, the firm forfeits the opportunity to plan for and clearly identify costs that will be incurred as it moves forward and may, therefore, fail to develop an appropriate pricing structure. Finally, privacy is good business, pure and simple, and, as we have argued, an *ex post* approach to the issue ignores this fact completely.

We have seen numerous environmental cases, as well as high-profile, high-dollar tobacco lawsuits, where such external costs can come back to haunt industries through an *ex post*, or after-the-fact liability, regime. As you will read in the next section, consumer litigation is gaining momentum as new legislation takes hold and consumers become more aware of their privacy rights. Consequently, the ability to impose these costs on businesses is increasing. We

---

[7] "Surviving the Privacy Revolution" (Forrester Research, February 2001).

believe that an *ex ante,* or proactive, model, in which a company internalizes privacy costs and thus takes them into account in its privacy policy, is preferable to an *ex post,* or liability, regime. In other words, the cost today for a company to implement a privacy infrastructure is less than the expected value of the cost that may (and most likely will) arise over time.

Implementing a proactive, build-it-in privacy plan will also be beneficial for the company in both the intermediate and long terms, which in turn, will maximize society's gains and best protect personal privacy. Michael Erdle, a privacy and Internet lawyer with Deeth Williams, told us that the benefits of such an approach will, over time, become much clearer. "It costs money, which is especially discouraging when there are downturns in the economy and people are reluctant to spend, but a lot of businesses are realizing that it's money well spent."

There is no doubt that a company will have to incur some upfront capital and ongoing costs to implement and maintain good information-privacy practices. To help minimize this cost, some of the initial work can be done internally and with the aid of free or inexpensive instructional software. At some point, depending on the size of your business and the complexity of its information requirements, you may feel it necessary to hire external consultants or buy more sophisticated security and information-management software. Some larger companies, particularly online business-to-consumer ventures, may even choose to hire a privacy point person, such as a corporate privacy officer, who can be held accountable for all data-protection initiatives. We believe all of these measures should be viewed, like any other operational or procedural measure, as a cost of doing *good* business — rather than a penalty imposed from the outside.

The Unpredictable Cost: Litigation

Dr. Alan Westin, for his bimonthly report on consumer privacy litigation, tracked more than 50 consumer privacy cases in the United States as of spring 2001. Seven of those cases had achieved class-action status. Overall, the companies involved in these cases have had to pay more than $60 million (U.S.) in settlements or judgments, with the lion's share of that money won by the Federal Trade Commission. According to Westin's report, nearly half of the cases dealt with companies that were charged with breaking a promise made to customers (i.e., violating a stated privacy policy) by disclosing their personal data. Nearly one-fifth of the cases were against companies accused of tracking online users without their consent or knowledge. This percentage was roughly the same for companies that disposed of or sold customer data after a bankruptcy or acquisition. "Companies can expect government agencies to continue their vigorous enforcement of consumer protection laws in these areas," states the report. Executives from the Information Technology Association of America, among others, have argued that legislation that provides for the private rights of civil legal action will invite frivolous lawsuits against companies. This is a sensitive matter that federal lawmakers will need to address as broad-based private-sector legislation is drafted. What is clear is that regulators, on behalf of consumers, will subject companies to legal action both at home and abroad when they do not comply with legislation.

A study released in 2001 by professional services firm Andersen found that U.S. multinationals doing business internationally have so far done a poor job of complying with minimum worldwide standards for privacy. Out of 75 Fortune 500 and medium-sized companies in the United States that conduct commerce globally, and which represent a broad range of industries, none met all six of the privacy principles of notice, choice, access, security, data integrity and enforcement that were established in the U.S.-EU Safe Harbor agreement.[8] Only two of the companies met five principles, and eight passed only one. The least complied with principle was enforcement. Only 5 per cent of the companies had mechanisms in place to assure compliance and provide a way for individuals to seek recourse. Less than half of the companies provided proper notice,

---

[8] "U.S. Multinationals Slow to Implement Emerging Global Privacy Practices, Andersen Study Shows" (Andersen press release, August 16, 2001). (Andersen based its finding on six of the seven privacy principles outlined in the U.S.-EU Safe Harbor agreement. The principle of "onward transfer" was excluded.)

access and security. By comparison, data integrity and choice scored the highest, with 74 per cent and 80 per cent in compliance, respectively. Kerry Shackelford, a principal with Andersen, said the European Union's "stand-still" on legal enforcement is not going to last forever. Shackelford warned that the EU could, at any time, move to block data transfer to U.S. companies that fail to meet all principles in its Directive on Data Protection. "Disruption to the conduct of business is a very real risk." And this doesn't include financial penalties, damaging reports in the press or tough questions from Lou Dobbs Moneyline on CNN.

A Comprehensive Approach

When FTC commissioner Mozelle Thompson said there were "too many holes in the Swiss cheese," he was referring to industry attempts at self-regulation. But his statement could just as well refer to individual organizations that neglect to take a comprehensive approach to privacy. Privacy isn't just about one department, one division, one project, one product, one marketing campaign, one database, one geographical location or one Web site. Alternatively, privacy isn't about reacting after the fact to systems breaches, glitches or mistakes. Organizations that take a Swiss-cheese approach will, as Thompson described, have holes throughout their strategy. Instead, a company should be analyzing and regularly assessing privacy risks across its entire operation. This means applying privacy principles to the following areas: marketing, human resources, sales, accounting, and communications departments; online and offline processes and procedures; all information systems; all offices and facilities; all products and services; all divisions and subsidiaries; and business partners that occupy significant positions in a supply chain. It also means building a cross-functional privacy team composed of a diverse group of individuals from across the enterprise, thus allowing the team leader to be aware of the needs and concerns of each department. In turn, each department could be assigned specific tasks and responsibilities.

The complexity of this process will vary depending on the size of the organization and the geographic markets it targets. Needless to say, smaller organizations that operate locally or domestically will have a much easier time charting out their information-management practices and data flows than global firms with offices and facilities in many countries. But again, privacy should not be thought of as an additional burden imposed upon you by government regulators. Instead of viewing it as merely a compliance issue, treat it as a business opportunity — the opportunity to improve your customer information systems and, in the process, achieve higher levels of customer partnership and service. It's good business, pure and simple.

How to Diagnose Privacy

Perhaps your organization, like many, has never given much thought to privacy issues. Perhaps your own awareness has increased considerably but you're not quite sure where you should start. You may want to self-administer a privacy diagnostic, a voluntary assessment of how privacy-friendly your information-management practices are. The United States Council for International Business (USCIB), whose membership includes more than 300 multinational corporations, law firms and business associations, recognized that companies needed to pay closer attention to their data-management operations if they wanted to avoid the wrath of privacy regulations and laws. In 1998 it released the USCIB Privacy Diagnostic, which amounted to a detailed checklist that companies could run through to help them become more familiar with basic privacy principles, the regulatory environment in the United States and their own information needs and practices. The USCIB Privacy Diagnostic was a simple tool — a seven-page, question-based document — but it served as a stepping-stone to creating internal privacy policies and procedures, which is always a good place to start. (A copy of the USCIB Diagnostic can be found at **www.uscib. org/privmin.asp**. Keep in mind that it was developed in 1998, so some elements — such as regulation — are likely to be outdated.)

Technology, as it always does, has made self-diagnosis much easier and user-friendly. In 2001, the Information and Privacy Commissioner of Ontario, in partnership with PricewaterhouseCoopers and security specialist Guardent, released its Privacy Diagnostic Tool, or PDT, easy-to-use software that is available free of charge to any organization that might collect, use, buy, trade, sell, share or disclose personal information in the course of doing business (**www.ipc.on.ca/english/resources/resources.htm**). Indeed, any business that uses the personal information of consumers for marketing, sales or customer-relationship management will find such a tool a valuable starting point. As well, any organization worried about existing and impending legislation — both at home and abroad — will want to find out whether its business practices are in compliance. "The PDT provides a platform for organizations to clearly understand fair information practices — which form the basis of privacy laws around the world," said Dr. Patrick Sullivan, vice-president of privacy and information policy at Guardent.

The PDT addresses 10 principles that are integral to the proper management of personal information: accountability, identifying purposes, consent, accuracy, safeguards, openness, individual access, challenging compliance, limiting collection, and limiting use, disclosure and retention. The software takes a company through a detailed explanation of each principle and highlights some of the risks of not adhering to that principle. It asks a series of "yes" or "no" questions along the way in order to gauge the company's level of compliance. Where compliance appears to be lacking, the PDT will instruct a company to review or amend its policies and procedures so that they meet either the "required" or, if desired, "best" practices.

The PDT is just one example of the various free or inexpensive self-diagnostic tools that are expected to enter the market over the next few years. Of course, such a diagnostic tool is not intended to replace a more detailed privacy audit or impact assessment. But a self-administered privacy diagnostic is a good starting point that will lead your organization in the direction it needs to go, as well as answer some basic yet essential questions. The PDT will provide a snapshot of your organization's privacy friendliness (or lack thereof), and will suggest what you can do to improve it.

You may also want to rate how exposed your company may be to the risks associated with privacy. A simple privacy risk assessment test, like the one appearing in Figure 5.1, will help you determine what your organization's level of attention to consumer privacy should be. It will also suggest a schedule for implementing a comprehensive privacy program.

The Privacy Impact Assessment

Are you planning to introduce a new data warehouse into your business? Or linking a handful of databases scattered throughout your organization? Perhaps you're interested in installing a video surveillance, biometric or smart card security system in the workplace. You may need to conduct a privacy impact assessment, or PIA, which helps ensure that the new technologies, information systems or policies you are considering comply with basic privacy requirements. A PIA is an assessment and analysis of the effects a major project may have on privacy. It identifies the risks and addresses how they can be mitigated. It's essentially the same as an environmental impact assessment, which determines how the actions of a company, industry or manufacturing program are likely to affect our water, soil and air.

According to privacy expert David Flaherty, former information and privacy commissioner of British Columbia, Canada, and now a privacy consultant, effective PIAs set off warning alarms during the early stages of an information system's introduction, redesign or modification. The goal is to describe an organization's personal data flows as fully as possible to determine how much they protect the privacy of customers and employees. "Ultimately, a privacy impact assessment is a risk assessment tool for decision-makers that can address not only the legal, but the moral and ethical, issues posed by whatever is being proposed," says Flaherty.[9] He adds that a PIA aims to describe, in as much detail as necessary, the key components of the information system being added or modified.

Figure 5.1 • *Privacy Risk Assessment Test*

COMPANY CHARACTERISTIC   SCORE

Importance of the brand (measured by advertising budget)

[1 (<$50 million); 2 ($51 milliion – $149 million); 3 (>$150 million)] ☐

Percent of sales to consumers

[1 (<30% of sales); 2 (31% – 50% of sales); 3 (>51% of sales)] ☐

Percent of sales to Canadian, European, and Australian consumers

[1 (<10% of sales); 2 (11% – 20% of sales); 3 (>21% of sales)] ☐

Number of separate customer databases

[1 (<10 databases); 2 (11 – 20 databases); 3 (>21 databases)] ☐

Existing US privacy regulation compliance

[1 (no statutes apply); 2 (one statute applies); 3 (two-plus statutes apply)] ☐

Number of direct-mail campaigns run annually

[1 (<10 campaigns); 2 (11 – 25 campaigns); 3 (>25 campaigns)] ☐

Company management structure

[1 (centralized); 2 (moderately decentralized); 3 (fully decentralized)] ☐

Percent of applications that are legacy systems

[1 (<10% of applications); 2 (11% – 25% of applications); 3 (>26% of applications)] ☐

Online marketing strategy includes; personalization,

email newsletters or promotions, third-party ad servers

[1 (no elements); 2 (one element used); 3 (two-plus elements used)] ☐

Offline marketing strategy includes: loyalty program, in-store date capture,

warranty cards, third-party data acquisition

[1 (no elements used); 2 (one element used); 3 (two-plus elements used)] ☐

Rate of employee turnover in call center, Web, marketing

[1 (<5% turnover); 2 (6% – 14% turnover); 3 (>15% turnover)] ☐

Number of external partners (customer service, Web operations, logistics, marketing)

[1 (no partners); 2 (one to two partners); 3 (two-plus partners)] ☐

                                                        Total Risk Factor ☐

SCORE ANALYSIS

>28	High Risk: Need to embrace whole-view approach to privacy within the next six months.
21–28	Above-average Risk: Need to embrace whole-view approach to privacy within the next 12 months.
13–20	Average Risk: Need to embrace whole-view approach to privacy in the next 18 months.
<13	Low Immediate Risk: Need to embrace whole-view approach to privacy in the next 24 months.

Source: 2002, Forrester Research, Inc.

Here are the types of questions to ask when conducting a PIA:

- What are the needs and goals of the system?
- What national or regional laws or privacy standards must be taken into account?
- What are the purposes of the data?
- What kind of data will be collected and stored?
- Which data is sensitive and which is nonsensitive?
- How will it be used?
- Where does the data come from?
- Where does it go?
- To whom will it be disclosed?
- Where will it reside?
- How long will it be retained?
- When and how will the data be destroyed when it is no longer required?
- How will the data inventory be tracked and managed as it flows through the new system?

[9] David H. Flaherty, "Privacy Impact Assessments: An Essential Tool for Data Protection" (presentation at "New Technologies, Security and Freedom," 22nd Annual Meeting of Privacy and Data Protection Officials, Venice, September 27-30, 2000).

- What will be the technical architecture of the system?
- Which employees will have access to it?
- What kind of security safeguards will be in place to protect the data?

These are just a few of the questions that need to be asked. "The hard questions must be answered and not glossed over," says Flaherty. "My fear is that it is always going to be difficult to find someone building any automated system who knows enough about data protection principles and fair information practices to be able to apply them in a sophisticated manner."

When in doubt, call in the experts.

Privacy Architects (Consultants)

Companies that lack internal expertise in designing privacy-compliant systems and processes may find it worthwhile to hire a consultant known as a privacy architect. The title is a fairly new one, but it promises to grow in popularity as demand increases for people with privacy-specific skills and a broad knowledge of technical and business issues. Peter Hope-Tindall, chief privacy architect of Toronto consultancy dataPrivacy Partners, is among the first to adopt the title. Hope-Tindall says being a privacy architect means working cooperatively with technical, managerial, business development, legal, audit and policy personnel, all at the same time, within an organization. Consider the average company: the chief executive officer doesn't have a strong grasp of technology, the chief financial officer is generally focused on income statements and balance sheets, corporate counsel is preoccupied with dealing with the law, and technical employees are fixated on computer code. "Privacy architects sit in the vertical shaft of an organization and they go up and down: they can function in the boardroom and they can function in the technical meeting," he explains.

According to Hope-Tindall, privacy must be baked into the cake; it shouldn't be added later as the icing. Specifically, he says a chief architect is responsible for the following:

1. Helping to identify and define privacy needs within an organization, based on fair information practices and taking into account any statutory requirements;
2. Explaining privacy concepts to key personnel within an organization, as well as exploring and introducing relevant privacy-enhancing technologies to them;
3. Analyzing each technological component, process and procedure of a proposed system to evaluate its privacy risk characteristics; and
4. Developing a privacy architecture, conceptually and technically, that is feasible, is cost-effective and meets an organization's privacy needs, yet works within existing computer and security architectures.

A privacy architect may be a privacy consultant, but not all privacy consultants are privacy architects. For example, many consultants have a business management background but lack the technology skills to verify whether technical implementation is addressing business and policy concerns. Other consultants come from network and computer security backgrounds, which are technical but not broad enough to address the full spectrum of fair information practices. Hope-Tindall highlights another difference between a privacy architect and a consultant with a security background: "The security architect focuses on access controls and authorized access as defined by the system owner. In contrast, the privacy architect focuses on the collection, retention, proper use and destruction of data as mandated by the law and authorized by the individual whose data it is." He says the system owner is not the ultimate authority where privacy is concerned. "In fact, the system owner may be one of the parties from whom the data must be held private." This latter point is a completely foreign concept to most businesses.

There are many companies today that specialize in offering privacy consulting services. Most of the big accounting and consulting firms have privacy-related business units that have grown significantly over the past several years. These privacy experts charge several thousands to several millions of dollars to fulfill a company's privacy needs, depending on the client's size, the complexity of its business and information systems, the depth of required work and the types of technologies needed to accomplish objectives. IBM's privacy consulting practice has also experienced substantial growth: the company's two-person operation in 1998 consisted of several *dozen* privacy experts by 2001. Firms such as Guardent, Zero-Knowledge Systems, PrivacyRight, the Privacy Council, Hewlett-Packard, NCR and Entrust all offer their own, sometimes unique, sets of consulting skills, services or privacy-management software. (Many of these products will be discussed in **Chapter 11**.) As businesses, consumers, investors and politicians become more aware of privacy issues, an increasing number of privacy consultants (and architects) will come on the scene to meet a huge demand. The privacy consulting market, estimated as a $300-million business in 1999, is expected to be a $1.8-billion market by 2003.

Privacy Policies and Statements

Once an organization gets a firm enough grasp of its data flows, information needs, privacy requirements and consumer-friendly information-management strategy, it should formally document them. But whether or not this has taken place, a business should fulfill the privacy principle of openness by drafting a privacy policy — a declaration of intent that is ideally matched by business practices. This policy should then be communicated to consumers and employees in the form of a privacy statement — typically posted on a Web site or, for employees, a corporate intranet. "There's no magic in a privacy policy, but it's an indicator of whether or not the organization that operates the Web site has really addressed the subject of data protection," says lawyer Michael Power.

The OECD says a privacy policy or statement is a "vital step towards encouraging openness and trust in electronic commerce among visitors to Web sites." Privacy statements tell online visitors what to expect, helping them to make informed choices about the Web sites they encounter, and giving them a better understanding of the companies behind them. Ultimately, this clarity helps to overcome uncertainty that might otherwise prevent a transaction from taking place.

Consumers' questions that should be anticipated and answered in a privacy statement include: Is my personal information going to be collected? If so, when and how will it be collected? How will it be used? Who will have access to it? Will it ever be shared, disclosed or sold without my consent? Will I be notified if the policy changes? How is my personal information secured? Am I allowed to review, update and correct my data? Whom do I talk to if I have a privacy complaint? As you may have noticed, these questions all relate directly to the OECD's fair information practices. In fact, companies that need some assistance developing their privacy policies or statements can use a free online tool created by the OECD called the Privacy Statement Generator (found at **www.ftc.gov/ privacy/index.html**, under the heading "Consumer and Business Education"). Sponsored by Microsoft and Daimler Chrysler, the Privacy Statement Generator will walk you through a list of questions that will help your company craft a policy statement suited to your particular organization.

When writing a privacy statement, it is important to avoid technical language and legal jargon that is difficult for most consumers to understand. It is also important to keep the statement as brief as possible. Tailor the statement to the audience expected to read it — that is, a privacy statement on a children's Web site should not read like one on a site geared toward business professionals or technical workers. Forrester Research suggests a two-tiered statement, in which the first Web page contains simple answers to basic consumer questions. Each answer, however, contains a hyperlink that can take the reader to a second, more detailed review of the privacy policy.[10] This layered approach addresses your lawyer's concerns, ultimately aimed at reducing risk for your company, while communicating your privacy policy in wording that is understood by the average consumer. Indeed, the U.S. government recognized the need for greater simplicity in December 2001, when the FTC held a workshop to help financial service providers draft understandable, plain-English privacy policies.

---

[10] Jay Stanley, John C. McCarthy, Michael J. Tavilla and Jeremy Sharrad, "Surviving the Privacy Revolution" (Forrester Research, February 2001).

Anup Ghosh, author of *Security and Privacy for E-Business*, says a Web site privacy statement should also tell consumers what technologies are being used, such as cookies or Web bugs, to collect their personal information and track their surfing on the Internet.[11] As well, we suggest that a privacy statement do more than simply express the privacy policy of a particular Web site or service; it should be harmonized with — and linked to — the general privacy policy for the entire company operating the site or service. Do not assume that your online and offline practices will be viewed separately. FTC consumer protection chief Howard Beales says the regulator would consider a Web privacy policy as representative of both online and offline privacy practices unless the policy specifically indicates it is strictly intended for the Web.[12]

There is no question that these days consumers are far less willing to entrust their personal data to organizations that, at a minimum, don't have a posted privacy statement. "Most e-businesses are keenly aware that it is politically correct, if not imperative, to have online privacy policies," states Ghosh.[13] Yet strangely, many companies still don't showcase their privacy policies. A survey of 750 Web sites from both the United States and Europe, conducted in 2000, found that only 58 per cent had posted privacy policies.[14] In Canada and Australia the numbers have been even less encouraging, as more than half of surveyed Web sites failed to post or did not have a formal privacy policy.[15]

Privacy Seals and Symbols

For companies looking to go the extra distance by emphasizing the privacy-friendliness of their Web sites, a privacy seal may be a good idea. A privacy seal

---

[11] Anup K. Ghosh, *Security and Privacy for E-Business* (New York: John Wiley & Sons, 2001), p. 190.

[12] Brian Krebs, "Online Privacy Policies Apply to Offline Data Practices — FTC" Newsbytes [online], December 10, 2001.

[13] Ghosh, *supra*, note 11, p. 189.

[14] Consumers International, Office for Developed and Transition Economies, "Privacy@Net: An International Comparative Study of Consumer Privacy on the Internet," January 2001.

[15] PricewaterhouseCoopers Privacy Survey 2000 (Australia), p. 8; Michael Geist, "A Troubling Snapshot of E-Privacy in Canada" *Globe and Mail*, December 7, 2000.

is a visual symbol that a Web site may use when its privacy promises have been approved by a third party. There are a number of privacy seals to choose from, but the most popular by far come from the Council of Better Business Bureaus (BBB) and TRUSTe, an independent, non-profit organization founded in 1997 by the Electronic Frontier Foundation and the CommerceNet Consortium.

The BBB, which has been protecting consumers for more than 90 years, has had significant success with its BBB*Online* Privacy Seal (**www.bbbonline.com**), launched in 1999. As of September 2001, about 850 Web sites had qualified to display the BBB's privacy seal. According to BBB*Online*, its seal "confirms that a company stands behind its online privacy policy and has met the program requirements regarding the handling of personal information that is provided through its Web site." Companies that are already *persona non grata* with the BBB automatically do not qualify for its privacy seal. To obtain the seal, a site operator must fill out a 10-page questionnaire, after which BBB*Online* attempts to verify the answers. If the applicant fails to meet BBB*Online*'s privacy criteria, it is told what it needs to do and is given a chance to apply again. BBB*Online* requires that Web sites provide adequate security and give consumers access to their personal information. Web sites must also agree to undergo an annual self-assessment of their online privacy practices. For sensitive information, such as that dealing with health, personal finance, religion, politics, sexual orientation and racial and ethnic origin, BBB*Online* requires collection only on an opt-in basis.

At the time of writing, the cost of obtaining a BBB*Online* privacy seal depended on the size of an organization. All businesses must pay an up-front $75(U.S.) application fee to do the Compliance Assessment Questionnaire. If approved, a business with less than $1 million a year in revenue is required to pay a $200 annual fee; for organizations with more than $2 billion a year in revenue the annual fee is $6,000. (A sliding fee scale can be found at **www.bbb online.com**.) BBB*Online* has a commendable dispute-resolution process. Consumers can file complaints against any seal-carrying member directly to BBB*Online*, which then posts the complaints — and any follow-ups — on its own Web site. As a result of such publicity in the past, some Web sites have chosen to improve their privacy policies. If a Web site decides that it doesn't want to participate in the dispute resolution, BBB*Online* can take back its privacy seal and send the consumer complaint to a regulatory body such as the Federal Trade Commission.

To broaden the reach of its privacy initiative, in 2000 BBB*Online* joined with the Japan Information Processing Development Center (JIPDEC) to create a transnational or "reciprocal" Web privacy seal that could be recognized by online users in the United States and Japan. Ken Hunter, president and CEO of the Council of Better Business Bureaus, said the BBB*Online* and JIPDEC initiative represents an important step in harmonizing online privacy standards globally. "It will no doubt be helpful to consumers to find a trusted and well-known mark on the Web site of a foreign, unfamiliar business," he said.[16]

The most popular online privacy seal is currently the TRUSTe seal, which appears on more than 2,000 Web sites, including most of the Internet's major e-commerce sites. Similar to BBB*Online*, TRUSTe grants its seal to Web sites that have conducted self-assessments of their online privacy practices. These practices must comply with the principles of notice, choice, access and security. A consumer on a Web site who clicks on the TRUSTe seal will be taken to the Web site's privacy statement. TRUSTe says it will conduct periodic reviews of member Web sites to determine whether they are complying with their stated privacy policies.

The cost of a TRUSTe seal also depends on the size of a company, but the scale differs considerably from BBB*Online*. Companies with less than $1 million a year in revenues are required to pay an annual fee of $299; businesses with more than $75 million a year in revenues have annual fees of $6,999. TRUSTe has a page on its Web site where consumers can voice complaints if a licensed member is believed to have violated the conditions of its privacy seal. If TRUSTe is convinced that a member has breached its seal-approved privacy statement, one of its auditors will carry out an investigation and will work with

---

[16] Better Business Bureau, "New Online Privacy Tool to Transcend Borders" (press release, May 18, 2000).

the Web site to address the concern. If a Web site fails to resolve the concern, the TRUSTe seal could be revoked.

TRUSTe is also working on a program called the Symbols and Labels Initiative. The idea is to take the incomprehensible jargon and complexity of a privacy policy — which few consumers actually read — and summarize it in the form of an easily understandable symbol. Such a symbol would be clearly displayed on a Web site as a way for consumers to quickly assess its data and privacy practices. Used in conjunction with a privacy seal, a privacy symbol would provide consumers with a snapshot of how their data is collected and used. Advocates of the system say it would be particularly useful on the mobile Internet, since the small screens of most wireless devices are impractical for reading full-length privacy statements.

Of course, no system is without its problems, and BBB*Online* and TRUSTe are no exceptions. There has been significant debate about the independent nature of both organizations, because of their affiliations with the private sector. TRUSTe and BBB*Online* are sponsored by big names such as Microsoft, Intel and America Online. TRUSTe, in particular, has been criticized for not adequately addressing consumers' complaints. Both organizations have been criticized for awarding seals to companies that are being investigated by the FTC for privacy violations. Sadly, weak enforcement and the perception of private-sector bias may, over the long term, undermine the purpose of these seals. Another problem with privacy seals is that they pertain strictly to Web sites, not to software or plug-ins that may be downloaded from sites. The concern is that online visitors who see a privacy seal will incorrectly assume that the Web site's privacy statement reflects all aspects of a company's products, services and operations.

Nonetheless, we believe that privacy seals have so far helped to create an environment of trust on the Internet. For example, Cheskin Research ranked TRUSTe as the most "trust-invoking" seal on the Web in an August 2000 report. According to Lawrence Surtees with International Data Corp., 58 per cent of online consumers said they would be more likely to hand over their personal data to a Web site if it carried both a privacy statement and a privacy seal from a "recognized" organization. He also found that 44 per cent of Internet users who are familiar with privacy seals spent more than $500 online during a six-month period, compared to 32 per cent who said they were unfamiliar with such seals.[17] It is for this reason that some Web sites, such as online travel store Expedia.com, have opted to display both the BBB*Online* and TRUSTe seals.

The Privacy Audit

Expedia.com has expanded its privacy compliance efforts beyond the BBB*Online* and TRUSTe seal programs. In May 2001, Expedia announced that, after a lengthy and rigorous audit, it had received a WebTrust privacy seal from Pricewater-houseCoopers. This made the popular site one of the first in the world to undergo a detailed third-party inspection of its Web site information practices.

The American Institute of Certified Public Accountants and the Canadian Institute of Chartered Accountants created the WebTrust seal in 1997. Unlike most Web seals, which tend to rely on self-assessment and the assumption of privacy compliance, WebTrust requires that a certified public accountant conduct an independent examination and verification of a Web site's business practices and procedures. These practices must fulfill established standards of access, accuracy, choice, notice and security before the WebTrust seal can be posted. The cost of the seal itself is $1,400, but additional professional fees can be substantially higher depending on the complexity and business dynamics of the site. WebTrust audits as of the end of 2001 had been conducted on nearly 30 Web sites, for companies such as B2B software and services firm Ariba, telephone giant Bell Canada and Zurich Financial Services Australia. These sites must be recertified at least every 90 days to keep their WebTrust seal. (For more information on WebTrust, visit **www.aicpa.org, www.cica.ca** or **www.webtrust.org**. For a list of companies that have the WebTrust seal, visit **www.webtrust.org/abtseals.htm**.)

An offshoot of the original WebTrust is the WebTrust Program for On-Line Privacy, launched in 2000. The WebTrust privacy seal is designed specifically to

---

[17] Lawrence Surtees, "Nowhere to Hide: Privacy Implications of Wireless Location Technology" (IDC Canada, August 2000).

compare a company's privacy policy with its actual practices. It goes into much greater depth and detail when measuring the policies and procedures of a Web site against established privacy principles. The first company to receive the WebTrust privacy seal was financial services provider H.D. Vest, followed a few months later by Expedia.com. Stuart McDonald, managing director of Expedia Canada, said the WebTrust privacy seal, in addition to the BBB*Online* and TRUSTe seals, makes the Web site much more inviting to online consumers, particularly first-time browsers. "We believe this is a worthwhile investment for us because it helps to reduce that perception of risk," McDonald told us, adding that the move is expected to spur growth on the site. "It turns lookers into bookers."

The WebTrust, BBB*Online* and TRUSTe seals apply only to the privacy practices of a Web site, not to the practices of an organization. Larger companies looking to do a thorough privacy audit of their enterprise-wide business processes and systems can start by consulting with the assurance division of a reputable accounting firm or a broad-ranged services company with a privacy practice, such as IBM. For small and medium-sized businesses, a growing number of boutique privacy consultancies can perform adequate but more affordable, smaller-scale audits. Whichever route you choose, you can expect your company's desktops, servers, databases, procedures and policies to be looked over with a fine-tooth comb. It's a process that can sometimes take months, but if it saves you the expense and controversy attached to a high-profile privacy breach, you will find it well worth the wait.

Privacy Culture and Training

Becoming a privacy-friendly business does not end with privacy diagnostics, impact assessments, policies, seals and audits. Perhaps the most effective way of creating a long-term privacy program, and gaining a trusted reputation in the marketplace, is by nurturing a culture and value system within your organization that is sensitive to, respectful of and attentive to the privacy concerns of consumers and employees. This is where strong doses of education and training become important. Bruce Phillips, privacy consultant and former privacy commissioner of Canada, told us, "The largest and most important part of privacy work is education and understanding, particularly when you're dealing with institutions that have been in business for a long period of time and have developed a set of business practices tailored to their own particular needs."

It has often been said that employees are an organization's weakest link when it comes to privacy and security. You can pay top dollar for computer and network security technologies, you can spend months conducting privacy impact assessments and audits, you can hire the most expensive information-management consultants and privacy architects, but all it takes is one employee who doesn't know any better to accidentally leak or give away customer information to somebody who shouldn't have it. A simple act such as this could hurt your company's brand and lead to civil litigation. For the employee, it can mean immediate dismissal. "A slip of the mouse has caused many privacy violations," Jason Catlett, president of privacy advocacy firm Junkbusters, told us. Catlett adds that employees who have access to sensitive consumer and corporate information may be tempted to share this information with friends, use it for their own purposes or even sell it unless they are properly trained and made aware of the consequences. "This isn't just about law and technology. It's a matter of training and developing an organizational culture that regards privacy as important and in need of training."

Many companies are starting to get this message. Bell Canada, the largest telephone, Internet, wireless and direct-to-home satellite service provider in Canada, is an excellent example of a company taking a comprehensive approach to privacy training and education. Bell released its new privacy policy and an updated version of its Code of Fair Information Practices in October 2000. In conjunction with a customer notice campaign, the company implemented a training program to familiarize employees with its privacy practices and to encourage greater respect for customers' privacy. Customer-facing employees, such as call center agents, were given training sessions on Canada's new e-commerce privacy law. Bell's privacy policy and code have also been incorporated into its Code of Business Conduct, which requires annual sign-off by all staff.

Some online companies have adopted even more aggressive approaches. PeopleFirst.com, the largest online automotive lender in North America, takes the issue of consumer privacy so seriously that in 2001 it held its first annual Privacy Week. During this five-day period, the company attempted to raise employees' awareness of the importance of customer privacy. It reviewed its privacy policy with staff and it trained all employees on what they must do to ensure the company is complying with this policy. Employees were also required to sign a privacy pledge. "We are making sure that every employee honors each customer's individual privacy rights," said Alan Amico, chief privacy officer with PeopleFirst.com and mastermind of Privacy Week.[18] During one activity, Amico asked employees random questions about the company's privacy policy. When an employee answered correctly, he or she was awarded a movie pass or other prize. According to Amico, a company can communicate its privacy policy to employees in a number of ways, including departmental meetings, e-mail, internal newsletters, corporate intranets and desk-side reminders. He says it is also a good idea to add privacy training to orientation sessions for all new employees. For existing employees, random privacy challenges can be held throughout the year to further nurture a culture of privacy.

Thornton May, chief psychographer with Toffler Associates and former chief awareness officer at security consulting firm Guardent, believes that privacy activities within an organization must be branded as important and desirable for them to be taken seriously — and internalized — by employees and executives. "Historically, security and privacy have been thought of as someone else's responsibility," wrote May in his regular column for *Computerworld* in July 2001. "Today, they must be embedded in an organization's behavior. The only way to make this happen is to reposition and re-brand security (and privacy) as something executives want to do vs. something they have to do."

This rebranding might not happen overnight, but now is a good time to start. You might want to raise this issue at your next board meeting.

---

[18] PeopleFirst.com, "PeopleFirst.com Launches First Annual Privacy Week" (press release, April 4, 2001). (Some information in this paragraph is also taken from a presentation by Alan Amico, chief privacy officer for PeopleFirst.com.)

Avoiding Window Dressing

One of the biggest mistakes businesses make when it comes to privacy is to not follow through on policy promises. "They'll say they do these wonderful and glorious things — and then they make no attempt to comply with their policies," says Dr. Larry Ponemon, chief executive officer of the Privacy Council, a Dallas-based consultancy.[19] As many businesses have found out, being all show and no action is a risky short-term strategy that, when it backfires, can have long-term repercussions. In 1999, when consumer privacy issues began to capture the attention of the mainstream media, many dot-com companies scrambled to find quick-and-dirty ways to jump on the privacy bandwagon. One Web designer in Toronto told us that clients would walk into his office and say, "Oh, by the way, we also need a privacy policy on the site." Some companies would merely snip excerpts from someone else's Web privacy policy and paste them on their own site, as if it were a formula for instant trust. It's no wonder that Forrester Research came out with a summer 1999 report that stated, "Most privacy policies are a joke."[20] Simply put, window dressing isn't enough for Net-savvy consumers.

Consumers want — and deserve — more than a privacy-friendly facade. Rather than half-hearted efforts that create a vague perception that their personal information is safeguarded and handled fairly, consumers want genuine assurances that privacy policies are going to be followed. Privacy should not be viewed strictly as a public relations tactic; it should be treated as an investment in customer trust, and in the long-term survival of your business. Besides, those that make privacy promises they don't keep risk falling on the bad side of the FTC and other industry watchdogs. "Having a privacy policy without implementing its stated practices is simply false advertising," wrote Anup Ghosh in *Security and Privacy for E-Business*.[21] As we have already discussed, the FTC is on the lookout for companies with deceptive business practices, and has also prom-

[19] Stephanie Stoughton, "Turning to Technology to Staunch Privacy Leaks" Boston *Globe*, August 27, 2001.
[20] Tyler Hamilton, "Privacy Policies Are a Joke," *Globe and Mail*, September 23, 1999.
[21] Ghosh, *supra*, note 11, p. 192.

ised to increase the enforcement of consumer protection laws. So don't cut corners; make it real. Put in the time that is required to make your company's privacy policy reflect your actual business practices.

A Top-Down Approach: Keep It Senior

Our final, and perhaps most important, word of advice in this chapter has to do with leadership. A company will make little progress with its privacy projects, initiatives and overall compliance efforts if it assigns such responsibilities to a team of low-ranking employees who may only get together once a month in a staff meeting room. A group such as this might be determined to make a difference, but if these employees don't have the ear, support and constant guidance of upper management, any hard work on their part is likely to go unappreciated and unimplemented. And that would be a complete waste of time and resources.

There is no question about it: senior management *must* buy into privacy if related policies, practices, processes and procedures are to be respected and followed by the entire organization. A top-down approach to privacy — starting with the CEO or the board of directors and ending with frontline staff — will also make it easier to obtain the financial and staff resources that are required to perform timely and comprehensive diagnostics, assessments and audits of your company's privacy and information practices. In the next chapter, we will take an in-depth look at the role of the chief privacy officer, or CPO, one of the newest and fastest-growing executive positions in corporate North America. The CPO is a high-profile internal executive who is accountable for all privacy issues touching an organization. Ideally, the CPO has enough clout to command the attention of the board of directors and influence corporate policy.

The Bottom Line

Privacy is a core business issue that, if handled correctly, can lead to competitive advantages and long-term savings. But any benefits to be achieved through privacy will not come from half-hearted efforts that could easily be revealed as window dressing. Before posting a Web site privacy statement for all the world to see or communicating a privacy policy to offline customers, it is essential that a company conduct a comprehensive review of its information-management practices, documenting all information flows and making sure that processes and procedures are in place to achieve privacy objectives and mitigate risks. But the work does not stop there. Once a privacy policy has been crafted, a genuine effort must be made to instill a culture of privacy within your organization, through a top-down approach that includes education and training. A sound privacy strategy will, in effect, create a business-consumer partnership that, like a joint venture, needs the trust and respect of both parties if it is to succeed.

We strongly believe that privacy is the next business imperative. It could very well be the distinguishing factor between old-world thinkers and the emerging leaders of the new economy.

Chapter 6

CPO: The Officer of the Future

"The growing number of chief privacy officers
points to a trend that government needs to
understand fully — management of [personal]
information has now become a standard
operating function for business."

Philip J. Bond, U.S. Undersecretary of
Commerce for Technology, 2001

The New "O"

When Web startup AllAdvantage.com opened for business in April 1999, its executives knew it was only a matter of time before privacy concerns emerged. AllAdvantage.com offered daily promotions, sweepstakes — even cash — to people who downloaded and used its Web browser to surf the Internet. In exchange, participants agreed to watch targeted advertisements through a special online viewer. It was a business model that partially relied on the collection of customer information, understandably piquing the interest of privacy advocates and creating some hesitation among consumers. To address these concerns, AllAdvantage.com decided to make a little history: in the summer of that year, it became the first company in North America — perhaps the world — to appoint a chief privacy officer, in this case a 30-year-old Internet guru by the name of Ray Everett-Church. The young executive was charged with overseeing the company's privacy strategy, with the goal of building more trusting relationships with customers.

Unfortunately, the business model underlying AllAdvantage.com — that is, paying people to watch advertisements — eventually proved faulty. By February 2001, the company had run out of cash and was forced to pull the plug on its online operations. Everett-Church, a pioneer in his field, moved on to become a privacy consultant and senior analyst with consultancy ePrivacy Group. While AllAdvantage.com, like many of its dot-com peers, is now a distant memory in the first chapter of the new economy, the position of chief privacy officer, or CPO, has lived on and, indeed, is burgeoning in corporate North America. Other titles for the position include corporate privacy officer, privacy officer, privacy manager and vice-president of data protection.

Privacy and American Business (P&AB), a CPO training organization headed by privacy veteran Dr. Alan Westin, estimates that there were well over 500 corporate and chief privacy officers in the United States by the end of 2001, though hundreds more carry out CPO duties part time. P&AB began its CPO training program only in 2000, but it now has well over 100 members representing organizations across a wide range of industries. Similarly, the Privacy Council, led by Dr. Larry Ponemon, has teamed up with the Cox School of Business at Southern Methodist University in Dallas to offer its own intensive three-day CPO training program. The Privacy Council has another program that allows smaller companies to essentially rent a CPO for six months, giving these businesses the expertise they need to carry out early-stage privacy risk and impact assessments.

Why Appoint a CPO?

New legislation in North America and around the world has created a need for privacy specialists who can interpret the rules (generally subsumed in fair information practices) and apply them across the enterprise in private-sector settings. These rules are contained in legislation such as the U.S. Children's Online Privacy

Protection Act (COPPA), the Gramm-Leach-Bliley Act (GLBA), the Health Insurance Portability and Accountability Act (HIPAA), Canada's Personal Information Protection and Electronic Documents Act (PIPEDA) and a plethora of regulations coming out of the European Union, Australia, New Zealand, Hong Kong and Japan. In many cases, such as with HIPAA, the rules in fact require organizations to appoint a privacy point person, someone responsible for privacy compliance and a contact person for public complaints. "As HIPAA regulations come in, every covered entity has to have a designated official who is in charge of implementing privacy policies," says Dr. Alan Westin.

Westin estimates that 30,000 health-care organizations are covered under the HIPAA regulations alone, creating the need for thousands of privacy officers in 2002 and beyond. This same requirement for a dedicated privacy point person exists in Canada under PIPEDA and under data-protection legislation in Europe. "My sense is that the job of privacy officer is becoming more and more institutionalized," says Westin. "The institutionalization of privacy through the privacy officer is the single most important development in terms of impact as we enter 2002, 2003 and 2004." Indeed, high-profile companies such as IBM, EDS, AT&T and Verizon Communications have brought momentum to the trend by paving a path that other companies and CPOs can follow. As the U.S. Federal Trade Commission steps up its enforcement of consumer privacy laws, and as privacy-related lawsuits grow in number, Westin adds that smart companies are finding privacy officers indispensable.

Legislation, of course, merely provides the minimum standards for protecting personal information. For organizations that want to show leadership and go beyond the letter of the law, a CPO can be invaluable in directing management toward best practices.

What Makes a Good CPO?

It is difficult to provide a complete list of responsibilities and required skills for the position of CPO because the role is a new one and it continues to evolve. The job description can also vary significantly, depending on the size of an organization, its type of business, the industry in which it operates, the laws and regulations it must comply with, the amount and detail of customer information it collects and the level of seniority it grants to the position. The job is also defined by the degree of top-level commitment an organization is prepared to give to privacy issues and the resources — both financial and human — that it allocates to the cause.

Although many privacy officers come from legal backgrounds, it is not uncommon for them to bring marketing, communications, management and technical skills to this broadly defined job — which is as much about business development, product design, employee relations and customer service as it is about regulatory compliance. One survey found that nearly half of all organizations with a CPO want to play a leadership role in the area of privacy as a way to win points with consumers and gain a competitive edge over industry rivals.[1] These companies view good privacy practices as a way of building stronger, more trusting relationships with the buying public and industry partners. It's a proactive approach — one that requires privacy to be built into all aspects of an organization, not applied as an afterthought simply to obey the law. This is consistent with our view that, for maximum gain, privacy should be treated as a core business issue, not a compliance issue.

For many companies, the CPO is a multidisciplinary officer who has the difficult task of protecting consumer and employee interests, satisfying government concerns, following the laws of many countries (not to mention states and regions) and advancing the business objectives of the company, all at the same time. A privacy officer must be someone who can oversee the mapping of information flows across an organization, the privacy-impact assessments of new technologies and the privacy audits of information systems that handle customer and employee data (which is where some technical knowledge is useful). It is typically the privacy officer's job to design and assure compliance with a corporate privacy policy that harmonizes business objectives

---

[1] Privacy and American Business and the Association of Corporate Privacy Officers, "New Survey Shows Privacy Officers Take Hold in Key Consumer Industries and Report to Top Management" (press release, December 6, 2001). (Based on a survey conducted by Opinion Research Corp. of Princeton, N.J.)

with customer interests. This policy must also be regularly updated to reflect the regulatory and business environment of the day.

But there's more. Not only should privacy officers know fair information practices like the back of their hands, they should be able to articulate these principles across their organization, from the customer-support agent who deals directly with the public, to the chief executive officer who ultimately approves and supports major privacy initiatives. The privacy officer usually works alongside other departments — marketing, legal, information technology, sales, public relations, customer service, human resources, research and development — to design a privacy strategy and culture that the entire company will embrace and promote. Employee training and education is a significant part of that effort.

To top it all off, the CPO, as privacy point person for an organization, acts as an ombudsman, responding to customer questions and helping to mediate complaints. The goal is to avoid lawsuits and scrutiny from an often overly critical media. Finally, if something unfortunate should happen, it is the CPO's job to manage whatever crisis might ensue.

Alan Amico, chief privacy officer with online auto lender PeopleFirst.com, told one industry magazine that he was caught a little off guard by the wide scope of his job. "You're dealing with laws, with technical issues, with marketing, with training issues. It goes across the company," said Amico. "I didn't appreciate how much time is involved, what a big job it is."[2]

The huge responsibilities that come with being a privacy officer, the broad range of skills that are required and the demand for such experienced persons make it a relatively highly paid corporate position. A survey of privacy officers commissioned by P&AB and the Association of Corporate Privacy Officers found that 57 per cent earned an annual salary of more than $100,000, while 11 per cent — likely high-ranking "chief" privacy officers — earned more than $200,000. Other interesting findings from the survey, the first of its kind, included:

[2] Connie Winkler, "Privacy Protector" Network World [online], March 26, 2001.

- 67 per cent of privacy officers had worked in the business for more than 10 years
- nearly half of respondents said they had at least one full-time staff member supporting them. Many had a team of three or more privacy staffers
- 40 per cent said they expect half of all U.S. companies will have a designated privacy officer before 2005, amounting to about 20,000 officers from a range of industries including retail, telecommunications, financial services, health care and the Internet
- 68 per cent said they did not think that the terrorist events of September 11, 2001, will have a significant effect on how they perform their duties or the way in which their company addresses privacy issues.[3]

More than Cosmetic

Considerable debate has emerged about the effectiveness of CPOs. Some privacy advocates argue that many companies use CPOs as a public relations smokescreen. In such cases, an organization considers the *perception* of being privacy-friendly to be more important than the reality. Here, a CPO tends to be given little clout and insufficient resources to effect any true change in the organization, or to protect customer information. "A lot of companies appoint chief privacy officers as a show trophy," maintains Jason Catlett, president of privacy advocacy group Junkbusters. "I often say that chief privacy officers are like corporate crash-test dummies."[4]

Catlett's view may be extreme, but it highlights the varying attitudes organizations have toward the general issue of privacy and in particular the position of the CPO. Larry Ponemon of the Privacy Council says a majority of companies that have CPOs don't give them enough financial and human resources, let alone the authority they need to perform their jobs properly. He tells a story of a privacy officer hired by one U.S. bank to implement, among other things, an opt-in database for keeping track of up to 20 million customer files. The privacy

[3] Privacy and American Business, "New Survey."
[4] Tyler Hamilton, "Experts Debate Importance of Chief Privacy Officer" Toronto *Star*, March 13, 2001.

officer believed she had a team of 11 technical staff that would carry out the requirements for the new system. Unfortunately, only two of the 11 implemented the necessary changes, while the other nine — clearly not under her direct authority — falsely claimed that the changes had been made. "This was reported back to her, and she was totally shocked, totally upset," Ponemon told us. "She had no budget and no direct authority to make this sort of thing work."

Ideally, a privacy officer not only should have adequate resources and authority within a given organization but should report directly to senior officials, preferably a vice-president, chief executive officer or, better yet, the board of directors. "Ultimately, this is a CEO and board-level issue," says Ponemon. "They have to buy into it and they have to believe in it and that it's working." According to the P&AB survey, an encouraging 82 per cent of privacy officers said they report directly to senior executives. It is a trend that we hope — and expect — will grow in corporate circles.

Our advice to any company that wants to hire a CPO for cosmetic purposes alone is simple: Don't do it. Sooner or later, the strategy will backfire, resulting in a loss of consumer trust and confidence that may be difficult, or impossible, to regain.

In the Trenches: CPO Profiles

To help you get a better handle on what it takes to be a CPO, including the day-to-day operational challenges of the job, we have gone directly to the source. What follows are work profiles of six privacy officers. Each is a pioneer in his or her respective industry or sector.

Name:	*Harriet Pearson*
Company:	*International Business Machines Corp.*
Official Title:	*Chief Privacy Officer*
Appointed:	*November 2000*

Computing giant IBM, or Big Blue, employs more than 300,000 staff worldwide and generates about $90 billion in annual revenues through a combination of hardware, software and services. Harriet Pearson took on the role of chief privacy officer at IBM in the fall of 2000, bringing with her more than ten years of policy, legal and technology experience. She was a lawyer and engineer before joining Big Blue in 1993. Before becoming CPO, she was the director of public affairs.

As CPO, Pearson reports to IBM's senior vice-president and general counsel. She says that the reporting structure works well, though other organizations might have different approaches that are similarly effective. "In my mind, the important thing is to have the person responsible for data privacy policies and practices at a high-enough level, and reporting through a high-enough level, to facilitate bringing all the necessary parties together quickly to get the job done." Doing so also sends an important signal to customers and employees that the company takes the issue of privacy seriously.

Pearson is quick to point out that privacy is not a new issue for IBM; the company has had a privacy policy in place since the 1960s. "The emergence of the Internet caused us to focus our attention at a whole new level," she explains. This new environment required a flexible management system able to quickly adapt to a changing marketplace. "Appointing a CPO was an important step in extending our leadership and responsiveness to this issue." In Pearson's view, the "Internet revolution" is only 5 per cent complete. She strongly believes that there is a business opportunity for companies that can maintain a balance between an individual's desire for privacy and an organization's need to gather information. "In the next few years, some predict that 3,000 per cent more data will be collected than is now," she says, adding that concern about how this data is compiled and used makes maintaining customer trust more critical than ever. "If any business loses a customer's trust, that business is not going to last long. This is especially true for any business or society that wants to take advantage of the efficiencies and conveniences of e-business and the Internet. Privacy has to be embedded into the fabric of our marketing strategies, how we act as a company and how our people with access to information behave and treat data. It's a crucial part of who we are and want to be. And it is crucial to defining and fueling the new age in which we live."

On a typical day, Pearson will talk with technology teams at IBM who are developing products and working with customers to fulfill their needs. She will also bring other relevant parts of the organization into the discussions so they can contribute to the company's broader privacy strategy. She often chairs teleconference calls or Web meetings with her team. Together, they focus their attention on the company's internal data-management system and privacy compliance needs. "I might speak with a government official, or engage in industry dialogue on data privacy practices; and I will talk with at least two outside organizations or customers facing challenges presented by privacy." Pearson devotes about 30 per cent of her time to what she describes as her "cross-functional, transnational" Privacy Management Team, a small matrix of specialists who work with hundreds of others in the organization on privacy matters. Another 30 per cent of her time is spent harmonizing IBM technology and research work with the company's privacy objectives; 20 per cent goes toward the privacy needs of IBM customers and partners; and another 20 per cent is typically set aside for public policy issues and industry initiatives related to privacy. Considerable time is spent with IBM's marketing department. In fact, one member of her team is a customer information policy manager who is part of IBM's sales and marketing organization.

One of Pearson's biggest challenges as CPO was assembling the right team of people and getting them up to speed on privacy issues. This was a particularly daunting task because of the immense size of IBM, which operates in 160 countries and works with hundreds of industry partners around the globe. "Getting the team focused on our current privacy objectives and quickly moving the agenda forward across multiple geographies and business units has been challenging," she says. "In such a large company, we need to work through multiple teams and channels to fully implement our strategy, and I get impatient because this takes time." Pearson is delighted with the outcome, however, and is proud of the way the company is able to advance the privacy interests and compliance needs of its customers. "We have a way to help them get started, assess their needs, decide which way they want to take their strategy and help them determine what role privacy plays in maintaining the trust of their customers and employees. And if they want technological solutions, we have that, too."

Looking forward, Pearson sees the role of CPO as invaluable for directing what is increasingly a very complex issue. But over time, she sees the job of CPO becoming less complex as systems are put in place to manage the issue. "I think the privacy issue will mature as e-business matures and comes into its own. When that happens, as long as we've laid the groundwork and continued our diligence, privacy as an issue should become more operationalized, internalized, part of the culture and a little less complicated."

Name: *Peter Cullen*
Company: *RBC Financial Group*
Official Title: *Corporate Privacy Officer*
Appointed: *September 2000*

RBC Financial Group — or the Royal Bank — is Canada's largest financial institution, employing about 58,000 staff and providing banking, investment, wealth management and insurance services to more than 12 million consumers, businesses and public-sector customers in 30 countries. Peter Cullen was named corporate privacy officer in 2000 to act as the "new gatekeeper" of the institution's 1987 privacy code. Cullen was senior manager of customer loyalty before taking on the CPO role. Since he joined RBC in 1976, the positions he has held have included manager of personnel services, customer service, branch operations and training. His educational background includes an MBA.

Cullen reports to a senior vice-president of e-business as well as a vice-president of customer information management. He says the job is somewhat unconventional for a large, established organization such as RBC, mainly because it deals simultaneously with the *risk* side of privacy, which relates primarily to compliance and governance, and the *opportunity* side of privacy, which addresses marketing and customer relationships. The right competencies from both areas help bridge the dualities of the position. Cullen's typical 12-hour day is anything but typical. "It is a mix of developing strategy, implementing things to accomplish this strategy and then dealing with the work required as a result of implementing," he explains. "If you have been successful with the implementation, answering questions and providing support becomes a big part of the day. All of this gets interrupted from time to time with privacy issues that require immediate attention."

Roughly 40 per cent of Cullen's time is devoted to RBC's personal and commercial banking operations, with an equal split between Canada and the United States. About 20 per cent of his attention is focused on the company's e-business strategy, and the remaining 40 per cent goes toward other business services — again, spread evenly between Canadian and U.S. operations. Crossing all boundaries is the task of aligning privacy protocols with information management and emerging business models. This, in turn, must all be aligned with marketing strategies and product/service designs that meet customers' needs and address their privacy concerns.

The position of corporate privacy officer was created at RBC for two reasons. First, the company wanted to differentiate itself from competitors by achieving competence in the privacy area. Demonstrating that it was serious about the first goal led to the second reason: RBC appointed a CPO to show regulators, advocates and consumers that it was solidly committed to the issue. "With the alignment of information use being core to the organization's strategy, we need to maintain our customer trust and the opportunity to achieve competitive differentiation."

Cullen's key challenge so far has been, he says, "managing the balance of time and resources." Over the long term, the idea is to get people in the organization playing their own parts with respect to privacy. "If anyone thinks they don't have to worry about privacy because someone else is, we are in trouble." He adds that it takes patience and diligence to transform the culture. "This is a change management process as much as anything else."

But he's satisfied with the outcome, pointing out that RBC Financial, backed by a history of strong privacy compliance, already has a culture and management discipline that makes managing privacy an important part of daily life. This has largely been accomplished by embedding privacy management into sales management. His next challenge, he says, is "turning privacy into a revenue part of the business."

Cullen says RBC has started to build a more comprehensive and expansive customer preference model that gives customers a greater level of control over how their information is used. "E-mail marketing is permission-based, and we are currently testing bringing a suite of privacy and security tools to our customers via a partnership with [software firm] Zero-Knowledge." The company is also measuring its customers' perceptions of privacy through surveys, and tracking customers' privacy complaints across a number of "listening posts," after which results are compared against the competition with the help of market research reports. The effort is producing results: customer complaints related to privacy have been reduced by 50 per cent.

Cullen believes that for many companies, the role of CPO over time will be as much visionary as operational. "The CPO will be able to demonstrate, in tangible ways, how privacy management delivers on shareholder value — not just cost avoidance but also revenue generation." Other organizations will choose to have privacy officers focused on managing business risk instead. "For us, this is a cost of doing business and needs to be part of the culture. Information use is the core part of our business strategy. Since privacy is about the use of information, the two are fundamentally linked, for now and the foreseeable future."

Name: *Jules Polonetsky*
Company: *DoubleClick Inc.*
Official Title: *Chief Privacy Officer*
Appointed: *March 2000*

Jules Polonetsky had his work cut out for him when he was hired for the position of CPO at DoubleClick, which runs the world's premier online advertising network. According to the company's press releases, DoubleClick "allows marketers to deliver the right message, to the right person, at the right time." As we discussed in a previous chapter, DoubleClick found itself in hot water after revealing in early 2000 that it was planning a service that would track the Internet surfing habits of consumers and simultaneously match the data to personally identifiable information. In February 2000, the U.S. Federal Trade Commission commenced an investigation into DoubleClick's activities — an effort that was subsequently dropped — and the company increasingly found itself the subject of negative reports in the media and from privacy advocates. Not surprisingly, the position of CPO at DoubleClick was created a month after the FTC investigation was launched, and Polonetsky, former consumer affairs commissioner for New York City, jumped into action. "I came in post-crisis," says Polonetsky, though he says the company had been considering the position much earlier as it transformed from being a pure technology company to an Internet data company. When he started, he says, "it was an uphill battle trying to regain and gain the trust of advocates and critics, many of whom had made up their mind that the company was wearing a dark hat, without having taken a hard, close look."

Polonetsky considers his role very similar to his job as consumer affairs commissioner. He sees himself as a kind of consumer rights "enforcer" at the company. "That helps guide my sense of mission and makes it easier for me to make tough decisions when there are business needs on the other side." His seniority within DoubleClick makes this possible. Polonetsky reports directly to the board of directors and also gives day-to-day reports directly to the chief executive officer. "It's a bit more of a degree of independence than sometimes one sees but it's the way the company thought it should structure the role and it's one of the reasons why I came in." For him, this independence is crucial when it comes to telling another employee or business partners — who may be motivated by a commission or revenue deadline — that a certain approach cannot be taken because it conflicts, from a privacy perspective, with DoubleClick's strategic direction. "The whole point of creating a chief privacy officer, even at companies where the reporting structure is somewhat different, is to invest responsibility in someone whose success is going to be judged less by revenue and operational concerns, but instead by the company's privacy reputation."

Wearing the CPO hat, Polonetsky calls himself a "jack of many trades" and a "master of some." Like his peers, Polonetsky juggles a number of responsibilities, from auditing and compliance, to legal counsel, to government relations, to consumer advocacy relations, to consumer ombudsman, to getting on the ground floor of product design. He also considers himself the corporate ethicist and moralist, "because today, some of the most challenging issues are the ones where we need to go beyond whether a practice is legally compliant." In a given day, Polonetsky may have to brush up on a country's privacy legislation, work with lawyers on an audit program or help train business clients on what they ought to be saying in their privacy policies. He might also join in on an industry conference call or two dealing with such issues as P3P specifications or the rules for using Web beacons (bugs). "There's always a mix of six or seven pieces of the job," he says. "It ends up being very much issue-driven."

Perhaps his biggest duty has to do with client education. DoubleClick doesn't interact directly with consumers. Rather, it deals with 15,000 business clients that use DoubleClick's technology to meet their online marketing and advertising needs. "A big part of my team is working with these clients to make sure they're appropriately describing what they do, giving choice to consumers and linking to our opt-out feature," says Polonetsky. "We're now the largest e-mail delivery service bureau in the world. There are lots of clients using our technology to deliver e-mail, so we help police their lists."

He estimates that about 30 per cent of his time is spent dealing with client education and compliance issues. Another 10 per cent goes to employee education, 10 per cent to internal privacy audits, 10 per cent to government relations, 10 per cent to internal product development, 10 per cent to mergers and acquisitions and 10 per cent to industry initiatives. The final 10 per cent is devoted to his role as consumer ombudsman. Polonetsky has a team of five privacy experts, not including outside consultants, and a budget in the "low millions" to help him get the job done.

The challenges for Polonetsky are many. One challenge is that the Internet moves at hyper speed, offering precious little time for thoughtful consideration and analysis of issues. A second challenge, where he believes more work needs to be done, is in convincing "the hardest-core privacy advocates" that the company is serious about privacy, defined in this case as a healthy balance between data protection and marketing opportunities. A third challenge is that DoubleClick's advertising network interacts with hundreds of millions of consumers around the world, but not directly. Instead, consumers deal with DoubleClick's business customers — Web portals, Web sites, Internet service providers and other clients. This puts the company in a difficult situation, because it is often held accountable for activities it cannot directly control. "It's somebody else's Web site, and somebody else's privacy policy," Polonetsky says. "But I'm the messenger who's killed when users don't like the e-mail or don't wish to have received that e-mail." In this situation, the objective is to educate, persuade, pressure and in some cases require clients and partners to comply with certain privacy standards. "We end up enforcing that in contracts and with audits and other processes."

It appears to be working. Polonetsky says he and his team have managed to change thousands of privacy policies on Web sites, which are now better at disclosing how they use information-tracking technologies on the Internet. He is also proud of the way the company now insists that data protection be the beginning element of product design. "We previously assumed it was our clients' responsibility," he says. "But that's not the case. When you understand the technology better than your clients, you're the creator of the technology and have to take responsibility for how it's going to be used. You, in structuring business models that others are going to use, are well served if you think of what you can build in down the line that will ensure clients follow a set of guidelines." Over time, and after a bit of nudging, DoubleClick's programmers began thinking about privacy ideas early on in the design process. "They've seen the reaction to not having privacy baked in," he says. "If I end up looking at their product at the end of the day, it's going to be a much greater inconvenience to them if they haven't scoped out a particular data-protection requirement early on." In this sense, DoubleClick has become an active "privacy partner" to its clients under Polonetsky's tenure.

Name:	*Kirk Herath*
Company:	*Nationwide Insurance Companies*
Official Title:	*Chief Privacy Officer/Associate General Counsel*
Appointed:	*May 2000*

Nationwide Insurance was founded in 1925 by the Ohio Farm Bureau Federation. Nationwide had only a handful of employees at the time, but the company has since grown to become the thirtieth-largest insurer in the world, with 30,000 staff managing more than 16 million policies and $117 billion in statutory assets in the United States, Canada and, through its affiliates, parts of Europe, Asia and Latin America. Kirk Herath was chosen chief privacy officer after senior management realized it needed one person who could coordinate the development and implementation of uniform privacy policies and procedures for the company. Nationwide is subject to the Gramm-Leach-Bliley Act on the federal level, in addition to state legislation. "There is a need to speak with one voice and create a high-bar policy that takes all of these laws and regulations into consideration," Herath says.

Herath reports to the senior vice-president and general counsel of Nationwide; previously, he also had to report to the company's vice-president of government relations. "Since my activities are primarily legal in nature, the current reporting structure is preferable," he says. Herath has also held the role of chief public policy officer at Nationwide, and before that was director of legislative policy at the company. He considers himself the "conscience of privacy" at Nationwide, and in carrying out that role, he often finds himself short on time. "I answer a myriad of phone calls and e-mails on privacy issues. I act as a consultant to the business and operating units. I also opine on the legality of certain products and services, and attend endless amounts of meetings in an attempt to get in front of all offices and business units," he says. "Managing information privacy consumes time quicker than any other activity I've ever observed. Perhaps because it's so big and touches everything." Fortunately, he has several staff who assist him directly and dozens of other people throughout the organization who form what he calls "my virtual privacy office." The job, he says, is ad hoc and unpredictable. Sales and marketing issues take up the vast majority of his attention.

But marketing initially did not want the attention. In fact, Herath says the marketing department at Nationwide was "one of the toughest nuts to crack" when he took on the CPO role. "I really believe that they thought I was trying to put them out of business," he says. "But that's not my job. My job is to help them facilitate their marketing activities within the parameters of the law. Once they realized that fact, my team has been involved in all of Nationwide's major marketing projects." He says the marketing people now bring their ideas to him well before the eleventh hour and they work together to craft a plan that fits both the law and the company's own privacy policy. "It has worked into a nice partnership," he adds. "I do not believe that marketing will be successful without addressing privacy issues contained in each campaign. I still truly believe that companies who ignore privacy will be damned to failure."

When Herath took on the role, his first duty was to map how policyholder information flowed through the company and its various operating units. It was a Herculean task, requiring dozens of interviews with people who worked in every corner of operations. His team needed to find out where information was coming from, what journey it took as it moved through the organization, where it ended up and whether it was secure and kept up-to-date when it got there. He hired a consulting firm to help him develop a strategy to comply with the Gramm-Leach-Bliley Act, then spent about 10 months drafting a privacy statement that was compliant. It cost the company more than $6 million to comply, an amount that covered everything from privacy-policy mailings to the upgrading of information systems. Since GLBA is not pre-emptive of state law, his team must always be aware of stricter rules — both existing or coming down the pipe — that may affect Nationwide. It is impractical to operate differently in each state, so the state privacy law with the greatest restrictions is often viewed as a de facto national standard. For this reason, another part of Herath's job is to lobby for legislation that is uniform with federal law.

Herath says one of his greatest accomplishments to date has been to sensitize company employees to privacy issues, as well as explain to customers how important privacy should be to them and how Nationwide is taking measures to protect their interests. Another accomplishment is that his privacy team is proving their worth to the company. "The fact we not only were created but that we continue to thrive in a tight budget year is a testament to the fact we've been able to keep senior managements' faith in us. Most companies do not invest in areas that provide no value to their customers." Where could he make improvements? "I'd like to have a nice book of policies and procedures that anyone could go to and use to help them navigate the privacy shoals. It will come in time, but we've not had the time to codify everything. We have a nice procedures manual for all our major business units and some of the areas have developed FAQs, but I'd like to find a place, probably on the Web, where we could catalogue these resources and make them more user friendly."

Name:	*Zoe Strickland*
Company:	*United States Postal Service*
Official Title:	*Chief Privacy Officer*
Appointed:	*Fall 2000*

When an organization has a 225-year history of dealing with the public, trust is absolutely essential. For the U.S. Postal Service, an organization that delivers mail to 134 million addresses and has nearly 800,000 employees, privacy, security and trust are at the heart of a good reputation. The amount of information handled by the U.S. Postal Service is staggering. It processes 46 per cent of the world's postcards and letters, amounting to more than 200 billion pieces of mail each year and contributing to $68 billion in annual revenues. It gets an average of three million visits to its Web site each month.

At the end of 2000, the privacy and security practices of industry and federal agencies came under increased scrutiny. The public began to question the ability of both government and industry to protect personal information. The deputy postmaster general understood that the postal service must continue to be a leader on privacy issues, in light of evolving business practices, new information technologies and heightened customer expectations. To maintain and enhance its trusted brand, the U.S. Postal Service took the ambitious step of appointing one of the first CPOs in the federal government. This position went to Zoe Strickland, who reports to both the vice-president of consumer affairs and the postmaster general. Strickland's privacy office has an annual budget of about $2 million, which goes toward resources for developing privacy-related policies and business practices, advising business units on privacy-related technologies and complying with the Privacy Act of 1974, the Electronic Communications Privacy Act, the Postal Reorganization Act and the Trade Secrets Act, all of which set limits on the disclosure of certain types of personal and business-sensitive information.

Strickland says her position is broad reaching and involves working with many internal and external groups. "It makes for interesting, though sometimes long, days," she says. "Establishing a new privacy program requires an extraordinary amount of personal attention because a new CPO must devote a significant amount of time building personal relationships throughout the organization, learning organizational responsibilities and becoming familiar with a wide range of management practices." It's not uncommon, she says, to log 12-hour days — even on the occasional weekend. Much of her day is spent reading about emerging issues, technologies and laws and regulations related to privacy; responding to up to a hundred e-mails; convening and participating in three or four meetings that bring together cross-functional teams to address compliance and strategy issues; and working with internal business leaders and external stakeholders (business partners, advocacy groups and government officials). A majority of her time is spent with departments that handle information security, marketing (including product development, sales and advertising) and information technology infrastructure. The rest of her time is divided between the legal department, public affairs, finance, operations, human resources and the Inspector General, which is an independent body that investigates and evaluates the integrity of the postal system.

One of Strickland's biggest challenges is updating and translating traditional notions of trust to those that can address modern privacy issues. "Ultimately, privacy must be built into the culture of a company," she says. But whereas business practices have been developed over time to protect the privacy of physical mail, new needs have emerged in today's digital environment. "We have done a significant amount of work to create business practices that help our employees address privacy throughout the product development process, rather than assuming that existing rules, regulations and business practices will be sufficient." She says public-sector organizations are under more pressure to respond quickly to consumers' privacy concerns. "It is not uncommon for policy leaders to impose very specific privacy practices on government organizations," she explains. "For example, when the use of cookies caught the attention of the public, the response from federal leaders was to strictly curtail the use of all cookies. Ultimately, the federal policy was revised to differentiate between session cookies and persistent cookies, but the series of policy changes focused attention on tracking devices on government Web sites for some time."

Strickland believes that as technologies change, public-sector organizations have a duty to deploy the latest business practices and technologies to protect personal information. However, she adds that CPOs in the public sector must also work hard to educate policy leaders about emerging technologies and business practices in order to drive broader policy guide-lines that can be implemented as quickly and easily as possible. The U.S. Postal Service is in a unique position among federal agencies, she says. Even though it is an independent establishment of the executive branch, it competes with private-sector firms and must therefore constantly monitor privacy business practices to stay at or above both government and industry standards. "That drove our decision to voluntarily comply with FTC best practices and other commercial guidelines, such as the Gramm-Leach-Bliley Act and the Children's Online Privacy Protection Act." Educating the public is another challenging goal. Strickland frequently addresses outside groups on privacy-related issues, but she believes that in general CPOs need to become better at articulating what constitutes best practices in privacy management. "We are all quick to point out that our companies are committed to protecting privacy, but how many people in the general public — or corporate leaders — can articulate what makes a company a leader in privacy?"

There have been many privacy-related accomplishments at the U.S. Postal Service since Strickland took the reins. In her first year as CPO, her team created and posted an enhanced privacy policy for the organization's Web sites that met or exceeded government and industry standards. The policy included an assurance that the organization would *never* sell person-ally identifiable information and would not collect it unless the user specif-ically or knowingly provided it. Consumers were also given the ability to review and correct their personal information. With respect to business partners of the U.S. Postal Service, a standard language was created for all vendor contracts. The contracts ensure that vendors doing business with the U.S. Postal Service obey the same restrictions on the collection of person-ally identifiable information and the use of tracking devices. For new prod-ucts, Strickland and her team developed business practices and a privacy toolkit that makes sure privacy is built into the business plan. The toolkit includes a manager's checklist that ensures compliance with specific privacy policies and statutes, and it helps to determine the sensitivity or privacy risks associated with new systems. Finally, regular audits are conducted to determine whether privacy practices are compliant with policies. Stickland's office, as well as an independent office of the Inspector General, conducts the audits. It should be noted that the U.S. Postal Service has adopted P3P technology for all its Web sites and uses Web audit software to monitor its sites for unauthorized cookies and other monitoring programs.

Strickland has five tips for newly appointed CPOs or those who are considering such a position.

1. Make sure you understand the organization's goals and the level of support for those goals. Then make a list of issues that will require executive backing and make sure you have the support you need.

2. Take time to identify the right departments or groups to be represented in your cross-functional privacy team. Your success as CPO will depend on how you work formally and informally with this team and how team members work with you. A strong, cross-functional team can get prompt results from senior managers.

3. Follow the data! Create a data map of your organization. Your information technology or marketing departments may already have the data sources you need to create that map. Companies with customer relationship management (CRM) systems may have already identified and catalogued the data. Ask around.

4. Focus on the product development process. It is much easier to build privacy into new products, services and contracts as they're being developed than it is to force compliance just before they go to market. (See "Build It In — Whenever Possible" in **Chapter 11**.)

5. When starting a new privacy program, it is important to meet people and develop strategic relationships throughout the organization. A new CPO should make the rounds, but should also establish processes that will help managers help themselves. "This, of course, becomes more important the larger your organization is," Strickland says.

Name: *Oliver Johnson*
Company: *Merck & Co.*
Official Title: *Chief Privacy Officer*
Appointed: *March 2001*

Merck is a research-driven pharmaceutical firm that has 69,000 employees throughout the world and is a Fortune 100 company. Merck's attention to privacy issues began when a number of people from various areas of the company took it upon themselves to investigate data-protection rules. Oliver Johnson, who had spent ten years at Merck as a lawyer for different operations within the company, was particularly interested in the European Union's Directive on Data Protection and the rules that governed the transmission of personal information to non-EU countries, such as the United States. "I raised that with my management, and through a series of interactions we became aware of what other people were doing about privacy at the company," says Johnson. "None of us had top-level coordination." He said the group got together and pitched a CPO position for Merck. Management asked Johnson to take on the role, which is administered through Merck's legal department. He reports to Merck's management committee, including the chairman, president and chief executive officer.

Johnson's typical day is not unlike his peers'. He meets with as many groups from within the company as possible to get a fundamental under-standing of how the business operates. He is in charge of a privacy team whose members have their own responsibilities and specialties. He manages outside law firms and consultants, internal staff, and organizations external to Merck, such as partners, who may have some influence on the company's privacy policies. A survey conducted in late 2001 by KPMG found that one-third of all U.S. pharmaceutical companies were "not serious at all" about privacy requirements in the Health Insurance Portability and Accountability Act (HIPAA) of 1996, which targets health-care organizations and certain drug makers. The survey also found that another 31 per cent were "not at all aware" of privacy issues and liabilities associated with HIPAA.[5] KPMG warned that the pharmaceutical industry should not leave the issue on the back burner. "I would tend to agree with KPMG," says Johnson. "Certainly, when we created the privacy office here, Merck took a position that was quite different than most in the industry. Privacy and data protection are major issues for pharmaceutical companies." He says Merck is directly covered by HIPAA because of its health benefits plans and onsite health clinics, which hold personal health information about individuals. HIPAA also indirectly affects Merck because the law covers other health-care entities through which Merck collects important information for marketing activities and clinical research. "The indirect impact is much more significant to us than the direct impact," he says. "The primary spirit of the law is to provide high-level protection to health data."

In addition to HIPAA, Johnson gives a lot of his attention to the EU Directive on Data Protection, which is important if a pharmaceutical company performs clinical trials in Europe and needs to import personal information back to the United States. Merck is a global company that does significant work in Europe. For this reason, the company became the first U.S. pharmaceutical company to sign the U.S.-EU Safe Harbor agreement, which allows the free flow of information between the two regions as long as certain privacy rules are observed. But Europe was just the start. "We are tracking legislation in a number of different countries," says Johnson. "Perhaps it's the lawyer in me, but I cannot be effective in a role if I can't understand the legal context in which those issues arise."

Likewise, context is necessary when dealing with Merck's various businesses. The company conducts basic research and clinical research, it manufactures drugs and it is a marketing organization. "You can't look at privacy in a single context. You have to look at it in all of these contexts." It helps, then, that his privacy team comes from a variety of backgrounds: legal,

[5] "Drug Makers Unprepared for HIPAA, Survey Finds," **www.drugstorenews.com,** January 17, 2002.

project management, research, marketing and administration. "A year ago we did not exist. Now we have people in the organization seeking us out and asking for our advice on a broad array of issues."

When it comes to training employees to be sensitive to privacy issues, Johnson prefers to spend his time with smaller groups of people rather than creating a headquarters-based program that is rolled out to the rest of the world. "What I have not done is create some large training program that every employee must go to for half a day," he says, adding that different approaches may work for different companies. "What I have done is communicate with people. A lot of people identify themselves and their own issues, then they ask me to come in and talk to them about those issues." In its first year, Johnson's privacy team gave about 50 different talks, by invitation, to people in every part of the company. "I have a rule," he says. "We do not turn down any internal speaking engagement. I don't care what it is, even if it's only three people making the request. It's one thing to have a generic training program, and a very different thing to have somebody from a clinical study call you up and say they have 30 or 40 people with questions. We will design a talk and give a talk to that group, and our talk tends to be very interactive."

Online Support

Many resources to help privacy officers stay on top of issues, trends, legislation and news are available free on the Internet. These resources are also available to anybody who has an interest in privacy, whether a concerned consumer or a CEO who wants to investigate the issue more seriously. Privacy and American Business (**www.pandab.org**) maintains a resource site at **www.privacyexchange.org**. The Privacy Council at **www.privacycouncil.com** provides an area on its site dedicated to the latest privacy news and issues. Both the Privacy Council and P&AB sites are geared toward a business audience, with a particular interest in serving the needs of CPOs. The Electronic Privacy Information Center and Privacy International jointly operate an information site at

www.privacy.org. Visitors can subscribe to free e-mail newsletters through all three sites.

The Privacy Foundation, a consumer advocacy group, maintains a site at **www.privacyfoundation.org** that provides research reports and news on privacy and technology. Although the site targets consumers rather than businesses, the information is insightful and representative of the top privacy concerns of the day. Similar information can be found at **www.privacy.net**, which gives consumers a crash course on privacy-intrusive technologies and their uses on the Internet. Another good resource is **www.privacyalliance.org**, operated by the Online Privacy Alliance, a diverse group of more than 80 corporations and associations that have joined together to promote an environment of trust on the Internet and to foster the protection of individuals' online privacy. In Canada, a firm called PRIVA-C has assembled a resource center with information from the U.S., Canada and Europe at **www.priva-c.com**. Presided over by Canadian privacy expert Brendan Seaton, PRIVA-C holds CPO workshops in several North American cities each year. The company also has a number of Web-based tutorials that a CPO can use to train employees about privacy issues and rules without the need for costly travel or in-house resources.

Dozens of other free and fee-based resources dedicated to privacy are available on the Web. A good search engine should locate them, though we are certain that what we have listed here will fulfill your day-to-day needs. If you prefer old-fashioned paper resources, subscribe to either Evan Hendricks' *Privacy Times* ($250 for 23 issues a year; **www.privacytimes.com**) or Robert Ellis Smith's *The Privacy Journal* ($125 for 12 issues a year; **www.townon line.com/privacyjournal**). If you have recently been appointed CPO, you might consider joining the International Association of Privacy Officers, a support organization resulting from the merger of the Association of Corporate Privacy Officers (an offspring of P&AB) and the Privacy Officers Association. The Conference Board of Canada has also set up a support group for Canadian CPOs called the Council for Chief Privacy Officers. The peer group meets three times a year to exchange ideas, share experiences and listen to expert guest speakers.

The Bottom Line

Privacy is a complex issue, one that is defined by legislation, simultaneously threatened and enhanced by technology, amplified by consumer fears and, more than ever, acknowledged in the business world through the creation of corporate policies and procedures. As a complex issue, privacy cannot be tackled in a haphazard manner — dedicated privacy officers are increasingly being called upon to bring coherency, consistency, compliance and continuity to the data-collection practices of organizations, creating a self-perpetuating culture of privacy that works to win the trust of consumers.

CPOs are not a fad. On the contrary, as information systems are increasingly populated with the personal data of consumers, CPOs will become a fact of life — another established "O" in the organizational hierarchy of our private and public sectors.

Chapter 7

We Didn't Mean It: Leaks, Glitches and Security Breaches

"Take a lesson from Watergate: It wasn't
the break-in that led to President Nixon's
demise; it was the cover-up."

Jonathan Gaw, research analyst,
International Data Corp.

Weak Defense

One of the eight principles of fair information practices (discussed in **Chapter 3**) is security safeguards: personal data should be protected by reasonable security safeguards against such risks as loss or unauthorized access, destruction, use, modification and disclosure of data. Security is not synonymous with privacy, but it is nonetheless an essential component of privacy, particularly in the online universe. KPMG's Mary Pat McCarthy and Stuart Campbell make this point very clear in their book, *Security Transformation: Digital Defense Strategies to Protect Your Company's Reputation and Market Share*. "If a company's privacy policy is to keep all personal information unshared, but its security architecture is so woefully lacking that outsiders were able to access clear-text customer records, then that company is both a security and privacy failure. In this case, its privacy failure is unwitting, but ignorance, as we all know, is no defense."[1]

---

[1] Mary Pat McCarthy and Stuart Campbell, with Rob Brownstein, *Security Transformation: Digital Defense Strategies to Protect Your Company's Reputation and Market Share* (New York: McGraw-Hill, 2001), p. 158.

Consider the following 12 security — and, as a result, privacy — breaches that occurred online during 2001:

- "A security breach at Travelocity exposed the personal information of thousands of the online travel company's customers, the company confirmed." (News.com, January 22)
- "Tax preparation site e1040 mistakenly switched off its encryption software … leaving customers' social security numbers and passwords exposed on the Web, a company spokesman said." (News.com, February 12)
- "Music company Columbia House left a hole in more than its CDs during the past week, when a security breach on its Web site exposed thousands of customers' names, addresses and portions of credit card numbers." (News.com, February 21)
- "Malicious hackers used a bug in PDG Shopping Cart — a popular e-commerce software tool — to break into a number of merchant Web sites and steal credit card numbers." (Newsbytes, April 10)
- "Lucent Technologies Canada got caught with its pants down yesterday after a visitor to its corporate Web site stumbled upon confidential files that contained the personal information of hundreds of customers." (Toronto Star, June 8)
- "Customers whose credit card details were exposed on the ComputerHQ site found it hard to believe that the company had not contacted them about the problem as soon as [a customer] alerted ComputerHQ about the security hole." (Wired News, June 18)
- "Several small online shops are exposing their customer order data, including credit card numbers, because of improperly installed online shopping cart software [DCShop]." (Newsbytes, June 19)
- "Customers of domain name registrar Network Solutions complained this week that private e-mail sent to the company's support department was being forwarded to others who had sent in requests for help. One e-mail … included an attachment that contained more than 200 private messages." (News.com, June 20)

- "Pharmaceutical maker Eli Lilly & Co. blamed a programming error for an incident last week in which it accidentally disclosed the e-mail addresses of about 600 medical patients." (The Industry Standard online, July 5)
- "Frequent fliers who logged onto United Airline's Web site got a look at other people's Mileage Plus account information for more than 12 hours thanks to a computer glitch." (Associated Press, July 25)
- "Detailed psychological records containing the innermost secrets of at least 62 children and teenagers were accidentally posted on the University of Montana Web site last week in one of the most glaring violations of privacy over the Internet." (L.A. *Times*, November 7)
- "Playboy.com has alerted customers that an intruder broke into its Web site and obtained some customer information, including credit card numbers." (News.com, November 20)

These examples are randomly chosen from the thousands of reported and unreported security breaches that took place in just one year on the Internet. In fact, the number of breaches reported in North America doubled between 1996 and 2001. According to the 2001 Computer Crime and Security Survey, an annual report from the Computer Security Institute and the FBI, 85 per cent of companies said they had been the victims of a security breach during the previous 12 months, compared with 42 per cent in 1996.[2] Of them, 70 per cent cited their Internet connections as a frequent point of attack, compared with 59 per cent only a year earlier. In a separate 2001 study by KPMG, it was found that hackers, poor implementation of security policies and lack of employee awareness ranked as the top three security threats to an organization.[3] The study also found that internal threats from current and former employees were a significant concern. (See Figures 7.1, 7.2 and 7.3.)

A big wake-up call came in October 2000, when Microsoft admitted that hackers, perhaps in Russia, had broken into the software giant's computer

---

[2] Computer Security Institute, "Financial Losses Due to Internet Intrusions, Trade Secret Theft and Other Cyber Crimes Soar" (press release, March 12, 2001; **www.gocsi.com**).
[3] KPMG, *2001 Global e.fr@ud.survey*.

Figure 7.1 • *Greatest Areas of Threat to E-Commerce Systems*

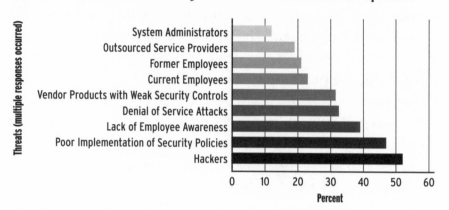

Source: *Provided by KPMG LLP.*

Figure 7.2 • *Customer Concerns in E-Commerce Transactions*

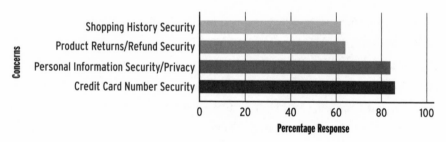

Source: *Provided by KMPG LLP.*

Figure 7.3 • *Factors that Prevented or are Preventing the Implementation of Full E-Commerce Systems*

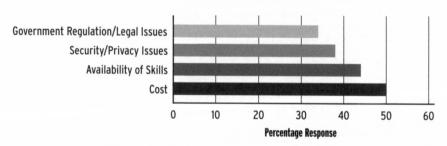

Source: *Provided by KPMG LLP.*

systems, where they had several weeks to snoop around before being discovered. The FBI was quickly brought in to investigate, but the event left people wondering: If a hacker can breach the computer systems of mighty Microsoft, a company that provides software that runs most of the world's computer systems, then how secure are the rest of us? How safeguarded is our privacy? How trusting can we be?

This chapter will explore these questions by looking at some common weaknesses in a security infrastructure, with examples of companies that have been caught "with their pants down." We will suggest ways that organizations can mitigate their security risks. What you will find is that technology itself is neutral — it is both the problem and the answer. Assurances of security and privacy will ultimately depend on the people and processes that put technology to work, and the choices that are made regarding its use.

Most sections in this chapter conclude with bulleted lists that offer tips on improving security and privacy for your customers. These are not comprehensive lists. Security is a critical component of protecting customer privacy, but an in-depth analysis of security per se is outside the scope of this book. We urge readers to seek out sources that are dedicated to security and include a higher-level overview of policies and procedures, attack and penetration, and network assessment.

Oops — It Was an Accident!

In the 12 examples of security breaches listed above, several reasons are given for the companies' problems. One was caused by a "security hole;" another was the result of a security feature being "mistakenly switched off." Software was "improperly installed" or contained a program "bug" or "programming error." One company simply blamed the breach on a "computer glitch," a blanket explanation that would seem to cover any problem.

But make no mistake: in most of these examples, the fault rests solely with an employee or a group of employees who did not follow proper policies and procedures or, perhaps more importantly, had no policies and procedures to follow. Still, judging by the frequency with which security problems are written off as "glitches," you would think that technology was the source of all unintended chaos on the Internet. The words "glitch," "bug" and "hiccup" have essentially become euphemisms for "Oops! We really messed up." When dealing with their public relations nightmares, companies often use these words to downplay the severity of a security problem and to transfer blame to a piece of software that doesn't have to report to a senior vice-president.

Cryptography expert Bruce Schneier, in his book *Secrets & Lies*, spends a great deal of time discussing "the Human Factor" as it relates to computer security. The way Schneier sees it, everything about a computer system — its hardware, software, network — can be protected with the latest and greatest security technologies, but everything can fall apart when we humans enter the picture, as we invariably must.

> When I started doing cryptographic consulting for companies, I would tell prospective clients that I could secure their digital data more or less perfectly, but that securing the interaction between data and the people would be a problem. Now I am more cynical. Now I tell prospective clients that the mathematics are impeccable, the computers are vincible, the networks are lousy, and the people are abysmal. I've learned a lot about the problems of securing computers and networks, but none of that really helps solve the people problem. Securing the interaction between people and just about anything is a big problem.[4]

While we do not wish to pin the blame exclusively on "humans" — software is sometimes full of bugs that are beyond the control of people — we do want to stress that human error is a factor that must be addressed. What is important is that companies identify matters within their control and then take measures to control them.

[4] Bruce Schneier, *Secrets & Lies* (New York: John Wiley and Sons, 2000), p. 255.

In the Travelocity.com example, the popular Internet travel site simply forgot to secure the personal information — names, addresses, phone numbers and e-mail addresses — of more than 44,000 customers who had entered an online contest. The mix-up occurred when the company moved its Web servers from San Francisco to a location in Tulsa, Oklahoma. During the move, an internal file that contained contest entry information was left in an online directory that could be viewed for more than a month by the public. "There were two or three chances for us to prevent the error," Jim Marsicano, Travelocity.com's executive vice-president of sales and service, told the Toronto *Star* a couple of days after the problem was discovered. "It was an eye-opener and, quite honestly, an embarrassing lesson to learn that something as simple as human error could cause this type of thing to happen."[5]

More and more companies are learning this lesson the hard way. Often, IT staff put too much trust in technology and don't know what to do when something goes wrong. Other times, an important yet simple task can be forgotten because procedures are not in place to guide employees through a particular process. Something as simple as "I forgot" can be prevented with "Here's a reminder." But that reminder is effective only if somebody listens and follows through. When it was revealed that Toronto-based wireless service provider Look Communications had left thousands of customer addresses, phone numbers and credit card numbers unprotected on the Internet, the company explained that a customer file was mistakenly left open by an employee who was testing a Web server. Hindsight may be 20/20, but this breach could have easily been prevented had a proper procedural checklist been followed.

Schneier points out that an employee, without appreciating the risks, will often ignore security procedures largely because they are seen to impose barriers on productivity or are thought to be inconvenient. "It has been said that the most insecure system is the one that isn't used. And more often than not, a security system isn't used because it's just too irritating," he wrote. "Even

---

[5] Rachel Ross, "Web Site Exposes Data on 44,000" Toronto *Star*, January 23, 2001.

today, when the deadline approaches and you have to get the job done, people don't even think twice about bypassing security."[6] Think about how many times you have stuck a password on the side of your computer or given it to a colleague simply because it's convenient. Now, think about how often your company's IT staff will temporarily turn off a security measure, such as a firewall or password-protection, because it is slowing down a project or interfering with another system feature. It happens more frequently than you might realize. Do they always remember to turn these features back on? According to the headlines, apparently not.

Of course, employees can also be tricked into bypassing procedures the low-tech way, through a technique commonly referred to in the hacker community as "social engineering." If you're the type of person who will hold the door for a stranger as you enter a staff-only area, then you could easily become a victim of social engineering, which exploits our nature as helpful, noncombative and generally trusting human beings. Let's face it: we generally don't like saying no — particularly to people we suspect are our superiors. Hackers and con artists take advantage of this tendency by pretending to be people they aren't and by claiming to have authority over something they don't. This need not be done in person — it can also be accomplished over the telephone or through electronic communications such as e-mail. On the phone, all it takes is confidence and a friendly yet persuasive persona. In person, props such as fake nametags, uniforms and business cards will usually do the trick. E-mail, which can easily be altered to look authoritative and official, is also an effective way to lure information out of employees.

Social engineers also thrive by putting people on the spot, which can be done by creating a crisis or some sense of urgency. Pressured to make a quick decision, panicky employees will often make the wrong one, by divulging passwords and account information to a complete stranger. After serving nearly five years in prison, well-known hacker Kevin Mitnick testified before Congress that organizations are throwing away their money as long as their employees can be

---

[6] Schneier, *supra* note 4, pp. 260 and 261.

duped. "Companies can spend millions of dollars toward technological protections, and that's wasted if somebody can basically call someone on the telephone and either convince them to do something on the computer that lowers the computer's defenses or reveals the information they were seeking."[7]

Humans are far from perfect, but that doesn't mean we can't strive for some improvement — or even a little common sense. Here are some tips for strengthening your company's security procedures:

- Promote security as a high priority that must be dealt with proactively, not as a secondary concern that tends to be addressed after the damage is done.
- If your organization has taken the time to set up security procedures, make sure all employees — from IT staff to frontline call center agents — have received adequate training and are made aware of how crucial these procedures are and how to avoid simple mistakes. In an *InformationWeek* survey, a third of companies admitted that less than 25 per cent of their employees were familiar with corporate security guidelines.[8]
- Discourage employees from bypassing procedures out of convenience or from being too slack with passwords by holding them more accountable, either through serious penalties or the threat of dismissal. Publicize these consequences.
- Guard against the dangers of social engineering by strictly limiting the number of people who have access to sensitive information and by making sure those people know, and can verify the identities of, the individuals to whom they can disclose that information.

The Inside Job

Procedural breakdowns that result from good people inadvertently doing not-so-good things are one problem. Another problem comes from malicious,

[7] Schneier, *supra* note 4, p. 267.
[8] "Beware of the Threat from Within" (*InformationWeek* survey of 2,375 U.S companies, October 16, 2000).

dishonest or disgruntled people intentionally doing bad things. Even though companies can attempt to screen the people they hire to make sure they're getting trustworthy, hardworking staff, in reality, you never know. Whether it's the bad seed that was planted the day he or she was hired, a desperate employee taking kickbacks to make some extra income on the side or an otherwise decent but disgruntled worker who is seeking revenge for being fired, the outcome can be devastating. Rogue employees can pose an enormous threat to security.

Consider the case of Nicholas Middleton, a computer administrator with a San Francisco ISP called Slip.net. In February 1998 Middleton quit, evidently unhappy with his job. The following month, he used another employee's name and password to access Slip.net's computer system, where he proceeded to create two fake accounts. Four days later, he used those accounts to destroy data on a Slip.net computer. He also accessed and altered customer accounts, killed a new billing system and severed service to a number of Slip.net's corporate customers. Middleton was caught, convicted and given three years' probation, but the damage was done. Slip.net's security, along with the privacy of its customers, had been irreparably compromised.

According to the Computer Security Institute/FBI, nearly 50 per cent of all network security breaches originate with insiders.[9] In another survey, conducted by *Information Security* magazine, 58 per cent of respondents said they had experienced security breaches resulting from employee abuse of computer access controls.[10] As well, nearly a quarter of respondents said that insiders were responsible for electronic theft, sabotage or intentional destruction or disclosure of proprietary data, which could include highly sensitive customer information. The threat from insiders becomes even greater during economic downturns. During late 2000 and into 2001, employees working in the technology sector witnessed a dramatic, and for some unexpected, reversal of fortune. Hundreds of thousands of people lost their jobs or saw their high-flying stock options plummet. For those lucky enough to stay employed, morale

[9] Computer Security Institute, *supra*, note 2.
[10] *Information Security* magazine, September 2000.

plunged and loyalties began to disintegrate. Security experts warn that during such periods, companies must be on high alert to prevent security breaches and sabotage. Companies that consistently have a high staff turnover should also take special precautions to protect themselves and their customers.

Here are some measures you can take to minimize inside threats:

- Education is the best deterrence. An employee will be less likely to take kickbacks or share corporate information with others if he or she knows the personal risks and consequences of doing so.
- If an employee has been fired or has quit on bad terms, politely walk the person out of the building. This pertains particularly to those who have had daily, high-level access to corporate systems.
- Immediately after an employee has been dismissed, close the employee's accounts and change system-access passwords. It is also a good idea to scan for viruses and other programs that may have been left behind as a way to sabotage a system or gain unauthorized access at a later date.
- Have proper audit trails in place to keep track of employee access to all systems and corporate data, and make sure that all employees are aware that such a tracking system is in place. The aim is to deter improper behavior and to foster respect for customer privacy.
- Install password-protected screen savers on all staff computers to reduce the chance that a rogue employee will breach security using a colleague's computer.

The Hack Attack

December 19, 2000, was a bad day for online electronics and computer retailer Egghead.com. That was the day the technical operations director notified executives that a hacker had broken into the company's computer system, where it was suspected that more than three million customer files, including credit card numbers and other personal information, had been illegally accessed. According to the reports, the hacker managed to penetrate deeply into the company's network and was able to launch a program targeted at its customer database. For nearly three weeks, neither the company nor its customers knew for sure whether there was a criminal on the loose with millions of active credit card numbers (and who knows what else) at his disposal. "This was a reasonably sophisticated job," Jeff Sheahan, CEO of Egghead.com, told one retail magazine. "I think this was a for-profit team of folks, not someone doing it for kicks or extortion."[11]

Fortunately, after several weeks of investigation, it was determined that no customer data had been stolen, mainly because Egghead.com's security staff had managed to shut down the system early enough, and the program launched by the hacker had failed. Still, many security experts and customers criticized the company's handling of the situation. Why was the customer database accessible from the Internet? Why did it take so long (the standard is less than a week) to find out what went wrong? Some analysts thought the length of the investigation suggested that the company had inadequate network monitoring and logging capabilities. The delay was costly — for Egghead.com, because its reputation was damaged (the company has since been sold as part of bankruptcy proceedings), and for a number of banks and credit unions who spent millions of dollars unnecessarily canceling and replacing credit cards. The costs to business are indeed high.

The attack on Egghead.com's systems could have been worse. In February 2001, Bibliofind.com, an online rare-book marketplace owned by Amazon.com, discovered that a hacker had breached its Web servers in October and had repeatedly gained access to its systems over the next four months. Unlike the Egghead.com case, the hacker who compromised Bibliofind.com managed to take thousands of detailed customer records, including standard information such as names, home addresses and credit card numbers. According to the 2001 Computer Security Institute/FBI survey, two in five respondents detected system penetration from outside intruders. Of those who cited attacks, 58 per cent reported ten or more incidents during a 12-month period.[12]

---

[11] Andee Joyce, "Egghead's Hacking Nightmare" RetailTech, April 2001.
[12] Computer Security Institute, *supra*, note 2.

We Didn't Mean It: Leaks, Glitches and Security Breaches

Examples of such breaches are in no short supply, but we will save some of these horror stories for the next chapter. The point is that hacker incidents are on the rise. The storage capability of computers is growing by as much as 70 per cent a year; as more personal information is collected, stored and circulated over the Internet, the risk to consumer privacy grows higher. Couple that with the proliferation of sophisticated and not-so-sophisticated hacker "scripts," quick and efficient programs that automatically sniff out vulnerable computer systems. By automating much of the process, hackers can find more systems to exploit in a shorter time. Companies must be more vigilant than ever in trying to secure their Web sites and computer systems from outsiders.

Consider the following steps to minimize the hacker risk:

- The Internet does not sleep — neither should your technical staff responsible for security. Companies should install intrusion-detection systems that continuously log all access and activity on the network. These systems should be monitored 24 hours a day and logs should be reviewed regularly for suspicious activity.
- If the data doesn't need to be on front-end Web servers, then take it offline.
- Make sure a firewall separates internal systems from the Internet.
- Securely encrypt all stored and transmitted data. If a hacker does manage to breach your systems, this additional layer of protection could prevent access to sensitive information.
- Patch it up. Many of the holes and vulnerabilities in computer systems can be easily sewed up if companies regularly communicate with their equipment and software vendors. Have a designated member of your IT staff regularly visit vendor Web sites to find out about new security patches for recently discovered software holes. A vast majority of security breaches through the Internet occur because of these holes, yet most companies do a poor job of plugging them up.
- Hack yourself. According to the National Research Council, companies should regularly try to penetrate their own systems as a way of discovering vulnerabilities before hackers do.

- Finally, if your company is hit by a hacker attack, tell you customers before they hear it from someone else. Explain what steps you are taking to rectify the problem. Above all: take responsibility. If your efforts to detect and catch the violator will be significantly affected by going public, plan the timing of your announcement carefully.

Virus, Worms and Trojan Horses

Melissa, Love Letter, Back Orifice, AnnaKournikova, Code Red, SirCam — the list of computer viruses seems almost endless, and it is growing exponentially. The 2001 Computer Security Institute/FBI survey found that 94 per cent of North American companies detected computer viruses on their corporate networks, up from 85 per cent the previous year. As viruses become smarter, stronger and more deceptive, you can expect that percentage to rise even higher. Generally speaking, a virus is a block of malicious code that is designed to infect computers. A virus spreads when infected documents or applications are transferred to another computer via floppy disk, CD-ROM, e-mail or some other electronic means. When the virus-infected application or executable document is launched, the virus is released into the new computer.

A quick-spreading class of self-propagating virus is known as a worm. Worms are different from viruses in that they do not attach themselves to programs. Worms are able to slither from one computer to another as long as these devices are connected to the same network, such as the Internet. A recent example is the Code Red worm, which threatened to slow down the entire Internet by flooding it with massive amounts of useless data. Code Red scanned the Internet looking for software security holes in Microsoft's Internet Information Server software, used to run e-commerce sites. The virus had a monthly cycle: it would aggressively spread itself for a couple of weeks, then it attempted to cripple the White House Web site with a barrage of useless data (known as a denial-of-service attack). After a few days, the worm would go back to sleep mode, only to wake up days later to start the cycle over again. The fear at the time was that Code Red would find enough ISS holes to replicate millions of times over. It was also discovered that Code Red had mutated, meaning there were now different versions of the worm to contend with. With so many worms scanning the Internet at the same time, it was believed that an unbearable amount of data traffic would slow down the operations of Web sites. The FBI, Microsoft and the White House stepped in and issued a warning that Code Red be stopped. The solution was simple: download a patch from Microsoft's Web site. But for some reason, it took a global press conference televised on CNN to spur organizations into action.

Code Red was not a privacy threat, but it does serve as an example of how organizations are not doing enough to plug security holes and eliminate system vulnerabilities. Without adequate protection, a company may find itself dealing with a worm that also threatens the privacy of its customers. The SirCam worm, which cropped up in July 2001, is a case in point. Like a great majority of worms, SirCam spreads by e-mailing copies of itself to all the addresses in the infected computer's e-mail address book, which tends in most cases to be Microsoft Outlook. If a recipient of this infected e-mail clicks on the accompanying attachment, the worm e-mails itself to a new batch of recipients. Left unchecked, this process can cause congestion on corporate e-mail servers. But SirCam causes much more harm than simply spreading itself; it also sends new recipients a random file that has been taken from the infected computer. These files can be anything — customer lists, love letters, employee payroll data, resumes, corporate memos. In one reported case, a Web site said it had received a secret document from the administration of Ukraine president Leonid Kuchma. The document included Kuchma's itinerary for an upcoming national event.

A Trojan horse is another virus-like program that has the potential to cause a serious privacy breach. Trojan horses are aimed at specific victims, who receive a malicious program that appears to be useful. Once a system is infected, the Trojan horse can erase or alter files, steal password data, capture keystrokes and break down security defenses so that somebody, a hacker for example, can later gain access to the system. Back Orifice 2000 is a well-known example of a Trojan horse. It allows a user to gain complete control over an organization's computer from a remote location.

Even when viruses don't cause excessive harm, they are almost always annoying and usually contribute to lost productivity. The majority start out as pranks aimed at defacing computer screens, adding political messages to the end of documents, or playing small sound files or cartoons. But a growing number of extremely destructive viruses, worms and Trojan horses are designed to erase data, confuse computers, slow down networks and break down the security defenses of organizations. These viruses come in many different flavors, and unless your organization takes the necessary steps to inoculate against them, it might just find itself in the middle of a major security and privacy crisis. You have to be proactive. "What people tend to do is patch today and then wait for the next big threat to hit," Michael Murphy, general manager of Canadian operations for anti-virus software firm Symantec, told us. Murphy says companies should be more disciplined and proactive when it comes to updating anti-virus software, instead of reacting after the damage is done.

Here are some helpful hints:

- Every organization that operates completely or partly on the Internet should use up-to-date anti-virus software, which can be bought through companies such as Symantec (**www.symantec.com**), Network Associates (**www.networkas-sociates.com**) and Trend Micro (**www.trendmicro.com**).
- Viruses spread and mutate quickly. Just as organizations should have someone dedicated to downloading software patches for known security holes, they should also assign someone — perhaps the same person — to monitor new threats from viruses, worms and Trojan horses. Again, vigilance is the theme. The latest updates can be downloaded from the anti-virus software sites.
- Employees should be warned not to click on attachments unless they are expected. Clever worms often customize e-mail to make it look as if attachments are coming from trustworthy sources. In such cases — or if ever in doubt — ask the sender to clarify the nature of the attachment.

Beware Wireless

A growing number of organizations are turning to wireless technology as a way to extend the reach of their internal data networks beyond the desktop. As well, many employees are using wireless technology to link various computers to their homes. There is no doubt that wireless networking has the benefits of flexibility, convenience and speed, but the tradeoff when using such technology may be the weakened security of your organization and the privacy of your customers. Currently, the most popular wireless local-area networks are based on the Wi-Fi (802.11) standard, which is built into equipment from vendors such as Cisco Systems, Compaq, Apple and Agere (Lucent). American Airlines offers Wi-Fi networks in most of its frequent-flier lounges so executives can work on their laptops while waiting for flights. Wi-Fi networks are now offered by many hotel chains that cater to the business crowd. Even Starbucks has begun installing Wi-Fi networks on its premises so hard working customers can stay connected while sucking back a grande latte.

The problem is, most of these wireless networks are not protected with encryption, or they use a security algorithm called wired equivalent privacy, or WEP, that can be overwhelmed and, worse, is rarely turned on. Consequently, wireless networks are highly vulnerable to a hacking technique called war driving. Ben Sapiro, senior consultant with the information risk management division of KPMG in Toronto, gave us a demonstration of war driving in August 2001. We hopped into a cab and began driving randomly through the streets of downtown Toronto. Sapiro, armed with a laptop, an antenna and a piece of software called Network Stumbler (there are others, such as AirSnort and WEPCrack), showed us how easy it was to pluck wireless networks literally out of the air, simply by driving to within a few hundred feet of a corporate or home user. In 15 minutes of driving, we picked up signals from 43 Wi-Fi networks, only nine of which had their WEP protection turned on. If these networks had belonged to law firms, consulting companies, hospitals or home users remotely connected to a corporate intranet, information up for grabs could have included confidential client data, intellectual property, medical records, customer lists and personal correspondence. Gaining unauthorized access to these networks is illegal, but Sapiro assured us that at any point he could have broken in with the click of a mouse. "It's like putting a phone jack on the outside of your building and inviting the public to plug in," Sapiro explained. "We could stop the car right now, get access to a company's network, and nobody would have any idea we got in."

Consider the following scenarios. An executive takes her laptop home with all sorts of sensitive corporate and personal documents on the hard drive. This executive connects her laptop to a home wireless network and begins to do some work. A war driver passes by her home and, by tapping into the home wireless network, gains access to the data being transmitted to and from her laptop's hard drive. A lengthy customer list and a number of confidential e-mails are taken.

In another scenario, this executive uses her laptop, which is still connected to her home wireless network, to access her company's corporate intranet. Again, a war driver parked on the street outside her home easily gains access to the company's intranet via the Wi-Fi link. A customer database full of highly sensitive personal information is taken and a destructive virus is left behind.

According to an August 2001 report from Gartner, three out of every ten organizations can expect to suffer some sort of serious security breach from a wireless local-area network by the end of 2002, unless measures are taken to secure such networks.[13] Gartner also estimated that one in five organizations already have so-called rogue wireless networks — that is, unauthorized wireless networks independently set up by employees without the knowledge of their employers. This situation is especially dangerous, since each employee represents a potential back door into a business's internal systems. Remember, all it takes is a $100 wireless LAN card and a piece of free software downloaded off the Internet for your company's wireless network to be breached.

KPMG and Gartner recommend the following measures when using wireless technology to extend the reach of your company's data network:

---

[13] Gartner Inc., "Firewalls Bypassed in Wireless LANs" (press release, August 9, 2001).

- Add as many layers of security as possible, such as file and transmission encryption, to deter hackers from targeting your company.
- Educate employees on the risks of using a wireless local-area network both at work and at home.
- Require employees to notify your company if they set up home-based wireless networks. Remote access to a corporate intranet should be done using VPN, or virtual private network, software. (This is also a good idea for cable modem or DSL connections.)
- Make sure that any sensitive information carried in company laptops is kept to an absolute minimum, password-protected and encrypted. Cab drivers in London, England, reported that 2,900 laptops had been left in their back seats during a six-month period in 2001. Imagine what that figure would be for an entire year, worldwide.

Sorry Isn't Enough

Customers have many expectations when they conduct a transaction with a company. They expect decent and reasonably speedy service. They expect to receive the product or service they paid for, at the agreed-upon price. They expect their transaction to be safeguarded. And unless they express otherwise, they expect their privacy to be respected. In a competitive marketplace, the likelihood is that dissatisfied customers will flee to the competition — or even worse, perhaps abandon e-commerce altogether. For most customers, hearing "sorry" after a "glitch" — that is, a major mess-up — may not be sufficient. They want to know in a timely fashion what went wrong as well as who, where, when, why and how. They also want to be assured that measures are being taken to prevent such "glitches" from happening again, and they will reward companies that follow through on their promises.

The message here is that your organization is ultimately responsible for unintentional information leaks, procedural breakdowns, employee sabotage, hacker attacks, malicious worms and other network vulnerabilities, wireless or otherwise. With existing and future laws requiring that consumer information be properly safeguarded, your organization might also be legally liable for security breaches that are the proven result of carelessness or negligence. There is also the unwanted public scrutiny and media attention that comes with these breaches. Avoid all the negative consequences by addressing the problem up front and introducing some preventive measures.

The Bottom Line

As one security expert told us, anyone would be able crack any network with the right amount of skills, resources and time. But the fact is, a majority of security breaches and privacy fiascos are simply the result of a mistake — someone not doing something they should, or somebody doing something they shouldn't. Your organization can take simple and commonsense measures to significantly minimize its security risks. Education, vigilance and awareness are a good start. Following the steps in this chapter will get you pointed in the right direction.

Chapter 8

Why Consumers Are Worried

> "Today, it is all too easy to imagine a world in which our digital autonomy has been stripped away, a world where our actions are monitored, our secrets are known, and our choices are therefore circumscribed."
>
> Simson Garfinkel, *Database Nation*

One-Way Mirrors

Picture a world where most of the mirrors you walk by are one-way mirrors, making it possible for unknown characters to surreptitiously watch your every step, monitor every building or store you walk into, see you as you try on clothing, as well as scrutinize your lifestyle and personal habits as you go about your day. Not only that, but the people behind those mirrors take notes on what you do and where you go, and they store these records indefinitely, often sharing them with other strangers so that a comprehensive — though not necessarily correct — profile of you can be created and repeatedly sold. And the mirrors are everywhere — in shopping malls, in bookstores, in video and music shops, at work, at the grocery store, at the bank, in your doctor's office, in your car and in your home. You can try breaking these mirrors, but there are far too many to count, let alone shatter.

The above scenario may be an exaggeration, but we believe the metaphor of the one-way mirror appropriately conveys some of the privacy fears that the average person has in a digital world, where surveillance remains a common practice. In our view, one-way mirrors are for police interrogation rooms, not for individuals who use the Internet to shop, entertain and inform themselves, or for those who conduct transactions with the expectation that their privacy is being respected. One-way mirrors — in the form of Web bugs, cookies, hidden cameras, interactive television and telematics — have made it increasingly difficult for customers to know who is watching them, where their personal information is flowing and whether the profiles of them are based on false, misleading or incomplete data. One-way mirrors are not only intrusive but they are bad for business, because they put consumers in a vulnerable position, creating a feeling of insecurity that ultimately steals confidence, breeds distrust and holds back the potential of e-commerce.

Dr. Larry Ponemon, chief executive officer of the Privacy Council and former head of PricewaterhouseCoopers' privacy practice, says there are far too many examples of companies that monitor and record the activities of customers without proper notification. He points to a privacy audit (among the hundreds he has conducted) he performed for a U.S. hotel chain that keeps lists of movie titles being rented by visitors. "While the name of the movie isn't on the bill, it is included in the customer profile," says Ponemon. "I saw one that said *Debbie Does Dallas Again*, right there with the customer's name. These data are shared with their many affiliates, including other hotels and restaurants. If you have a history of watching porn in their hotels, you may notice that they're offering you a greater porn selection, geared toward your tastes."[1] In another example, Ponemon describes an online career-search service that operated a chat room for disgruntled employees. The people who visited this chat room often criticized their employers, assuming that their online postings were private and confidential. It turns out that the search firm was monitoring the chat postings and trying to

---

[1] Larry Ponemon, "Gospel of Privacy Guru: Be Wary; Assume the Worst," interview by Dana Hawkins, *U.S. News and World Report*, June 25, 2001.

sell the information to employers as part of a tracking service. Perhaps the participants of the chat room should have been more aware of the risks. Nonetheless, the actions of the search firm were deceptive and intended to mislead. After nearly 300 audits over a three-year period, Ponemon was discouraged by what he found. "As an auditor, you reach the conclusion that it's pretty awful out there."

There is no doubt about it, Internet users worldwide are disturbed by such covert practices, even though most businesses have good intentions and are generally unaware when they've stepped over the line. A study by the Pew Internet and American Life Project found that 54 per cent of Internet users believe that the online tracking of consumers is a harmful activity, and 84 per cent of online users were concerned that strangers would somehow obtain information about them or their families.[2] Such concerns and fears will surely increase as existing tracking techniques are perfected and as new surveillance and data-collection technologies enter the marketplace. We are at a crucial moment in history, where high-tech gadgetry, affordable supercomputers, data-mining and -analysis software, powerful electronic storage systems and ubiquitous wireless and landline communications have converged to give businesses and governments an unprecedented ability to shadow, record and dissect the movements of consumers. Never before has snooping been so easy, or so potentially dangerous to the values we cherish and, so often, take for granted. Simson Garfinkel, author of *Database Nation*, wrote that the e-mail messages we create, the telephone calls we make, the credit cards and frequent-flier cards we use, and the bank machines we frequent all make up a "data shadow" of our lives — a term, he points out, coined by privacy expert Dr. Alan Westin of Columbia University.[3] Garfinkel argues that a person's data shadow is largely beyond his or her control.

---

[2] Susannah Fox, "Trust and Privacy Online: Why Americans Want to Rewrite the Rules" (Pew Internet and American Life Project, August 20, 2000).

[3] Simson Garfinkel, *Database Nation: The Death of Privacy in the 21st Century* (Sebastopol, Calif.: O'Reilly & Associates, 2000), p. 70.

> Scattered across the computers of hundreds of different companies, my shadow stands at attention, shoulder-to-shoulder with an army of other data shadows inside the databanks of corporations and governments all over the world. These shadows are making routine the discovery of human secrets. They are forcing us to live up to a new standard of accountability. And because the information that makes up these shadows is occasionally incorrect, they leave us all vulnerable to punishment or retaliation for actions that we did not even commit.[4]

Hundreds of technologies in existence today are capable of shadowing the lives of consumers. What follows is a list of some of the more popular — and perhaps notorious — applications and services that your business may be tempted to use, if it isn't using them already. Our discussion includes cookies, Web bugs, biometrics, satellite-tracking services, online passports, spyware and a number of other data-collection tools that threaten to create more one-way mirrors in our digital society. Our goal is not to criticize the use of these technologies but rather to point out their controversial nature and to suggest ways to minimize their intrusion on, or threat to, personal privacy. Excluded from this group are government systems that can tap into e-mail, telephone calls, voicemails and other modes of communication. The FBI's Carnivore system, for example (which was renamed DCS1000), is able to sniff out suspicious e-mail messages as they pass through Internet service providers. Meanwhile, a much larger and more powerful spy system, the mysterious Echelon network, has been called a communications "vacuum cleaner" because it can suck up and analyze all sorts of electronic communication signals in the name of national security. (The existence of Echelon has never been officially confirmed, but the system is believed to be shared by the United States, the United Kingdom, Canada, Australia and New Zealand. In the U.S., the National Security Agency would be the military intelligence body overseeing Echelon surveillance. The European Union has long suspected that Echelon is used to steal corporate secrets from non-member nations.) Though these government systems are as

---

[4] *Ibid.*

fascinating as they are controversial, our focus here is on technologies that are easily available and increasingly affordable in a commercial context.

Later in this chapter, we will detail the problem of identity theft, the fastest growing form of consumer fraud in North America, one that is feeding off the mountains of personal information that sit unprotected in the online reservoirs of our information economy.

The Cookie Monster

Most users of the World Wide Web would agree that there is nothing convenient or personal about visiting a favorite e-commerce site to buy some merchandise only to find that the transaction information provided during a previous visit — including name, address, shipping information and credit card number — must be re-entered for the umpteenth time. Such a time-consuming experience is akin to going to work every morning and having to identify yourself to a forgetful boss whenever you enter the office. Netscape programmer Lou Montulli was only 24 years old when, in 1994, he decided to give the Web something it was seriously lacking: a memory. Within no time, he developed online tracking tools called cookies that fundamentally changed the nature of the Internet by allowing Web sites to remember those who visited.

A cookie is a small file that is automatically placed on your computer's hard drive when you visit a Web site. Cookies can contain several elements: a unique user ID number, the name and address of the Web site, information about your activity on the site, information about your computer (e.g., browser and computer type) and an expiration date for when the cookie should deactivate. When you revisit the Web site, the site reaches into your computer, reads the information in the cookie and instantly identifies a previously assigned ID number, making it possible for the site to remember you and what you did at the site.

Why is this important? First, Web surfers no longer need to manually enter their user ID information when they return to a site. Second, cookies allow customers to leave a Web site in the middle of a transaction — say, with a shopping cart full of CDs and books — and return later to complete the purchase.

With cookies, the Web site remembers what's in the shopping cart and the customer shipping and payment information that was entered at the first visit. Without cookies, all would be forgotten. Third, cookies make it easier for Web sites to "personalize" the user experience. They track where customers go on a site and then match advertising, news, promotional offers and other services to the customer's interests.

But there is a dark side to cookies when they are used improperly. Before cookies were created, surfing the Internet was largely an anonymous activity. In the age of cookies, it has become far too easy for companies to intrude on the privacy of consumers without their knowledge or consent. Many companies simply don't inform online visitors that their Web sites use cookies, meaning customers are typically unaware that their hard drives are receiving tracking files. Indeed, surveys suggest that a majority of online consumers haven't a clue of what cookies are, let alone how cookies invade their privacy. Net-savvy consumers may figure out how to set their browsers to announce or outright reject cookies, or they can use special "cookie-crusher" software to accomplish the same goal, but even then, a growing number of Web sites — particularly financial sites — are making cookies a requirement for entry. Online auction giant eBay.com, for example, announced in September 2001 that all users of its site would be required to accept cookies if they wanted to use the service. Increasingly, consumer choice is being nibbled away.

Many supporters of cookies argue that the tiny files are harmless. They explain that cookies don't contain personally identifiable information, such as names, addresses and e-mail addresses. While this is true, it is easy for a Web site to match the user ID number embedded in cookies with site registration information, allowing companies to create a detailed profile of any customer's Web site activities. This becomes an even greater threat in the case of third-party cookies, which are common cookies that are disseminated through a large network of member sites, such as the online advertising network run by DoubleClick. A company such as DoubleClick is capable of tracking Internet users as they move between thousands of Web sites because a common third-party cookie connects the online dots. In other words, users drop cookie crumbs as they navigate the Web, making it easy for DoubleClick to follow their trail. DoubleClick, in turn, can use the information to better manage and target the online advertising of its customers, if it chooses. *New York Times* technology writer John Schwartz explains the potential danger of third-party cookies:

> If a Web surfer visited a large number of sites about AIDS treatment, for example, and if that data were tied to information that identified him — say, registration at one of the sites — an insurance company could, conceivably, collect the cookie data from an ad network and use it in a quiet decision to decline an application for a policy.[5]

Despite these risks, even privacy advocates recognize that cookies are a necessary evil on the Web, and that they're here to stay. Of course, privacy-friendly Web sites that choose not to use cookies should promote this fact to customers and use it to their competitive advantage. For those Web sites that choose to use cookies, a number of things can be done to reassure consumers and ease their concerns. A Web site's privacy policy should indicate whether cookies are in use and, if they are, should explain to consumers how cookies are relevant to the operation of the site. Assurances should be given that the information collected through the cookies is adequately safeguarded and kept separate from identifiable registration information. Web sites might also want to consider the use of temporary cookies that expire after a short period, rather than permanent cookies that allow for the tracking of consumers indefinitely. Finally, consumers should be given the choice of not accepting cookies, even if it means explaining to them how to block or screen incoming cookies through a browser's preference settings. After all, giving people a choice doesn't mean they will say no. Many won't — and you might just earn their trust in the process. If, in the end, you can't persuade them to say yes, then perhaps your business model needs a second look.

[5] John Schwartz, "Giving Web a Memory Costs its Users Privacy," *New York Times*, September, 4, 2001.

Bugging the Web

An increasing number of Web sites use a technology called Web bugs — tiny, essentially invisible graphics that are placed within a Web page for the purpose of tracking online visitors. Web bugs are also called clear GIFs or 1x1 GIFs, because they are usually so small — a single pixel on your computer screen — that they are unnoticeable with the human eye. Web bugs can collect much of the same information as cookies, such as computer IP addresses, the address of the Web page being looked at, the time and date the Web page was viewed and the type of browser doing the viewing. The bugs can be linked with site-specific cookies — however, one of the largest differences between a Web bug and a cookie is that consumers have absolutely no way of turning off Web bugs.

A study released in August 2001 by Cyveillance, an Internet analysis firm, found that the use of Web bugs is increasing at an average rate of 80 per cent each year. Over a three-year survey period, the company found that the number of Web pages that contained Web bugs increased by nearly 500 per cent and that 8 of 50 major brand names had Web bugs on their home pages. Another study indicates that top brands such as Yahoo and America Online regularly benefit from the use of Web bugs.

According to Cyveillance, companies not only need to worry about their own responsible use of Web bugs but also must be aware of whether business partners are using Web bugs, because association with these partners could pose a privacy risk.

The proliferation of Web bugs combined with the explosive growth of the Internet and vast online partner networks multiplies the risk to the average company of association with privacy concerns. When affiliates, suppliers, distributors, agents, etc. represent themselves as approved partners, there is an implied association that can set an expectation in the consumer's mind both regarding the experience they will have and a level of trustworthiness of the company. Some mechanisms that both authorized and unauthorized partners employ to secretly gain consumer information, if exposed, run the risk of being perceived by the consumer as a violation of their privacy.[6]

The key words here are "if exposed." Does a company really want to take that chance? While it is true that consumers can't turn off Web bugs, there are more and more ways for consumers to detect whether Web bugs are in use. For example, the Privacy Foundation, a consumer privacy group, released free software (an Internet Explorer add-on) in the summer of 2001 that gives users the ability to uncloak hidden bugs. The software, called Bugnosis, makes an "uh-oh" noise when a bug is detected. It also provides a way for people to send e-mail complaints directly to the company that created the bug. Richard Smith, who at the time was chief technology officer of the Privacy Foundation, said his goal was to get companies to "fess up" when they use Web bugs. "Any company that uses Web bugs on their site should say so clearly in their privacy policies and explain the following: why they are being used, what data is sent by a bug, who gets the data, and what they are doing with it."[7]

Openness and transparency are again key — be straight with your customers.

Biometrics

In the Stanley Kubrick sci-fi classic *2001: A Space Odyssey*, there is a scene in which two astronauts lock themselves inside a space pod to avoid being heard by HAL 9000, the homicidal supercomputer that has hijacked their spaceship. The two astronauts whisper to each other as they plot to take HAL offline. But HAL, watching through a window in the pod, identifies each astronaut, reads their lips and uncovers the content of their secret plan. This chilling scene was filmed in the late 1960s, but it accurately reflects the ways technology today can detect, scan, process and understand the identities and activities of human beings. This is in many ways what biometrics is all about.

[6] Brian H. Murray and James J. Cowart, "Web Bugs: A Study of the Presence and Growth Rate of Web Bugs on the Internet" (Cyveillance Inc., August 2001).

[7] Stefanie Olsen, "Privacy Group Shines Light on Web Bugs," CNET News.com [online], June 7, 2001.

Simply defined, biometrics is the identification or verification of individuals through their unique biological characteristics, such as a fingerprint or handprint. Other unique characteristics could include a person's palm, voice, eyes (iris or retina), signature or DNA. The International Biometric Group, or IBG, estimates that sales of biometric technologies will reach about $600 million by 2003, arguably a conservative figure in light of the terrorist attacks of September 11, 2001. "The market size right now is very small, but the market potential has barely been scratched," says Raj Nanavati, a partner with IBG.[8] For obvious reasons, the ability to accurately identify someone through biometrics makes the technology a compelling online and offline security tool. It provides an effective way of authenticating individuals who are authorized to access buildings, computer networks and online accounts or who want to perform secure Internet, mobile or in-store purchases.

Companies such as Bioscrypt and Indivos have developed systems that allow consumers to pay for groceries, clothing and other goods by having their finger scanned at a checkout counter — passwords, cash or plastic cards are not required. Once the person's identity has been authenticated against a pre-established customer account, the payment can be instantly processed. Likewise, on the Web, mouse devices with built-in thumb scanners and wireless phones with voice-recognition software may soon be a common way for consumers to securely engage in mobile and Internet commerce. Biometrics can also be combined with passwords or smart cards to enhance security for electronic transactions. For example, some ATM machines combine customer fingerprint scans with a PIN number to reinforce secure access to accounts.

But the sophistication of biometrics doesn't stop there. Biometric technologies have already made it possible for computers to spot our faces in a crowd, recognize us through our own unique odors and identify us through the rhythm of our walk. More than that, biometrics becomes an exceptionally powerful tool when the ability to identify a person is combined with the ability to analyze and understand that person's behavior. A computer scientist at Carnegie Mellon

[8] Tyler Hamilton, "Big Brother Goes Digital," Toronto *Star*, November 5, 2000.

University in Pittsburgh recently taught a computer how to read lips — just like HAL 9000. Another experimental technology developed by IBM, called BlueEyes, can record and interpret eye movements and facial expressions to determine somebody's emotional reaction — boredom, curiosity, excitement — to things like product displays and in-store promotions. Consumer advocates fear that one day these programs will be linked to face-recognition or other biometric systems, taking customer profiling to the extreme. "Once identity is established, it will be cross-referenced to capture that person's income and buying preferences. It's only a matter of time," Barry Steinhardt, associate director of the American Civil Liberties Union, told the MIT *Technology Review*.[9] In the U.K., popular bookstore chain Borders has already experimented with face-recognition software called FaceIt, provided by Visionics, in Minnesota. Borders said it installed the system to reduce shoplifting, but the company quickly suspended the project when privacy concerns were raised.

Biometric technologies can be categorized as active or passive, depending on how much control is given to the subject of a biometric scan. Active biometrics typically includes fingerprint, thumbprint, handprint, iris and voice scans, because an individual is required to participate directly in a transaction. (Iris scans, however, are soon expected to become passive.) In other words, nobody can force you to put your finger on a scanner, but if you do, this demonstrates you are aware of the technology and your direct participation implies some degree of consent. By contrast, passive biometrics — exemplified by face-recognition systems — do not always require an individual's participation, meaning the technology can operate in stealth. Remember the one-way mirror? With passive biometrics, people who believe they are walking anonymously through a crowd, in a shopping mall or in a store could easily be snapped, scanned, matched and profiled within seconds of being spotted by a hidden camera.

This was the case in January 2001, when 100,000 fans and workers attending the Super Bowl in Tampa Bay, Florida, had their faces secretly scanned as they passed through the stadium turnstiles. The photos were matched against a data-

---

[9] Claire Tristam, "Innovation: Behind BlueEyes," MIT *Technology Review*, May 2001.

base of known criminals and terrorists as a security measure. Similar systems have been used at casinos, airports and driver's license offices to detect undesirables or deter fraudulent activity, but use of the technology at the Super Bowl — which has since been nicknamed Snooper Bowl — was particularly controversial because fans were not notified of the intrusive measure. The terrorist attacks on New York City and Washington, D.C., have understandably sparked even greater interest in face-recognition technology, which is increasingly being used in airports and other crowded public places to spot known terrorists and dangerous characters. For example, planners of the 2002 Winter Olympics in Salt Lake City, Utah, used face-recognition technology as part of their overall security plan.

We believe that such technologies, as a complement to other security procedures and processes, are an important way of improving public safety and reducing fraud. But in their present form, biometric technologies can be extremely invasive unless strict controls are in place with respect to the storage and secondary uses of the biometric templates (see **Chapter 11** for more on this). The general guidelines for selecting and implementing biometrics are as follows: the system should have a proven benefit, it should be deemed necessary and its use should be limited to its original purpose — e.g., public safety, crime prevention or fraud detection. It should also be determined whether the system as designed violates any privacy laws. Can another system be used that is nearly as effective but less intrusive to individual privacy? If not, then the system being considered should be transparent, meaning individuals should be notified that a biometric surveillance system is being used. The goal here is to avoid one-way mirrors, by taking the "passive" out of biometrics and by giving privacy the respect it deserves. (Of course, it is important to acknowledge that transparency isn't always desirable. In matters involving police investigations, an organization may find it necessary that a covert approach be taken to catch known perpetrators. In such cases, users of the technology must rely on good judgment.)

Another major privacy concern with both passive and active biometrics is that a biometric measure, such as a face or fingerprint scan, can easily be stored with a person's identity in a database, which in turn can potentially be accessed by a number of third parties and used for a variety of intrusive or secondary purposes. This facilitates surveillance, by making it easier to track people's movements and obtain information about them. Thus, the threat to privacy comes not from the positive identification that biometrics provides but from the ability of others to access this information in identifiable form (i.e., with your name on it) and link it with other personal information, aiding the development of detailed personal profiles.

We believe that the potential for abuse could be reduced if the biometric itself was used as an encryption key — called biometric encryption, invented by Dr. George Tomko. Take the example of a fingerprint scanner in a grocery store. A customer sets up an account containing his name, address, telephone number, credit card number, expiry date, debit card number and PIN, which is encrypted by the unique characteristics of his fingerprint image. When the customer enters the store to buy groceries, his fingerprint is used only to confirm his eligibility for an automatic-payment service by decrypting his PIN — it is not used to divulge his identity, thereby eliminating the potential for secondary uses. The experience would be the biometric equivalent of using cash, but without having to carry any notes and coins. People can carry out their transactions privately in a "blind manner" without the electronic tracing of their activities. At the same time, fraud is virtually eliminated.

We believe that your biometric should serve as your private key, unique to you and you alone, for carrying out authorized, yet at times anonymous, transactions, which leads to both enhanced privacy and improved security. In the case of an airport biometric system designed to search for known terrorists, the digital image of your face or fingerprint should reveal nothing about you if it does not match up with information in a criminal database. Your biometric key would not open the door to the database — unless you happened to be on the FBI's Most Wanted list.

Satellite Tracking

In 1974, the U.S. Department of Defense launched the first of 24 satellites that, from an orbit 11,000 miles (17,600 kilometers) up, could pinpoint foreign military targets and steer ships through mazes of icebergs. By the early 1990s, the

U.S. military realized that its space-age navigational system — called the NAVSTAR Global Positioning System — could meet many commercial and personal needs as well. Today, civilians have free access to GPS signals, which, through a method called triangulation, can determine the location and velocity of any GPS-enabled device to within several yards. On its own, GPS is ideal for telling *you* where you are. However, when combined with wireless, Internet and mapping (Geographic Information System) technologies, GPS is perfectly suited for telling *somebody else* where you are or where something you own is located. This latter capability has spawned entire market segments, including child tracking, pet tracking, asset tracking, enhanced 911 for mobile phones, location-based mobile commerce, and telematics (vehicle navigation, stolen-vehicle location, fleet management and tracking).

Telematics is perhaps best exemplified by General Motors' pioneering OnStar service, which provides navigation, information and roadside assistance services to owners of luxury cars such as Oldsmobiles and Cadillacs. In a few years, it is expected that a majority of consumer vehicles will be equipped with an OnStar-like service, which can be used to find the nearest gas station, the fastest traffic route or directions in a foreign city. The service can also track down your car if it is stolen. Other companies, such as AirIQ and Fleetrak, are making great headway with commercial telematics applications that assist companies in managing and keeping track of moving assets. For example, a small trucking firm called Cam-Scott Transport in Ontario, Canada, uses a subscription-based telematics service from AirIQ to track a fleet of 84 trucks over the Internet. Not only that, but Cam-Scott is alerted if any truck strays from its course, speeds, overheats, is stolen or runs out of fuel. If a driver locks his keys in the truck cabin, Cam-Scott can ask AirIQ to remotely pop the locks.

Needless to say, telematics is a fascinating technology that has quickly become a multibillion-dollar industry. But with any technology that is designed to track people or "things," privacy concerns are inevitable. If GPS can pinpoint locations and compile information about the movements of people or vehicles, the routes taken and the length of trips, then it doesn't take much to predict — and pass judgment on — a broad range of personal habits or behaviors. This became immediately apparent to James Turner, a resident of New Haven, Connecticut, after he rented a minivan from Acme Rent-A-Car that was equipped with AirIQ tracking technology. Upon returning the vehicle, Turner discovered an extra charge of $450 on his rental bill. It turns out that Acme had monitored Turner's driving behavior, fining him $150 on three separate occasions for driving his rental vehicle faster than the legal limit. While Acme did state in its contract that it was using GPS and would fine speeders, Turner claimed the contract was too unclear on what the technology was and how it was being used. Turner's lawyer called Acme's policy "sort of creepy." Connecticut's Attorney General also stepped into the debate, accusing Acme of turning consumers into "unknowing victims of Big Brother tactics."[10] Meanwhile, the state's Department of Consumer Protection considered Acme's practices a violation of Connecticut law. No doubt, Acme never wanted or ever thought it would be thrust into such a controversial spotlight. But by moving perhaps too fast with a new technology without fully understanding or appreciating its privacy implications, the company inadvertently attracted a lot of negative press and government attention — bad for business, bad for market share.

Telematics offers just a taste of what GPS technology is bringing to our new economy. The wireless industry is gearing up for a slew of new services that will customize and target news, traffic reports, maps, directions, business information, advertising, retail promotions and other specials directly to where a person is located. The ability to track people on their mobile devices and offer them "geo-coded" services is expected to kick-start the market for mobile commerce, or m-commerce, particularly after new high-speed 3G wireless networks are introduced to the marketplace. According to Analysis Research, the global market for mobile location-based services will be worth $2 billion by the end of 2002[11] and as much as $18.5 billion by 2006. Part of what is spurring the creation of location-based technologies and services is a U.S.

---

[10] Michelle Delio, "Rent-a-Car Motto: Speed Bills." Wired News [online], July 12, 2001.

[11] Analysis Research, "Mobile Location Services to Generate US$18.5bn Global Revenues by 2006" (press release, February 14, 2001).

government mandate that all wireless service providers have the capability of locating a mobile phone user who has made a 911 emergency call. Today, it is difficult to track the precise whereabouts of a person who has called 911 on a mobile phone. At best, a person in distress can be tracked to a segment of the nearest radio tower, but this could still be miles away from the scene of an accident. Most wireless carriers in the United States have been slow to meet the government's mandate, but by 2005, all new mobile handsets are likely to be equipped with GPS technology or locatable through some other alternative, such as the land-based wireless tracking system developed by Canada's Cell-Loc.

Heather Fleming Phillips, a reporter with the San Jose *Mercury News*, nicely summarizes the issues surrounding location-based services and how they are expected to evolve:

> That technology will be used for emergency purposes at first, but will open the door for companies to send targeted ads on products, stores and restaurants. The location-tracking technology is a marketer's dream, and potentially a consumer's nightmare. It has the potential to track a shopper as she walks down the street, stops in at The Gap, and eats lunch at the McDonald's around the corner. Companies then could use the information to compile a detailed profile of that consumer's habits and buying preferences, and send targeted pop-up ads to her mobile phone for 50 cents off a Big Mac or two-for-one sale on T-shirts at The Gap. Wireless phone companies are eager to put the technology in place to generate additional revenue, but they're also aware that any privacy missteps could scare off consumers.[12]

You will recall our discussions near the end of **Chapter 2** of location-based technologies and m-commerce, and how decisions will need to be made today that preserve the privacy of consumers — and the reputation of the industry — tomorrow. The issues at hand are worth repeating: Will mobile consumers have the option to turn off the location-based feature of their handsets? Will consumers

---

[12] Heather Fleming Phillips, "Wireless Industry Treads Carefully on Privacy," San Jose *Mercury News*, February 7, 2001.

be given the choice to opt in or, at the very least, opt out when it comes to receiving location-specific advertising, promotions, coupons and services over a mobile device? If you are a company planning to use location-based techniques in your marketing and advertising strategy, how will you reflect this intention in your privacy policy? If you are a company operating a wireless network that collects the movements and mobile habits of consumers, how do you plan to safeguard that information and prevent it from falling into unauthorized hands? The potentially intrusive nature of location-based technologies must be addressed before companies that embrace it fumble their way into a major privacy controversy. Otherwise, laws will be passed to keep the use of such a powerful technology in check. Indeed, it appears that laws are already on the way. How can you, as a company, protect yourself and your customers? The answer is simple: Follow fair information practices.

Online Passports

Online passports — also known as e-wallets, Net IDs, single sign-on or "iden-tity" services — are exactly what they sound like: digital passports that allow registered users to move freely between a network of "member" Web sites, which in turn are able to identify who these users are, where their purchases should be delivered and what method of payment they prefer. Online passports save people from having to re-enter that information at the Web sites they frequent most. Single sign-ons can increase security by eliminating the need to remember multiple passwords, and also by allowing a single password change to protect all accounts at the same time. Passports often work with the help of cookies, and can contain as much personal information as necessary to facilitate Internet transactions and the delivery of various Web services. Basic personal information that may be contained within an online passport or e-wallet includes passwords, addresses, e-mail addresses, age, sex, language, credit card numbers and shipping information. Since the information in an online pass-port is stored on the Internet, the benefits of using such a service can be extended beyond personal computers to a variety of Web-enabled devices. The objective is to streamline e-commerce and enhance convenience, whether or not a person is using a PC, a laptop, a smart phone, a dashboard Web terminal, a public kiosk or a household Internet appliance.

Microsoft Passport is by far the largest and most popular passport service, with (as of 2002) more than 170 million registered accounts and more than 250 online merchants spanning as many as 40 countries. Microsoft cites convenience as one of the main benefits of Passport. "Passport simplifies sign-in and registration, lowering the barriers to e-commerce for the millions of consumers who are Passport members," the company states on its Web site. But Microsoft is not alone. AOL Time Warner, one of Microsoft's biggest rivals, had reportedly been working on a project called Magic Carpet that would essentially provide the same type of identity service. As well, a coalition of companies called the Liberty Alliance, led by Sun Microsystems, has announced plans to compete head-to-head with Microsoft in the area of online passports. Since the announcement, more than 35 companies have joined the broad-based group, among them General Motors, Nokia, Bank of America, RealNetworks, Cisco Systems, Sony, MasterCard International, American Express, eBay, NTT Docomo, Fidelity Investments and United Airlines. Even AOL Time Warner has since joined the group. Some experts say these three major passport initiatives may one day interact or merge with each other, ultimately creating an Internet super-passport with near-universal application.

But passport services have come under intense scrutiny by those who fear that too much personal information will be held by too few companies. Microsoft, in particular, has faced much criticism for Passport, largely because the popular identity service forms the core of the software giant's new Internet strategy, named .Net, and is a central feature of its Windows XP operating system. Microsoft's .Net strategy aims to create a vast world of Web services — for example, financial, medical, shopping, travel, scheduling and entertainment services — that can interact with, and be accessed through, a variety of Web-enabled devices. One Web service might send an e-mail alert to a person's pager whenever his favorite baseball player hits a home run. A second might alert an individual that the item she posted for auction on eBay has received a new bid.

Another could automatically schedule doctors' appointments or book airline tickets by interacting with a person's online calendar. Computers and devices using Windows XP are optimized for the .Net environment, meaning any XP device connected with the Internet will presumably — over time, of course — work in harmony with the Web services offered through .Net. However, the glue that binds all of this together is Passport, which contains the personal information that identifies who's who within this potentially massive, and so far exclusive, online marketplace being constructed by Microsoft. Indeed, anybody who uses Windows XP is strongly encouraged to register for Passport or else miss out on this fast-flowing future of e-commerce services and Internet applications.

But this vision doesn't sit well with many consumer groups and privacy advocates, who maintain that the long-term repercussions of having a universal ID system for the Internet are a direct threat to individual privacy. Microsoft has defended Passport and .Net, asserting that it does not plan to sell or trade the personal information of consumers. It also says that consumers will have more control when using Passport, because they will be able to manage who gets access to their information as well as how much of that information is passed along. Nonetheless, privacy watchdogs such as Marc Rotenberg, executive director of the Electronic Privacy Information Center (EPIC) in Washington, D.C., have their doubts. In an interview with the *New York Times*, Rotenberg said Microsoft has not proven itself trustworthy enough to be the gatekeeper of what amounts to tens of millions of consumer dossiers. "Microsoft has not established itself as the Fort Knox of Internet privacy," said Rotenberg, a day before EPIC and other consumer groups filed a complaint against the software titan with the Federal Trade Commission.[13] In its complaint, EPIC alleged that "Microsoft has engaged in and is engaging in unfair and deceptive trade practices intended to profile, track and monitor millions of Internet users." In Europe, at least one consumer threatened to file another complaint with the FTC, this time asking the federal trade regulator to investigate whether Microsoft's Passport system was violating the U.S.-EU Safe Harbor agreement.

[13] Steve Lohr, "Privacy Group Is Taking Issue with Microsoft," *New York Times*, July 25, 2001.

According to a survey from Gartner Group, 83 per cent of those who use Microsoft's Passport service do not feel comfortable enough to hand over their credit card numbers, suggesting that the company has a long way to go before it earns the trust of consumers. "Consumers are primarily concerned with their privacy and security, and they are not willing to sacrifice privacy in exchange for advanced Web interaction services, such as those offered by Passport," said Avivah Litan, research director at Gartner, which also found that one-third of online consumers are "very concerned" that Microsoft will have a difficult time keeping their personal information secure, or will be tempted to sell their data without asking for consent.[14] Litan said that Microsoft's strategy of bundling Passport with Windows XP may encourage tens of millions more people to subscribe to the service, but he said a lack of trust in Microsoft will likely result in people confining their use of Passport to the most basic features. It should be noted that Microsoft isn't the only large technology company that is struggling with its image with regard to consumer trust issues. Gartner also found that 37 per cent of online consumers have a high level of distrust for AOL Time Warner, compared with 29 per cent for Microsoft.

Only the future will tell whether Microsoft, AOL and the companies in the Liberty Alliance will be able to overcome these trust issues with passport-type services. Clearly, the hurdles are high — but not necessarily insurmountable. Microsoft has already started with the announcement of their new major strategy focused directly on privacy and security. One step in the right direction is to have a trusted third party serve as an independent guardian of the enormous information databases that feed Net ID services. In other words, outsource the job to the experts. VeriSign, one of the largest providers of Internet trust services, has already struck early security deals with Microsoft and is a member of the Liberty Alliance. Some industry observers say VeriSign may ultimately become a kind of privacy/security utility for the digital economy, holding information for profit-driven companies such as Microsoft and

---

[14] Gartner Group, "Gartner Survey Shows Consumers Largely Disinterested in Microsoft Passport, But They Sign Up Anyway," (media release, August 23, 2001; **www.gartner.com**).

keeping it protected — perhaps in encrypted format — from prying eyes. Consumers could then be given the key to their own safety deposit boxes in these databanks, unlocking their personal information only when needed at the time of a transaction.

So what does this mean for you? The important message here is that businesses looking to become member merchants of passport services, or even Microsoft's larger .Net initiative, will have to ask themselves how doing so will impact their own privacy policies as well as their relationship with old and new customers. By becoming part of such a large online membership, is your company's credibility or brand at risk if something goes wrong? It's a question worth asking.

Spyware

Also known as adware, media plug-ins, backdoor Santas and trojans, spyware is any piece of software that uses a person's Internet connection to secretly transmit information about that person's surfing — such as clicked-on banner ads — back to its parent company. Spyware is often bundled with freeware, software that can be downloaded at no cost from a Web site. The spyware is usually downloaded without the knowledge or explicit consent of the user because it piggybacks on a larger program. Once installed, the spyware runs in the background, quietly uploading information about a user's surfing back to its "mothership." For example, many digital file-swapping programs contain spyware that can tell a company and its advertisers that a person downloads a lot of rock music, pornographic pictures or action movies.

Most of this data is not personally identifiable, but many experts fear that such data could potentially be linked to personally identifiable information, allowing for the creation of detailed personal profiles that can be sold, shared and combined with other databases. If a user looks deep into the small print of a licensing agreement, he may find a vague reference to spyware, but this is insufficient at best. Whenever spyware is piggybacked onto a program, it is only good business practice to clearly notify users. This will give them a chance to cancel the download if they do not approve. Companies that fail to provide clear notification do far more than put their reputation on the line; they also risk being taken to court — and losing. As one U.S. federal trial judge said in a case against Netscape, "downloading is hardly an unambiguous indication of assent."[15] This is particularly the case when people don't know what they're truly downloading.

Electronic Tags

Tiny tracking devices, called electronic tags or transponders, are increasingly being used to speed up transactions. Electronic tags are one component of radio frequency identification, or RF/ID, systems, which use radio signals to identify packages and people as they pass through conveyor belts, checkout counters and store lineups. Exxon Mobile has more than five million customers using a device called Speedpass, a tiny transponder that fits on a keychain. The Speedpass is matched to a preregistered customer payment account. When Speedpass users fill up with gas, they simply wave their keychain in front of a reader on the gas pump, and the purchase is automatically billed to their account. Similar applications have been introduced throughout North America. McDonald's is experimenting with electronic tag technology at many locations in Chicago. Customers using the tags are billed automatically for the hamburgers and fries they buy as they coast past the restaurant's drive-through window — giving new meaning to the term "fast food." Increasingly, electronic tags are being used to manage warehouse inventories, track parcels, recover stolen vehicles and monitor the flow of airline passengers and their baggage as they move through airports.

Another application for electronic tags is "intelligent transportation systems," which employ advanced information and communications technologies to improve road safety and manage traffic flow. Transportation authorities, by monitoring the movement of your electronically tagged vehicle, can create more effective traffic-management programs and reduce congestion.

---

[15] Eric J. Sinrod, "To Make Legal Terms Stick, Make Web Users Click," USA Today.com (Law.com [online], August 23, 2001).

But like tags that track our purchases, tags that track our movements pose privacy risks. To work effectively, such systems must collect a considerable amount of transaction-generated information, which can be used to create profiles of consumers' travel patterns and spending habits. The possibilities grow more alarming if data from electronic tags is later linked with law-enforcement, medical, insurance, lifestyle or credit data. The challenge is to design these systems so that they can achieve the primary purpose of data collection, but no more. Privacy must be built in at the design stage to ensure that limitations are placed on secondary uses, not added later as an afterthought, which is far less effective. After all, who wants their daily activities to be bar-coded? We suspect very few of your customers would.

Interactive TV

New digital television services that provide Web surfing, e-mail, e-commerce, interactive advertising, interactive programming and customized viewing experiences are taking home entertainment to a new level. But in exchange for these high-tech TV features, consumers may be unknowingly giving away a great deal of personal information about their viewing, shopping and surfing habits. Interactive TV not only allows users to watch TV but it also makes it possible for the TV to watch back. A company called TiVo, for example, has been accused of making personal video recorders (PVRs) that can collect viewer data. PVRs let home users pause live TV shows and record favorite programs to a hard disk on a set-top box. The idea is to allow people to "time shift" programs and view them at a more convenient time.

According to a report from the Privacy Foundation, TiVo gathers information about user viewing habits and has the ability to match this data against personally identifiable records. TiVo says it is interested only in aggregate viewing behavior and that it has no intention of using data for direct marketing purposes.[16] Groups such as the Privacy Foundation fear that privacy policies could change

---

[16] David Martin, "TiVo's Data Collection and Privacy Practices" (investigative report for the Privacy Foundation, March 26, 2001).

after hundreds of thousands of subscribers are already locked in to the service. For its part, TiVo is aware of the privacy concerns and risks associated with the service. The company's 2000 annual report warns about uncertainty in the marketplace related to privacy concerns, as well as the risks involved with altering privacy policies: "Changes in the privacy policy could reduce demand for the TiVo Service, increase the cost of doing business as a result of litigation costs or increased service delivery costs, or otherwise harm our reputation and business." TiVo allows users to opt out of all information collection by calling a toll-free number. For the benefit of the entire industry, the hope is that TiVo, its peers and any newcomers to the field will continue to make privacy a top priority.

Your company may already be using one or more products that capture customer data, or may be considering implementing such technologies. We urge you to ask yourself: Is there a more privacy-protective option? The best option from both a privacy and a business perspective — and in some cases it may be the legal requirement — will be to have fair information practices put in place that minimize the threat to individual privacy. Consumers' fears will continue if a genuine effort is not made to address their privacy concerns in an open and responsible manner. As with any data collection, customer consent and notification is a must. Businesses should also have a clear purpose for using the technology, as well as a specific purpose for the data being collected. Both should be clearly communicated to the customer. As well, businesses should make every attempt to limit their use of this data, safeguard it from disclosure to unauthorized parties and assure its accuracy.

The aim here, as before, is for openness and transparency — stay away from covert activities and one-way mirrors, or else consumers are unlikely to give your company a second look.

Identity Theft
"Why steal from someone when you can just become that person?"

Bruce Schneier, *Secrets & Lies*

With so many surveillance and data-collection technologies gathering so much information about consumers, and with huge pools of this information stored in unsecured databases that are vulnerable to unauthorized access, it is no surprise that identity theft has become the fastest-growing crime in North America. Identity theft is the use of another person's identity, usually by acquiring identifying pieces of information, to commit criminal acts — mostly consumer fraud. Picking through garbage cans, picking pockets and raiding mailboxes are no longer the only way for fraudsters to steal an individual's personal information. In the digital age, identity theft has gone high-tech: criminals can use Internet search engines, do-it-yourself hacker kits and online "private-eye" search services to do all the dirty work for them — for a nominal fee or even for free. "The boom in e-commerce has created fertile ground for fraud," said Eileen Harrington, associate director of the division of marketing practices with the FTC's Bureau of Consumer Protection. "Internet technology is the latest draw for opportunistic predators who specialize in fraud. The rapid rise in the number of consumer complaints related to online fraud and deception bears this out: in 1997, the commission received fewer than 1,000 Internet fraud complaints; a year later, the number had increased eight-fold."[17] Often, all it takes is a bit of social engineering or "pre-texting" for criminals to get the information they need. A smooth-talking con artist can easily persuade a call center agent to reveal passwords and other account information about a particular individual. "Identity theft is a crime perpetrated both by individuals and organized groups," wrote Richard Power, author of *Tangled Web* and editorial director of the Computer Security Institute in San Francisco. "It is also a global phenomenon."[18]

---

[17] Eileen Harrington, "Internet Fraud" (presentation before the Subcommittee on Commerce, Trade and Consumer Protection of the House Committee on Energy and Commerce, May 23, 2001; **www.ftc.gov**).

[18] Richard Power, *Tangled Web* (Indianapolis: Que. Corp., 2000).

Here are some statistics showing the magnitude of the problem in the United States:

- The U.S. Federal Trade Commission reported 31,103 victims of identity theft in 2000, nearly half of which were related to credit card fraud. The U.S. states affected most were California, Texas, Florida and New York, and most victims were between the ages of 19 and 50.[19]
- According to the U.S. Treasury Department's Financial Crimes Enforcement Network, the number of identity theft cases reported by banks and other financial institutions in 2000 more than doubled from the 267 cases reported in 1999.[20]
- Credit-reporting agency Trans Union reported that identity theft has been increasing by 40 per cent annually since the late 1990s.[21]

Make no mistake: if the data goes into a computer system, there's no telling where else it might end up. The Privacy Foundation warned in a September 2001 report that online career services that store millions of resumes could be a potential target for identity thieves, who would find such information invaluable for creating false identities.[22] Privacy advocates are also concerned about bankrupt Internet ventures that attempt to sell their consumer databases to the highest bidders. Defunct companies such as N2H2, NSI, eTour, Boo.com and Toysmart.com were the subjects of public controversy when it became clear that the consumer databases they once promised to protect had become saleable assets. While this is essentially a "fair use" issue, it does have implications for identity theft.

---

[19] FTC Identity Theft Data Clearinghouse, "Identity Theft Complaint Data: Figures and Trends on Identity Theft, January 2000 through December 2000," **www.consumer.gov/idtheft/ reports.htm**.

[20] "Bank Identity Thefts Doubled in 2000," Associated Press, June 19, 2001.

[21] Carrie Kirby, "Identity-Theft Victims Struggle Against Rising Tide of Abuse," San Francisco *Chronicle*, February 10, 2001.

[22] Pam Dixon, "A Report on the Privacy Practices of Monster.com" (report for the Privacy Foundation, September 5, 2001).

Online contests or loyalty programs are another hot button, particularly if the Web sites gathering this information are not properly secured. In Canada, music TV station MuchMusic was forced to send an e-mail security advisory to thousands of individuals under the age of 18 who had entered an online contest. Many of these contestants had received "strange" phone calls from someone claiming to be a station employee. MuchMusic eventually determined that its Web site's database had been compromised. In another Canadian incident, a security flaw on the Web site of popular loyalty program Air Miles left 82 categories of personal information about nearly 50,000 members easily accessible on the Internet. To its credit, Air Miles went to great lengths to later secure its site and has subsequently developed some of the strongest privacy policies and practices in the industry.

Needless to say, though, there is a goldmine of unsecured information sitting unencrypted on the Internet that identity thieves would be more than happy to exploit. As search engines and surveillance tools become more powerful, it has become easier for criminals to aggregate information about a person and create detailed profiles that can be used for purposes of impersonation, purchasing goods, opening and accessing bank accounts, renting vehicles or, as we learned on September 11, 2001, to commit acts of terrorism. Soon after that day's attacks, the FBI named 19 hijackers that were believed to have crashed passenger jets into the World Trade Center Towers, the Pentagon and a Pennsylvania field. But the FBI later realized that the identities of some of those hijackers were false. "Identity theft, which was seen as an irritating consequence of modern life before September 11, is now seen as a potential threat to national security," wrote Farhad Manjoo, in an article for Wired News.[23]

Most times, however, identity theft is done for the purpose of fraud. Raphael Gray, a teenage hacker from Wales who called himself the Saint of E-commerce, was sentenced to three years of community rehabilitation and psychiatric treatment after he broke into hundreds of computer systems and stole more than 20,000 credit card numbers. Among the victims was Microsoft chairman and

[23] Farhad Manjoo, "Another Thing to Fear: ID Theft," Wired News [online], October 1, 2001.

billionaire Bill Gates. Gray used Gates's credit card number to order the executive a large package of Viagra. Gray managed to make nearly $3 million worth of fraudulent credit card charges before being caught.

In another famous incident, Abraham Abdallah, a high-school dropout from Detroit, used library computers in New York City to go online and obtain personal financial information about more than 200 of the richest and most powerful people in the United States. Abdallah used this information to steal $22 million from high-profile figures such as Warren Buffett, George Soros, Oprah Winfrey, Martha Stewart, Steven Spielberg, Paul Allen and Larry Ellison. These people were reportedly targeted because they appeared in the Forbes magazine list of the wealthiest people in America. How did Abdallah do it? He allegedly used pay phones and library computers to contact credit reporting agencies, such as Equifax, from which he obtained credit reports that allowed him to impersonate his victims and access their financial accounts.

But it's not only the rich and famous who are the victims of identity crimes. Far from it. In one case, Mari Frank, an attorney from Laguna Nigel, California, discovered that someone had purchased a sports car, spent more than $10,000 at Toys "R" Us, damaged a rental car and accumulated tens of thousands of dollars in debt using her personal information. In another case, an identity thief using the social security number and driver's license number of Kimo Crossman, a computer consultant in San Francisco, was able to spend up to $10,000 through existing or fraudulently opened credit card accounts. Imagine yourself becoming such a victim: you wake up one day and find that your bank account is empty, your credit cards are run up to their limit, your credit record is shot and you've been wrongfully linked to a number of criminal offenses. Worse still, trying to clear up such a mess and restore your reputation creates untold amounts of emotional, psychological and economic suffering. According to one study, the average victim of identity theft will spend 175 hours over two years attempting to get his or her life back in order.[24] The damage to the victim cannot be overstated.

---

[24] Carrie Kirby, "Identity-Theft Victims," *supra.*, note 21.

In the United States, the Identity Theft and Assumption Deterrence Act of 1998 was passed to strengthen existing criminal laws governing identity theft. The Act makes it a federal crime to knowingly transfer or unlawfully use another person's identification with the intent of committing, aiding or abetting a crime. The Act also gave the FTC more powers and resources to investigate complaints and study the nature of identity theft. But no matter how much legislation is put in place, or how diligent law-enforcement authorities are, a significant part of the problem is the ease with which someone can gain access to personal information. As one media report suggested, all it takes is $40 for a criminal to buy someone's social security number on the Internet. That number can then be used to collect more information, which in turn can be used to open and access bank accounts, buy expensive merchandise and obtain sizable loans. "It's risk free," said James Huse, social security inspector general, speaking at a U.S. House Ways and Means subcommittee hearing. "Why wouldn't criminals do it?"[25]

In California, an identity-theft law passed in 2001 aims to restrict the use and availability of social security numbers and credit records. Also that year, the U.S. Federal Deposit Insurance Corp. created guidelines to help financial institutions avoid the inadvertent release of customer information. Essentially, the FDIC is pressuring banks to put procedures in place that, among other things, prevent false change-of-address requests and prevent new accounts from being opened under false names. The guidelines also call for procedures that protect against pretext callers, who try to trick bank employees into releasing information about customers.

This is all a step in the right direction. But across all industries, both online and offline, businesses need to do a better job of safeguarding the information they hold about consumers. Otherwise, identity thieves will thrive, and consumer fears will be heightened.

---

[25] "Identity Theft Runs Rampant on Net, Inspector General Says," USA Today, May 23, 2001.

The Bottom Line

Consumers have good reason to be concerned and afraid. Everywhere they turn, one-way mirrors are covertly monitoring their movements, analyzing their purchases and creating detailed records of their lives. Consumers have a right to know whether their actions are being monitored, what information about them is being collected and, to a certain degree, how that information is being used. They also deserve to have that information protected, without fear that identity thieves or other strangers will access their information to commit crimes in their names or to harm their reputations. Legislation can help, but good privacy practices within the business community are the first step to preventing such problems at the source. And remember: a privacy payoff for consumers is a payoff for business as well. The two go hand in hand.

Chapter 9

The Impact on Marketing

"Direct marketing is an industry built on
customer trust ... Privacy is essential to good
business to establish trust with customers."

Robert Wientzen, president and CEO,
Direct Marketing Association

Database Marketing

In the previous chapter, we explored the various technologies that can be used to gather personal information about consumers, including cookies, Web bugs, online passports, spyware and mobile tracking technologies. In the offline world, customer surveys, contest entry forms, telephone surveys, magazine subscription inserts and loyalty swipe cards are a few of the more traditional methods of extracting both aggregate and identifiable data from consumers. When online and offline methods are used in conjunction with each other, companies have a potentially powerful marketing weapon: they can know who individuals are, where they live and work, what they eat and drink, how much they earn, whether they own a pet, the types of cars they drive, what medications they are taking, where they bank and hundreds of other potentially useful nuggets of data.

You might notice that we say *potentially* powerful and *potentially* useful. Like gold nuggets, data nuggets are random pieces of raw information that have little value until they are brought together and molded into something with a desirable structure and form. This is the key to a successful database marketing strategy, which might rely on data warehousing technologies to bring structure to data, business intelligence tools to give the information context and meaning, data-mining techniques to discover co-relations and trends, and customer relationship management applications to provide consistent and personalized interaction with customers. Only then do marketers truly get to know the person behind the customer.

In this chapter, we will discuss the power and the pitfalls of database marketing in the context of consumer privacy. We examine some of the false assumptions that often underlie marketing campaigns, the debate surrounding opt-in versus opt-out, the benefits of permission-based marketing and personalization, and the crucial relationship between data protection and information accuracy.

Database marketing is nothing new, except that today much more refined techniques are used to identify expressly targeted sectors and individuals. These methods have been called many things: niche marketing, one-to-one marketing, relationship marketing, target marketing, dialogue marketing and loyalty marketing. Much faster computers and networks, combined with parallel computing and new information-gathering and -analysis tools, enable marketers to identify smaller and smaller "niches" of the population, ultimately zeroing in or "drilling down" to the individual level. This represents considerable progress from past mass marketing, through which undifferentiated consumers all received identical solicitations. It even goes further than market segmentation, which organizes consumers according to common demographic features.

The problem with mass marketing — whether through the mail, the Internet, television, radio or roadside billboards — is that a large and diverse group of people is essentially drawn into opening, reading, watching or listening to the same message. All it takes is a delete key, a TV remote control, a twist of a radio dial or a nearby trash can to eliminate the message. Thus, mass marketing is ultimately an inefficient use of resources for a company, and an unnecessary intrusion into the lives of consumers, who typically view such marketing tactics as a time-consuming nuisance.

But when a company gets to know its existing and potential customers better, it can target its marketing efforts to individuals who will be more likely to see value in the products and information being presented. This, in turn, creates a need — and corresponding desire — for advertising with more substance and less tease. Technology guru George Gilder predicts a future where data-marketing techniques will significantly elevate the quality and usefulness of advertising. "In a world where advertisements are read only by people who choose to read them, the quality sharply improves," writes Gilder in his most recent book, *Telecosm*. "The hokiness and swarm we associate with Madison Avenue dissipates and the advertiser makes an honest effort to convey as much information as possible in as compelling as possible a style. Advertising becomes an art of trust rather than an art of deceit."[1] The key word here is "trust," and precisely how to build it with your customers.

False Assumptions

Gilder disputes the notion that consumer privacy is violated when an advertiser gains knowledge about that consumer. He says breaches of privacy are a reflection of *inadequate* knowledge, not excessive knowledge. "In a sense, telemarketers and other advertisers fail to invade our privacy enough. Someone calling you at the dinner hour to sell you a product of no interest is intruding on your time out of ignorance."[2] It is for this reason that Gilder believes that laws which restrict a company's ability to collect information about customers will contribute to private-sector ignorance, thereby increasing — rather than reducing — intrusions on privacy.

[1] George Gilder, *Telecosm: How Infinite Bandwidth Will Revolutionize Our World* (New York: The Free Press, 2000), p. 254.
[2] *Ibid.*

While we agree with Gilder that database marketing, in an ideal world, may elevate the quality of advertising and create better business-to-consumer relationships, we also believe that his general view of privacy is somewhat limited. Privacy is not just about transforming an intrusion into a welcome experience (through better knowledge); privacy is also about how much control consumers have over their information and the ways in which that information is used. You may be in the market for a red Corvette, but this doesn't mean you want Corvette car dealers bombarding you with faxes that use up valuable paper, e-mail that slows down your Internet connection, telephone calls that disrupt your private time and mail that litters your mailbox. Gilder's assumption is that with enough information about you, Corvette dealers would communicate with you using only the modes you wanted and at the times you preferred. But in order to gain that type of knowledge, they would first have to earn your trust and form a partnership with you. The Corvette dealer should not assume that you want the details of your personal interests, in Corvettes or anything else, sold to anyone and everyone who is willing to pay for it. Everyone has their reasons for guarding their personal information to varying degrees, and these reasons should not be dismissed by the assumptions of others. Do not presume to know what others are thinking — always ask.

As well, assumptions can inadvertently lead to negative outcomes for an individual. Imagine a situation in which a hospital sells the name and address of a pregnant woman to a direct-marketing company that proceeds to add her information, without her knowledge or consent, to dozens of online and offline mailing lists. The baby is stillborn, yet soon the woman is inundated with junk mail and spam aimed at new mothers. Sadly, an already difficult situation is made even worse. Even if there was no lasting harm to the grieving mother, it is neither a kind nor humane way to treat people — and it's simply bad business. The situation is no different with online banner advertisements that are targeted at users, whose seemingly harmless aggregate surfing data is secretly collected through cookies and Web bugs. A gay teenager who is not yet out of the closet might use the family computer to surf the Web for gay and lesbian books or chat groups and products targeted at the gay community. Web site tracking data that is collected through cookies is passed on to an online advertising network, which soon begins associating gay-culture banner ads to the IP address on that computer. A week later, the boy's father uses the computer to surf the Web and is inundated with those banner ads, causing him to suspect that his son is gay. A family dispute ensues, creating an embarrassing and potentially hurtful situation. Or consider interactive TV, which allows service providers to customize advertising based on viewing habits. It is conceivable that the private viewing habits of one person in a household could be revealed through personalized commercials that are viewed by another person in the household. Therefore, aggregate viewer data can still significantly intrude on someone's privacy. In a society where free choice is respected, people should be given the option of rejecting or accepting the ways in which they participate in the world — assumptions should not be made on their behalf. Take away a person's ability to exercise his or her choice and you earn yourself an adversary, not a customer.

This brings us to Gilder's position on privacy laws. Contrary to what Gilder implies, privacy rules generally do not prevent companies from collecting information about their customers. They can actually enhance data collection by ensuring that the data is relevant and, most important, accurate. Privacy rules and practices simply aim to give more control back to consumers by giving them an opportunity to decide whether to participate in marketing campaigns. Even if they do not, a company will ultimately save money from being misspent on wasteful contacts. "Data mining (and database marketing) is neither proscribed by law, nor is it bad for privacy," says privacy architect Peter Hope-Tindall. "It just has to be done with the individual's knowledge and consent."

Unfortunately, many consumers are in the dark with respect to how some marketers use their data. In Canada, for example, a 2001 survey by EKOS Research found that 54 per cent of people who participate in loyalty programs have no idea that their personal information — including their detailed buying habits — is being shared and sold, even though about 20 million Canadians have loyalty cards. "Overall, the findings reinforce the importance of obtaining meaningful consent from consumers to the collection, use and disclosure of individual consumer information for secondary marketing purposes," the study concluded.[3] Many marketers cite high participation rates in loyalty programs as an example of how consumers, while concerned about privacy issues, generally have no problem with their personal data being collected in exchange for reward points, air miles or some other perk. We believe this is a false assumption. Philippa Lawson, a lawyer with the Public Interest Advocacy Centre in Ottawa, said consumers may voluntarily participate in such programs, but they often don't know what they are joining and that their purchase trail is being followed and analyzed. "Clearly people cannot consent to practices to which they're unaware," said Lawson.[4]

Some marketers argue that in a free market economy, it is "buyer beware." And in an established market where the rules of operation are clearly known, they could say that consumers have to take responsibility for their choices. But when more than half of consumers don't know that their personal information is being sold, or their purchases tracked and profiled, then the "buyer beware" model is just a formula for annoying and alienating your customers when they eventually find out.

Our message to business: Don't assume anything — you will be putting your company at a disadvantage. Consumers have a right to make choices, and to know the implications of their choices. Knowledge and consent go hand in hand.

What Marketers Think

In 1993, the Canadian Marketing Association made it compulsory for members to comply with its industry privacy code, which required that consumers be given a "meaningful opportunity" to decline to have their personal information shared with third parties. According to the code, consumers should also be given access to their information and an opportunity to correct inaccuracies. John Gustavson, president and CEO of the CMA, said the rules were created because people have

---

[3] EKOS Research Associates, "Business Usage of Consumer Information for Direct Marketing: What the Public Thinks" (study commissioned by the Public Interest Advocacy Centre, August 2001).
[4] "Survey Suggests Consumers Don't Want Businesses Using Private Information," Canadian Press, September 6, 2001.

the right to control their personal information. "The Americans were horrified," Gustavson recalled. "They could not in their view require their members to comply with any principles." The CMA has more than 800 members, including major banks, insurance companies, publishers, telephone firms and Internet service providers. About one in five members are American companies operating in Canada. In 1995, the CMA went one step further, becoming the first direct-marketing organization in the world to support the creation of privacy legislation. Gustavson called on the Canadian government to pass comprehensive national privacy legislation that ensured that all private-sector organizations adhered to the same rules for the handling of consumer data. "Again, Americans were very upset because they didn't like the idea of privacy being legislated," said Gustavson. On January 1, 2001, Canada's Personal Information Protection and Electronic Documents Act went into effect, making many of the principles in the CMA's privacy code a legal requirement and creating a level playing field for all. In a guest column that appeared in the *Globe and Mail*, Gustavson explained the benefits of the new law:

> Business should view the privacy law as a business opportunity rather than a hindrance — at least for those who have done their homework and are prepared to respond. The law will certainly help build consumer confidence in using new technologies, and that in itself should be comforting to Canadians and for Canadian business. Without consumer confidence, privacy fears could effectively cripple growth in the marketplace.[5]

By the late 1990s, the Direct Marketing Association (DMA) in the United States had joined the chorus, making its privacy rules compulsory for its members. In 1997 the DMA's board of directors made a "Privacy Promise" to American consumers, and by 1999 all members of the DMA were required to follow four basic privacy-protection practices to fulfill this promise, similar to the self-regulatory rules put in place by the CMA and partially fulfilling the OECD's privacy guidelines. National privacy legislation in the United States,

---

[5] John Gustavson, "New Privacy Law a Win-Win for Consumers, Business," *Globe and Mail*, December 14, 2000.

however, is unlikely in the short term. Instead, marketers are forced to follow bits and pieces of privacy provisions buried in other state or federal statutes. In Gustavson's view, this fragmented approach in the United States puts an even greater burden on U.S. marketers, and is not as effective as national legislation in easing consumers' privacy concerns. However, there is no question that privacy is top-of-mind for most DMA members, which number nearly 5,000. According to a DMA survey, nearly seven in ten members have a top-level executive who is responsible for privacy within the organization. Nearly half of these members have sought consultants to help them develop their privacy practices.[6]

The good news is that marketers, whether in Canada or the United States, are increasingly embracing fair information practices to build stronger and more trusting relationships with customers. As well, new database marketing technologies are allowing marketers to focus their messages and better target their audiences. There is still a long way to go, but there is also much to gain. According to privacy expert Dr. Alan Westin, more than half of all consumers would happily accept direct marketing if they could also maintain control over their personal information. "Some people will opt out of everything if you provide them with the means. If direct marketing could really satisfy the other 75 per cent, that's where the future of direct marketing will lie."[7] As one prominent research firm once said, the low-hanging fruit of online customers has been picked, and if the e-commerce pie is to grow even further, online retailers will have to address the privacy concerns of a much larger, more demanding audience.

Opt-in Versus Opt-out

As we have established, there is general recognition in the marketing community that consumers should be given some control over where their personal information flows and how it is used, including whether or not they wish to receive

---

[6] Direct Marketing Association, "New DMA Survey Shows Privacy Issues Get CEO Attention" (press release, September 5, 2001).

[7] Claudia Montague, "Privacy: Getting the Information You Need Without Offending the Customers You Serve," *Marketing Tools*, November/December 1994.

unwanted advertising or direct-marketing solicitations from third parties. Exactly how this control should be granted, however, is the topic of immense debate. Should the onus be on consumers to opt out of a marketing program? Or should the burden be on companies to persuade consumers to opt in?

Opting in requires people to say "count me in" if they wish to receive marketing information from other companies or to have their information collected in the first place. This is also known as positive consent. Without such a positive indication, an organization must assume that individuals do not wish to have their personal information collected or given to other companies for other purposes. The second method, opting out, also permits a person to make a choice, but there is a subtle difference. Opting out means an organization assumes that people *want* to have their information collected and passed on to others *unless* they express otherwise, usually by checking off an opt-out box that appears on an online registration form or offline application or survey. If the box is not checked off — if individuals don't say "count me out" — the organization considers itself free to gather the information and use it in any way it wishes. But in many cases, organizations do not even provide an opt-out box, making it difficult for consumers to exercise control over their personal data. This is a business practice that should be discouraged and avoided.

From a privacy perspective, the ideal choice for a consumer is the positive consent, or "count me in," option. People can't opt in by accident; they must specifically request solicitations in order to receive them. We believe that businesses should strive to make opt-in a default setting, at least when they gather sensitive personal information on consumers – and, more importantly, if they plan to share that information. By using an opt-in approach, a company can signal to consumers that it respects their privacy and is willing to earn their trust and their business. Many marketers worry that positive consent may become a widely accepted standard; they fear that it will hurt their business. It stands to reason that if a consumer wants to hear more about a product or service, this consumer will ask to receive information about it. Indeed, a study by Ipsos-Reid, a global marketing research firm, found that four out of five Internet users in Canada opted into an average of 5.2 online marketing campaigns in 2001.

"There is no doubt that this medium can be effective when used appropriately," said Marcie Sayiner, senior research manager at Ipsos-Reid.[8] If a business can't persuade a consumer to opt into its marketing program, then it may want to consider whether that individual is worth the time and expense of pursuing.

In the EKOS Research survey mentioned earlier, seven out of ten Canadians said they considered opt-out approaches unacceptable. They preferred that companies ask for explicit positive consent to use their information for marketing purposes. But when businesses did use an opt-out approach, 82 per cent of those surveyed said it was "highly important" that the opt-out choice be brought to their attention in a clear way. Nearly 90 per cent said the opt-out option should be easy for them to exercise.[9] Americans generally share the same attitudes and concerns of Canadians when it comes to privacy and marketing. U.S. politicians, meanwhile, have struggled with the opt-in/opt-out debate. The general consensus in the privacy and data-protection community is that medical, financial and other sensitive information should be protected with an opt-in approach. Less-sensitive personal information can be gathered and shared on an opt-out basis, as long as the opt-out clause is clear and accessible to consumers.

In our view, a balance must be achieved between the two approaches. There may be a risk associated with imposing too high a standard for all types of information, as not all information or uses of information are privacy-sensitive. Requiring companies to use an opt-in approach across the board for every type of information they collect and for every use may be an overly costly and labor-intensive exercise. As a baseline standard, a better approach may be to use opt-in for times when it's truly needed — either when dealing with more sensitive information, such as medical and financial data, or when the third-party sharing of personal data could result in highly undesirable customer intrusions (e.g., rampant spam). In the next section, you will read why companies may choose to raise the bar even higher through permission marketing.

[8] Ipsos-Reid, "Email Marketing: What the Future Holds" (special supplement to *Canadian Interactive Reid Report*, March 2002).
[9] EKOS Research, *supra*, note 3.

As the debate over opt-in and opt-out proceeds, millions of consumers continue to be denied either option, a situation that reflects negatively on all marketers. Clearly, the industry must move quickly to develop a privacy-friendly standard that is acceptable to all and followed by all. Companies that take a progressive approach to implementing fair information practices today will be far ahead of the game tomorrow, especially when legislation is introduced.

The Benefits of Permission

Opt-in marketing is often referred to as permission marketing, particularly in the context of the Internet and other electronic media. Advocates of permission marketing argue that information overload has become the enemy of traditional "interruption marketing," through which consumers and small businesses are constantly and indiscriminately flooded with spam e-mail, automated telemarketing and fax broadcasting.

A marketing company in Toronto has taken interruption marketing to the extreme by developing sophisticated software that can plant unsolicited advertising messages in a customer's voicemail service. The software is able to sneak through a back door on the telephone company's network switches without being detected and without ringing the recipient's telephone. Although "back-door messaging" may seem less intrusive, advertising voicemail can quickly fill a person's voicemail box, leaving no room for legitimate and possibly crucial messages. This is similar to the way that junk faxes and e-mail use up valuable paper and network bandwidth, not to mention the time it takes to filter through and eliminate what amounts to electronic clutter. On the Web, this clutter continues to spread like wildfire. Pop-up advertisements, which open up new browser windows that block other Web pages, are a recent online annoyance, along with banner advertisements that expand in size when a mouse is inadvertently moved across a banner image. A company in Australia is even experimenting with "admail," a technology that can embed advertising messages directly into the text of an incoming e-mail, making it nearly impossible for a person to detect or filter out such advertisements in advance.

According to Internet-marketing guru Seth Godin, the author of *Permission Marketing*, people no longer have the time or patience to tolerate interruption marketing, which can easily turn potential customers into frustrated consumers. Godin's advice to businesses: Do a better job of persuading people to become volunteers in your marketing programs. Tell them why personal information is required. Will it be used in a way that benefits the individual? Why should this person care about a particular company's products and services? The answers to these questions must ultimately convince consumers that there is a benefit to receiving promotional e-mail and online advertising geared toward their specific interests and needs. "You tell consumers a little something about your company and its products, they tell you a little something about themselves, you tell them a little more, they tell you a little more — and over time, you create a mutually beneficial learning relationship," explained Godin in an interview with new-economy magazine *Fast Company*:

> The first rule of permission marketing is that it's based on selfishness: Consumers will grant a company permission to communicate only if they know what's in it for them. A company has to reward consumers, explicitly or implicitly, for paying attention to its messages. That's why the Net is such a powerful medium ... You can use e-mail to communicate with people frequently, quickly and unobtrusively — so long as they've given you permission to do that.[10]

Permission marketing is not expected to completely replace interruption marketing. For example, some degree of interruption marketing may be needed to get people's permission in the first place. However, from a privacy perspective, permission marketing offers several advantages. For one, the nuisance of unsolicited calls, e-mail and regular mail can be minimized, if not avoided altogether. The goal is to provide information that a consumer has voluntarily solicited

[10] William C. Taylor, "Permission Marketing," *Fast Company*, April 1998.

— a method of marketing that shows greater respect for consumers' choices. Permission marketing also places greater control in the hands of consumers, who are given the option of consenting and later withdrawing consent, and who can determine themselves whether their information should or should not be shared with third parties. Companies that embrace a permission-marketing strategy usually have an opt-in page on their Web sites, where consumers can voluntarily provide their personal information, including their likes and dislikes, lifestyle interests and demographic data.

Tessa Wegert, a media planner with Internet advertising agency BAM Solutions in Montreal, says that spam marketers have tarnished the reputation of the direct-marketing industry and that some regulatory or legislative measures may be needed to protect consumers and reward those companies who produce legitimate permission-based marketing campaigns. "For consumers, spam means dodgy e-mail messages from unknown sources, costly minutes of downloading time and an infuriating invasion of privacy," wrote Wegert in a column on the topic. "For advertisers, particularly those who fully recognize the negative connotations of the word, it represents potentially irreversible damage to the positive brand image that they have worked so hard to create ... As long as we can find a way to stomp out spammers before they corrupt this industry beyond repair, there is no end to e-mail marketing's potential in sight."[11]

To help calm consumer fears about online privacy, the Interactive Advertising Bureau, backed by companies such as DoubleClick, Yahoo and Terra Lycos announced an "awareness" advertising campaign worth more than $10 million in fall 2001. Banner ads on the Web instructed consumers how to protect themselves and their privacy on the Internet. Although this was a worthwhile public relations campaign, more must be done than shifting the burden to consumers. Ultimately, it will be the privacy practices of marketers themselves — not the surfing tactics of consumers — that will make the greatest difference.

[11] Tessa Wegert, "E-mail Marketing and the Fight Against Spam," *Globe and Mail*, October 10, 2001.

The Perks of Personalization

A study by Cyber Dialogue, an Internet marketing intelligence firm in New York, found that more than 95 per cent of online users have received spam and were annoyed by the experience.[12] On the other hand, the company found that people show a willingness to hand over a certain amount of personal information — most notably their name, e-mail address, level of education, age and special interests — if they feel they will receive a personalized surfing and shopping experience in return. Personalization is a method of marketing that uses technology and customer data to tailor advertising and services to an individual's personal wants, needs and interests. According to Cyber Dialogue, 65 per cent of Web users want personalization, to the extent that a Web site will remember their preferences and interests on each visit.[13] This figure was even higher in a study conducted by the Personalization Consortium, which found that 73 per cent of consumers consider it helpful and convenient when a Web site remembers their basic information.[14]

Personalization, when balanced with privacy, leads to online purchases. In another survey conducted by Cyber Dialogue and sponsored by the Personalization Consortium, it was discovered that 63 per cent of Web surfers would be more likely to register on a Web site that tailors content and services to their needs, and 56 per cent said they would be more likely to buy something from a site that allows personalization — as long as the personal data collected for this purpose was properly safeguarded and held in strict confidence. It was even found that 28 per cent of consumers who seek a personalized experience on the Web spent more than $2,000 online in 2000, compared with 17 per cent who did not take advantage of personalization.[15]

---

[12] Kevin Mabley, "Part III: Privacy vs. Personalization" (study, 2000).

[13] *Ibid.*

[14] Personalization Consortium, "Survey Finds Few Consumers Unwilling to Provide Personal Information to Web Marketers in Exchange for Better Services" (press release, April 5, 2000).

[15] Larry Seben, "Survey: Privacy Plus Personalization Equals Sales," CRM Daily.com [online], May 10, 2001.

Jonathan Gaw, an Internet research analyst with International Data Corp., is among a growing legion of researchers, thinkers and entrepreneurs who view personalization and privacy as complementary goals that can improve the overall performance of the electronic economy. According to Gaw, online firms need to do a better job of mixing the two ideas, rather than treating them as incompatible ingredients in two different recipes.

> The false dichotomy of "privacy or personalization" clouds the debate over the handling of customer information. It prevents online firms from addressing the issue in a balanced manner. Online firms need to clarify for customers the tradeoff of information and functionality. They should then allow customers to "dial up" or "dial down" the degree to which they accept the exchange. Online firms also need to better address issues of security, access, and enforcement of privacy policies. None of these issues necessarily impedes personalization functions, and instead can help generate trust with customers.[16]

And that trust should extend to the offline world, where many marketers still choose to target their customers by regular mail. Generic and seemingly anonymous junk mail campaigns are likely to create more suspicion or irritation than interest at a time when anthrax scares through the postal system, once unimaginable, echo in our memories. By contrast, more personalization and less envelope trickery may help ease consumer concerns. After the anthrax scare of fall 2001, the Canadian Marketing Association and other groups around the world advised their members to "stress the importance of security" in all direct-marketing campaigns.

Mobile (and Location) Marketing

In a mobile world, marketing and advertising becomes a much more sensitive subject, considering the new ways in which marketers can track down consumers and deliver highly personalized messages. Location-based mobile services, while

---

[16] Jonathan Gaw, "Online Personalization in an Era of Privacy Enforcement" (study, October 2000)

still in the early stages of development, have already made it technically possible to track the precise whereabouts of wireless phone users. Geographic coordinates can be combined with personally identifiable information and other descriptive data to create a consumer profile with unprecedented, and alarming, detail. Who collects this data, who they share it with and how it is used and safeguarded will be of immense concern for consumers, privacy advocates and government watchdogs as this nascent industry unfolds. The fear is that the mobile Internet will, as one newspaper report describes, become a "third-world bazaar, bombarding mobile phone users with confusing and annoying messages," all promising terrific deals, discounts and a slew of special promotions. This is further complicated in regions such as North America, where consumers have to pay for each message received, even if it's unsolicited.

The privacy-protective measures that are put in place today could very well make or break the success of mobile and location-based marketers. The wireless carriers that stand to become the gatekeepers of these services cannot afford a single misstep. "It has to be permission-based, otherwise it will be far too annoying and people will completely rebel," says Robert Blumenthal, vice-president of wireless Internet services at Telus Mobility of Burnaby, British Columbia.[17] Already, consumers view such services with suspicion. According to Forrester Research, 61 per cent of consumers believe it is likely that personal information collected through location-based mobile services will fall into the wrong hands if a business has access to it. The survey also found that 43 per cent of people believe that location-based advertising threatens their privacy, while only 10 per cent said they would find so-called push ads useful when delivered to a mobile phone.[18]

The above all depends, of course, on whether or not a person is granted the opportunity to opt into a mobile advertising campaign, rather than given the burden of opting out. Another survey, this time conducted by U.K. research firm the ARC Group for the Wireless Advertising Association, discovered that 65

---

[17] Kevin Marron, "Ads That Track You Down," *Globe and Mail*, June 8, 2001.

[18] Jay Stanley, "Surviving the Privacy Revolution" (Forrester Research, February 2001).

per cent of consumers who have opted into a mobile advertising program are willing to some degree to provide their personal information for marketing purposes. Nearly a quarter of those surveyed said they would be "very" or "extremely" willing, provided that the advertising campaigns are carefully targeted and relevant.[19] Both organizations also found that 77 per cent of consumers believe that mobile advertising must be opt-in.

What's certain is that, given *no* choice, consumers are going to protest. One wireless service provider in Toronto experimented with some of its mobile Internet customers by sending a single unsolicited text message to promote a local concert. The move caught customers by surprise, causing a small protest that forced the company to offer a public apology. "This is horrible marketing," said one outraged subscriber, who described the service as "ad pollution." A spokesperson at another Canadian wireless carrier said the company has already been forced to reimburse some customers for airtime charges that were incurred because of unsolicited mobile advertising — often referred to as wireless spam or "airspam." It should be noted that text-based advertising is just the beginning. New third-generation, or 3G, wireless services will make it possible to send multimedia commercials, advertising images and audio and video messages directly to a customer's mobile handset. The potential for clutter will be significant unless proper controls, preferably through a combination of self-regulation and regulatory rules, are put in place.

Some wireless industry groups have already taken steps to address these anticipated privacy issues. The Wireless Advertising Association, or WAA, whose membership includes top mobile device manufacturers, carriers, service providers, marketers and retailers, issued guidelines in 2000 dealing with the ways that personally identifiable information should be handled and spam should be avoided in a wireless environment. Most of these guidelines are based on fair information practices, with the WAA advising its members to provide marketing on a "confirmed" opt-in basis, meaning that the customer

---

[19] ARC Group, "Privacy Is Not a Barrier to the Success of Mobile Advertising" (press release, October 15, 2001).

would be given the choice up front to accept a mobile advertising campaign by giving a positive reply (such as pressing a specific key on the dial pad). The WAA's rules are not, however, compulsory for its members. Furthermore, though the organization has expressed its intention to develop guidelines for the use of information that is not personally identifiable (e.g., anonymous location data, log files and Web browsing activity on a mobile device), it has yet to implement these plans.[20]

Meanwhile, the Wireless Location Industry Association (WLIA) has drafted its own privacy policy standards to guide members with services specifically related to tracking the owner of a mobile device. Again, the good news is that opt-in consent underlines a set of fair information practices designed to ease consumer fears before, not after, the mobile-commerce industry grows up. Obviously, people who sign up for a location-based wireless service understand they'll be tracked, since this is the whole purpose of the service. Subscribers maintain control because they retain the ability to activate and deactivate location-based features at will. According to the draft policy, "WLIA members should (will) notify, and seek standard opt-in consent, from new subscribers of new services," and users will be given clear instructions on how to opt out or disable such services at a later date. Still, similar to the WAA guidelines, these standards apply strictly to personally identifiable information and are applicable only to WLIA members on a voluntary basis.

There is little doubt that the wireless industry and the location-based/m-commerce technology firms participating in this emerging market have learned from the privacy mistakes of their dot-com cousins. However, despite early efforts among these participants, it remains unclear that self-regulatory initiatives will be enough, or will be followed consistently enough, to satisfy customers. There must be more detailed analysis of the privacy implications of new mobile and location services. At a minimum, fair information practices should be considered the baseline privacy standard implemented by all

---

[20] The WAA is now the Mobile Marketing Association following its merger with the Wireless Marketing Association.

players. This is about far more than marketing and spam, this is about a future where the physical movements of millions of consumers will be tracked, stored, analyzed and shared. Can consumers truly be expected to trust such sensitive information to a new generation of private-sector organizations, companies without brand recognition or reputable track records? This has nothing to do with good corporate intentions, and everything to do with consumer perception. Common sense suggests that consumers have good reason for feeling insecure. In turn, marketers have a strong reason to eliminate this insecurity, by supporting the compulsory application of industry-wide privacy rules that will ultimately unleash the potential of mobile marketing and m-commerce.

False Data, False Choices: The Real Costs

An opt-in marketing strategy does more than simply earn the trust of consumers. By allowing consumers to control the uses of their personal information, permission marketing increases the likelihood that the customer data being collected and used is accurate and up-to-date. Both consumers and businesses suffer when data is full of errors. When an individual's personal profile is inaccurate or incomplete, there is a greater likelihood of that person being judged out of context or treated unfairly. Meanwhile, there is a high cost to businesses when their customer databases are riddled with errors. A wrong name or address can lead to misdirected advertising, ineffective marketing and wasted resources. Likewise, incorrect customer information can skew the results that are generated from data-mining and business intelligence software, applications that are often used to make critical business and marketing decisions. "It is a truism to say that data analysis can only be as good as the data itself," Bruce Slane, privacy commissioner of New Zealand, once said. Do you want the decisions being made at your company to be based on skewed data?

Sadly, privacy fears in the online world have driven many consumers, when they're given no other choice, to falsify the information they submit to Web sites and services. Studies suggest that between 20 and 50 per cent of online users have resorted to falsifying their information when attempting to use a Web site or gain access to an online service. A 2001 survey from Statistical Research of Westfield, New Jersey, found that one in five Web users have entered incorrect information to protect their privacy while trying to gain access to a Web site.[21] Technology consulting firm Accenture revealed in its own 2001 survey that 40 per cent of respondents gave false information to Web sites (similar to the 42 per cent reported by *Wired* magazine in previous years).[22] This figure is even higher for teenagers, of whom 53 per cent have given false information to Web sites to guard their privacy, according to a 2001 research brief by Forrester Research.[23]

It may be easy to understand why consumers falsify their information, but it is much more difficult to pinpoint the consequences of their doing so. The risks are many. Businesses may look at that incorrect information and make inaccurate assumptions about a person's lifestyle, likes and dislikes, age, income range, buying preferences and other personal habits that define this individual as a consumer. Once unleashed, incorrect information can "infect" other databases and other businesses, where it may lead to negative consequences: it could prevent someone from getting a job, obtaining a loan, securing an insurance policy or qualifying for a mortgage — and the person being rejected would never even know it. Even though the individual may have been responsible for the false information (such as when registering to gain access to a Web site), from a utilitarian perspective, it diminishes the benefit to both the company and the individual when they are presented with "false choices" that do not reflect their desired intent.

But even when personal information isn't intentionally falsified, databases still have a high margin of error. This margin of error increases as databases get larger and when more sources of data are relied on for collection purposes. An

---

[21] Statistical Research, "How People Use the Internet 2001" (study, June 2001).

[22] Paul F. Nunes and Ajit Kambil, "Internet Privacy: A Look Under the Covers" (Accenture Institute for Strategic Change, no date; **www.accenture.com**).

[23] Michael Antecol, with Becky Bermount, "Wired Teens Aren't Naïve About Online Privacy" (Forrester Research, July 24, 2001).

enormous amount of information is gathered on us every day — from the book purchases we make at Amazon.com to the contest forms we fill out at the grocery store or on a travel Web site. Many businesses rely on data-entry staff to enter this information, and electronic retailers must now ask their online customers to double as data-entry clerks. In both cases, hired staff and customers are equally prone to making typos and other mistakes, and there are often no processes in place for a business to verify the information or to prevent it from being doctored later. The potential for error is amplified when you consider that many of these customer databases are blended together and cross-matched in an attempt to make more complete — but not necessarily more correct — profiles. "The more databases involved, the greater the risk that the data is old or inaccurate and the more difficult it is to cleanse," writes Slane.[24]

Large databases are notorious for their error rates — conservative estimates range from 20 to 30 per cent. Larry Ponemon, CEO of the Privacy Council, estimates that there is an 85 per cent error rate in customer profiles, meaning that in each profile at least one piece of information is inaccurate. "That's huge," says Ponemon. He gives an example of how inaccurate data can lead to damaging assumptions: "One of our clients was a national diagnostics laboratory that sells the results of medical tests, blood work, biopsies, DNA screens. From the results, they try to determine your healthcare needs. Say you don't have AIDS but are taking a drug that's also used to treat it. They could incorrectly conclude you have AIDS, put that in your profile, and sell your data to a hospice. Their profiles were riddled with those kinds of errors."[25] And in the age of the Internet, this misinformation can travel around the planet in seconds, finding its way into other databases and to other people. The worst thing is, most people haven't a clue that inaccurate information about them is being stored or circulated. And most people have no idea of when or how they are

---

[24] Bruce Slane, "Data Mining and Fair Information Practices: Good Business Sense" (June 1998; **www. privacy.org.nz**).

[25] Dana Hawkins, "Gospel of Privacy Guru: Be Wary; Assume the Worst," U.S. News & World Report, June 25, 2001.

being misrepresented, or that decisions are being made without their knowledge that can negatively influence what happens to them.

So what can be done to eradicate this plague of misinformation? As we have already discussed, marketers and other businesses can first discourage the intentional falsifying of information by embracing a permission marketing strategy that lets consumers take control. When consumers feel they are in control, and when the information they provide gives them highly personalized and rewarding service, it is in their best interest to tell the truth. "Be patient," advises Accenture analysts Paul Nunes and Ajit Kambil. "Users are more comfortable revealing information gradually; they become more open to sharing as the perceived value in sharing increases."[26]

But the fact remains that customer database information can still be full of errors because of data-entry typos or the malicious alteration of data, as well as through the acquisition of erroneous data from third parties. This is why marketers should embrace fair information practices, giving special attention to the privacy principles of security, purpose, accuracy and access. Customer data should be properly safeguarded to make it more difficult to erase, alter or distort. The collection and use of this data should be limited to a specific purpose, thereby preventing any existing errors from spreading to third-party databases and making it easier to track and correct the errors. Accurate, complete and up-to-date information should be pursued by regularly verifying the source data. Finally, customers should be given access to their personal information, through protected forms of access, as they are the only ones who can truly verify its accuracy. They should also be given the opportunity to challenge the accuracy of their data and have it corrected, to prevent any future misrepresentation.

Although these privacy principles are aimed at protecting consumer rights, businesses will benefit enormously by ultimately reducing errors in customer databases and eliminating the wasteful use of marketing resources. Who wants to base their business and marketing decisions on inaccurate information? For businesses and consumers, increasing data accuracy is a win-win situation.

[26] Nunes and Kambil, *supra*, note 21.

The Bottom Line

Marketers will get more "bang for their buck," and will create more trusting and longer-term relationships with customers, if they choose a permission-based approach to their direct-marketing campaigns. Businesses should never assume that people want to have their personal information collected and used in marketing programs. Instead, they should simply ask, promising in return a more personalized and fulfilling online experience. Personalization plus privacy equals profit. If companies can get this formula right, the information they collect will be more accurate, their resources will be more efficiently allocated, and their customers will be more responsive. This is the future of effective marketing in an age of privacy awareness. Why settle for less?

Chapter 10

Workplace Privacy: The Boss Is Watching

"When invasions of privacy occur, employees
often feel that self-worth, morale, and the
overall quality of working life are eroded. The
ensuing negative impact of invasions of
privacy on work quality and productivity
is hidden human and real costs, not
often calculated by employers."

Ontario Privacy Commissioner, 1993

Judged at Work

Nobody seems to like being monitored and judged in the workplace — and U.S. federal judges are no exception. In the fall of 2000, the U.S. Administrative Office of the Courts ordered that the computers of all federal court workers be monitored. The office cited the need to improve network security and deter inappropriate computer use, such as playing Internet games or watching streaming video while on the job. Court staff didn't know the surveillance was taking place until a memo began circulating a few months later. Several judges from the Ninth Circuit Court of Appeals in San Francisco were outraged that they, their staff and 30,000 other court workers were being placed under a magnifying glass. In an act of defiance, on May 24, 2001, the judges ordered their own systems staff to temporarily shut down the surveillance and Internet-filtering program that had been installed, a move that affected about 10,000 court computers. "We are concerned about the propriety and even the legality of monitoring Internet usage," wrote Chief Judge Mary Schroeder in a memo-randum strongly criticizing the policy.

Judge Schroeder pointed out that use of the monitoring software was possibly a breach of the Electronic Communications Privacy Act of 1986, a law that makes it illegal for any person to knowingly intercept "any wire, oral or elec-tronic communication." She added that many court employees had already been disciplined as a result of such monitoring, though none of them had been given proper notice of the court's policy for computer use.[1] Needless to say, a highly charged debate ensued. Judge Edith Jones wrote in a letter to the Judicial Committee on Automation and Technology that such snooping tactics were unacceptable. "No one condones using government computers to download pornography, to gamble, to conduct personal profit-making business during office hours, or to achieve illegal or immoral goals. But to subject every judicial employee to random snooping and wiretapping of Internet communications is a drastic measure that should only be justified by proof of the most serious and systemic misuse."[2] In September, the 27-member Judicial Conference, a group of federal judges that governs court policy, announced that workplace privacy concerns merited further review and that a recommendation on giving "notice" would be evaluated "in light of developments in technology and recent concerns raised on privacy."[3]

Corporate America is no stranger to workplace surveillance, but unlike influ-ential federal judges, the average employee in the private sector has little recourse. A 2001 report by the American Management Association found that eight out of ten businesses in the United States electronically monitored their workers to some degree, more than double the number in 1997. The report, based on a survey of 1,627 organizations, discovered that 63 per cent of businesses monitored employee Web surfing, 47 per cent reviewed e-mail, 40

---

[1] Neil A. Lewis, "Rebels in Black Robes Recoil at Surveillance of Computers," *New York Times*, August 8, 2001.

[2] Matt Berger, "Judges Take on Digital Snooping Tuesday," *InfoWorld*, September 11, 2001.

[3] Administrative Office of U.S. Courts, "Judicial Conference Approves Recommendations on Elec-tronic Case File Availability and Internet Use" (press release, September 19, 2001).

per cent blocked inappropriate Web sites, 43 per cent tracked telephone use, 38 per cent used video surveillance for security and 27 per cent fired employees for "misuse" of office e-mail or Internet time.[4] Another study, this one by the Privacy Foundation, calculated that 14 million Americans — or more than a third of the people who have regular Internet access at work — are under constant electronic surveillance by employers who keep tabs on worker e-mail and Web use.[5] The rise in workplace monitoring has spawned an industry of software makers that specialize in surveillance and Internet filtering products. Technology research firm International Data Corp. estimated that organizations spent $62 million (U.S.) on Internet filtering and surveillance software in 1999, a figure that is expected to increase to $561 million by 2005.[6]

There is a long tradition of employers watching over employees to supervise their activities, supported by the belief that employees should be prepared to check their privacy at the door upon entering the workplace. After all, employers hire people to do a job, not to make personal phone calls, send e-mail to friends or use the Internet to search for summer vacation specials. The fact that employers own the equipment and space that employees use is for many enough to justify unrestricted workplace surveillance. Today's advancing technologies permit a far greater ability to monitor employees electronically and to probe more deeply into their lives. Computers, massive databases, networked communications, listening devices, video cameras and interception software all make it easier to monitor employees' actions, often covertly. But it is not clear whether such techniques enhance the performance of staff and advance the bottom line. One argument is that surveillance activities against employees are generally counter-productive, accomplishing the opposite of what is intended by increasing levels of workplace stress, decreasing motivation and trust, destroying worker morale and straining employee relations. Some

[4] American Management Association, "2001 Electronic Monitoring and Surveillance" (annual survey, April 18, 2001).
[5] Andrew Schulman, "The Extent of Systematic Monitoring of Employee E-mail and Internet Use" (report for the Privacy Foundation Workplace Surveillance Project, July 9, 2001).
[6] Jeffrey Benner, "Privacy at Work? Be Serious," *Wired News*, March 1, 2001.

studies have shown that employees experience higher rates of both physical and psychological problems in the presence of relentless monitoring.[7] Ultimately, it may come down to a question of fairness: Should employees be placed in a fishbowl?

That some U.S. federal judges, within the context of their own work environment, have become outspoken critics of employee surveillance suggests that employees should not have to check their privacy at the door. The expectation of privacy in the workplace may not be the same as elsewhere, but it does not — and should not — disappear. These days, more employees than ever are working longer hours, with less personal time. This affects their family life and challenges their health. Often, there is little distinction between work and home, since telecommuting and new technologies have blurred old boundaries. While there is certainly the potential for abuse, employees are often forced to do their online banking, shopping and personal communications during normal work hours. Are these personal activities not deserving of the same privacy that is expected outside the workplace? This is a matter of considerable debate. But one thing is clear: both employers and employees have legitimate concerns and needs. Balancing those needs in a fair and clearly disclosed corporate policy will go a long way in achieving internal workplace harmony.

The rest of this chapter will look at why companies monitor their employees' activities, the various ways in which they do this, and the legal implications of going too far. We will conclude by discussing how an organization, in implementing its workplace privacy policy, can balance the need to protect itself while respecting the privacy rights of its staff.

Why Companies Do It

There are many good reasons why employers feel compelled to monitor the electronic activities of their staff. One major concern, discussed in **Chapter**

---

[7] Karen Nussbaum, "Workers Under Surveillance," *Computerworld*, vol. 36, no. 1 (January 6, 1992), p. 21.

7, is computer/network security and the potential for corporate espionage. Employers are increasingly giving their employees open access to sensitive corporate and customer information. Increasingly, companies are monitoring their employees so they can know who is accessing this corporate information, when it is being accessed and where that information is being sent (e.g., to a business partner or an unauthorized third party). Proprietary data, corporate secrets and confidential customer data can often be mistakenly or intentionally released to outsiders, unless proper audit controls and monitoring measures are in place. Ironically, intruding on the privacy of employees is often necessary to protect the privacy of your customers.

Another reason for employee surveillance is to monitor staff performance, and at the same time to discourage activities that lower workplace productivity and efficiency. Use of company telephones, computers, Internet connections and e-mail to perform personal tasks, procrastinate or gossip with employees can become a drain on corporate productivity if left unchecked. Should an employee really be running an online auction on eBay during working hours? Is playing a game of solitaire or interactive Quake an appropriate use of workplace time? Not only do these activities distract employees from the job at hand but some of them can also use up considerable network resources. Likewise, e-mail messages with large image attachments can absorb a significant amount of network bandwidth. The huge popularity of Napster, MusicCity.com (Morpheus), Limewire (Gnutella), AudioGalaxy and other peer-to-peer file-swapping sites have caused considerable problems for companies, whose employees often spend the workday downloading massive picture, music and movie files to their desktops. Others prefer to choose audio and video broadcasts that stream a constant supply of online news, sports and entertainment to their screens. Such activities can slow a corporate network to a crawl, or shut it down altogether, preventing any real business from taking place.

But productivity, security and network efficiency concerns tell only part of the story. Perhaps the biggest reason why companies monitor their employees is to create a comfortable and safe working environment for all staff, by deterring harassment, discrimination and other questionable forms of Internet and e-mail behavior that could lead to expensive lawsuits. Indeed, one of the top reasons for workplace surveillance in corporate America is to avoid the legal liability resulting from the inappropriate online conduct of staff. According to the American Management Association, the results of an electronic policies and practices survey revealed that seven out of ten companies that monitored their employees did so to prevent and defend against workplace lawsuits.[8] Monitoring involved screening for obscene content, blocking pornographic Web sites and monitoring e-mail for workplace discrimination, sexual harassment and defamatory comments.

Unfortunately, in an effort to detect unacceptable employee communications and behavior, some employers cast a large net that captures *all* communications and behavior. From a privacy perspective, this is where workplace surveillance can cross the line, from monitoring legitimate workplace activities to monitoring activities that are *not* workplace related. "The potential exists for employers to know about all aspects of their employees' lives, including their health, genetic and psychological makeup, finances, schooling, past experience, how they spend their private time, and how they behave in the workplace from minute to minute," states a report from the Information and Privacy Commissioner of Ontario. "In effect, employees may become transparent to their employers."[9] Technological advances are steadily blurring that line further and further.

The next four sections describe the many ways electronic monitoring of employees can be conducted and, at times, overused. As you will find, some forms of electronic monitoring are more intrusive than others.

Least Intrusive: Spot Checks, Filtering and Blocking

It is important to distinguish between constant, systematic surveillance of employees and less intrusive ways of discouraging or preventing inappropriate

---

[8] American Management Association, "Beware Workplace E-mail, a New Survey Says" (press release citing results from 2001 Electronic Policies and Practices Survey, August 10, 2001).

[9] Information and Privacy Commissioner of Ontario, foreword to Workplace Privacy: A Consultation Paper (Toronto: Information and Privacy Commissioner of Ontario, June 1992), p. 2.

use of electronic communications. Some companies prefer to do spot checks of individual employees or groups of workers, either randomly or in response to specific complaints. In many respects, this method is no different from the way that police do random drinking-and-driving checks, pulling people over and asking them a few questions.

Sometimes, however, a complaint will be lodged against a particular employee, forcing the employer to monitor the e-mail and Web surfing of that individual over a specific, yet temporary period of time. In the summer of 2000, Dow Chemical spent a week monitoring employee e-mail use after a complaint was lodged. In the end, 50 people were fired and 200 faced disciplinary action. Complaints can vary: many are related to charges of sexual harassment or racial discrimination; others concern inappropriate Web use, such as visits to online gambling sites or viewing and disseminating pornographic, obscene or hateful materials. "By far the greater share of monitoring is performed on a spot-check basis," said Eric Rolfe Greenberg, director of management studies for the American Management Association (AMA).[10] According to a poll conducted by *CIO* magazine in 2001, 38 per cent of companies monitored the e-mail and Web use of employees only after a complaint had been lodged. The survey also found that 11 per cent focused their surveillance efforts on "problem employees," and 17 per cent conducted "sporadic" e-mail checks. Another 16 per cent said they never monitored worker e-mail.[11]

Two other forms of monitoring involve filtering software that can detect viruses and unwanted (obscene) attachments in e-mail messages, and blocking software that can prevent employees from accessing Web sites deemed inappropriate — such as pornographic, gambling and entertainment sites. Rather than record and store the electronic activities of employees, filtering and blocking programs simply prevent certain activities from taking place. Ideally,

---

[10] American Management Association (press release of annual workplace monitoring survey, April 18, 2001).
[11] CIO KnowPulse (*CIO* magazine press release reporting poll of 200 chief information officers, April 25, 2001).

all other forms of electronic communications or activity outside of predefined criteria would not be monitored and would therefore be kept private.

Blocking Web sites is a popular practice. As mentioned, the AMA found that four out of every ten companies use software that prevents employees from visiting specific Internet destinations. The leading company in this area is Websense, whose software of the same name is used by 13,000 organizations worldwide and monitors the Internet connections of more than 8.25 million workers. Websense can restrict access to nearly 80 categories of Web sites, ranging from the obscene and pornographic to harmless entertainment and travel-planning sites. "In its default configuration, Websense merely blocks certain Web sites, and does not keep any record of attempts to visit these sites," wrote Andrew Schulman, chief researcher for the Workplace Surveillance Project at the Privacy Foundation, in a report on the subject.[12] Some of Websense's biggest customers include Compaq Computer, IBM, AT&T Wireless and American Express. Of course, it is up to the companies using the software to determine the categories of Web sites they wish to block. Some companies may choose all categories, whereas others may pick one or two. Organizations that exercise discretion when deciding on categories, limiting the selection to only those that are necessary, will win the trust and respect of their employees.

In our view, workplace surveillance strategies limited to employee spot checks and Internet blocking and filtering software demonstrate a greater degree of sensitivity to the privacy of workers. This is particularly true when clear privacy policies are in place and a genuine effort has been made to notify employees of these practices. Employees who have been properly informed are likely to agree that such protective measures are required to maintain a hospitable, secure and productive business environment.

[12] Schulman, *supra*, note 5.

Parallel effort

Most Intrusive: Blanket Surveillance

Increasingly, companies are choosing to take advantage of the full surveillance capabilities that new technologies make possible, without regard for privacy concerns. In Schulman's analysis of Websense and its customers, it was found that 70 per cent used a more invasive version of the technology, called Websense Reporter, which can record *all* Web site access requests, blocked sites or otherwise. "Monitoring all Internet activity and e-mail correspondence of all employees, rather than looking over the shoulder of just those employees of whom one has a reasonable suspicion, is essentially a dragnet-style 'sweep,' a blanket, suspicionless search that carries with it grave privacy concerns," wrote Schulman.[13] In December 1999, it was revealed that Xerox engaged in blanket surveillance after the company fired 40 workers for visiting inappropriate Web sites.

The vendors that supply this technology — also known as e-mail or Web site "sniffer" programs — continue to emerge, with product names such as MIMEsweeper, Tumbleweed MMS, Elron Internet Manager, I-Gear/Mail-Gear, SurfControl SuperScout and eSniff. Prices range from about $200(U.S.) for small businesses to several thousands of dollars for medium-sized and large organizations. In general, a company can expect to pay between $5 and $10 per employee per year. Another network interception program, SilentRunner, is powerful enough to be used by the FBI, but was created by defense contractor Raytheon for use in the commercial sector. SilentRunner is undetectable and can capture and analyze all electronic communications by employees, including Web surfing, e-mail messages and attachments, database access, collaborative computing and even documents being sent for printing. According to a report in *Wired News*, SilentRunner "captures all the information on a network, in any code or human language, and translates it into easily decipherable three-dimensional diagrams of network behavior."[14] A basic version of the software reportedly sells for $25,000, but a turbo-version can cost more than $65,000.

[13] Schulman, *supra*, note 5.
[14] Jeffrey Benner, "Nailing the Company Spies," *Wired News*, March 1, 2001.

A feature found in many of these programs is keystroke tracking, which keeps a record of every single keystroke an employee makes. This means that *all* typing – of passwords, e-mail, instant messaging, word processing, spreadsheets — can be captured and stored for analysis. Nothing is left unrecorded, including personal Web-based e-mail through services such as Hotmail and Yahoo (mistakenly considered safe havens for personal communications at work), as long as the employee accesses the account through a work computer. Even words that are typed but immediately deleted can be kept in memory, including that profanity-filled e-mail to the boss that was typed in the heat of the moment but never actually sent. Adavi is one company that specializes in keystroke-tracking software, through its popular program Silent Watch. Software such as this can be bought for as little as $40, making it far too easy — and perhaps tempting — for companies to implement overly intrusive workplace surveillance programs.

The ability to monitor employee communications will only get easier as more companies merge their separate voice and data networks into a single network based on Internet protocol (IP), which makes it possible for voice, video, e-mail, Web pages and software to be carried over the same infrastructure. In an article on workplace monitoring that appeared in *Network Computing*, author Sean Doherty explained that voice-over-IP networks could spell even greater trouble for privacy.

> As enterprises adopt VoIP (voice over IP) on the corporate network, voice traffic will be as easy to monitor as Internet traffic, such as e-mail, FTP, HTTP and telnet. Voicemail will be stored in the same medium as e-mail and susceptible to the same tools now used to scan e-mail messages; the potential to infringe on employees' privacy will be greater than ever. Unfettered and unannounced monitoring that scans both voice and data traffic on the network may cross the lines of respectability and infringe on employees' rights to privacy.[15]

[15] Sean Doherty, "Monitoring and Privacy: Is Your Head Still in the Sand?" *Network Computing*, June 25, 2001.

For this reason, it has become more important than ever that good judgment and good faith prevail in any employee monitoring. Surveillance, if it is to be conducted, for the most part should be targeted, not blanketed. (There may be limited times when blanket monitoring of employees is warranted, such as at airports or nuclear power plants. Such things as the sensitivity of the job, dangers to public safety and the likelihood of serious harm if misconduct occurs should be the deciding factors.) Surveillance should also been done to confirm suspicions or follow up on specific complaints, rather than treating every employee in the workplace as a suspect in a crime not yet committed. There is no question that employers have the right to see what their employees are doing and how they are spending their time on the job, but at the very least, employees should be told this is happening and the manner in which it is happening. Employees should be given a chance to act accordingly under such circumstances, without being unfairly caught in what may appear to be a covert dragnet operation.

Every Move You Make: Video, Biometrics and E-Tags

Computer and network security may be a key requirement in today's workplace, but physical security is no less important. This has become particularly true in the aftermath of September 11, 2001. In addition to more traditional security concerns, companies must today consider the possibility of anthrax in the mail, sabotage and other acts of terrorism that were unheard-of in the past. An increasing number of companies are using video surveillance, biometric checkpoints and electronic tags to keep track of employee movements, keep intruders out and prevent theft and vandalism. Sometimes, however, the courts are ruling that the use of these technologies may exceed security purposes.

Take video cameras, for example, which have dropped significantly in price, can be purchased over the Internet and are now tiny enough to be installed in inconspicuous places. A company might have legitimate reasons to place surveillance cameras at main building entrances, along certain corridors and in parking lots, for both employee safety and security reasons. But some businesses have gone so far as to set up cameras in locker rooms, washrooms and other areas where employees can clearly have a reasonable expectation of privacy. Twenty employees, male and female, took their employer to court over precisely this type of surveillance. The employer, a power company in West Virginia, felt it had the right to videotape its employees anywhere in the building. The state court did not agree. The employees obtained a permanent injunction against their employer and they were awarded $80,000 in damages. This case is not the only one of its kind. In *Consolidated Freightways v. Cramer*, the U.S. Supreme Court cleared the way for employees at a trucking company to pursue an invasion-of-privacy suit against their employer, which had secretly installed video cameras in staff bathrooms. In 1997, an employee discovered one of the hidden cameras behind a mirror in a men's room. More cameras and a microphone were subsequently discovered, including a camera in a women's room.

Whether video surveillance is used for legitimate security purposes or for monitoring job performance, its all-embracing sweep captures every action, even those totally unrelated to the job. Because video surveillance can cast such a wide net, it gathers information well beyond that related to work performance and observes people without any suspicion of wrongdoing. Since this form of broad surveillance can be so invasive and may capture actions unrelated to the job, it should not be conducted covertly without reasonable cause. Unless surveillance is conducted as part of an investigation into possible wrongdoing, employers should notify their employees when and why video surveillance is taking place. Such notification should be done through a company privacy policy. In addition, notice should be provided through clearly posted "video monitoring" signs. Camera placement should be restricted to security-sensitive entrances and other areas where employees would likely find such monitoring reasonable. They may question, on the other hand, the need to videotape activities around the water cooler, the staff kitchen or washroom entrances, so make your case, if there is a case to be made.

Another high-tech method of monitoring — and controlling — access to buildings and offices uses biometric technology, which is more secure and resistant to fraud than traditional swipe-card or key-pad systems. As discussed in **Chapter 8**, biometrics is the identification or verification of individuals through their unique biological characteristics. Iris, handprint, fingerprint, face and voice scanners are already being used in some workplaces in North America and Europe, but the market for these products is still small. Biometrics is less invasive than video surveillance because, with the exception of face scanning, the employee needs to be an active participant. With biometrics, unauthorized outsiders can be denied entry to private buildings and facilities, but in order to use such a system, a company must require every employee to provide a sample scan of their iris, fingerprint, handprint or whatever other biometric is chosen. How will these employee biometrics be stored and secured? Will they be capable of being matched with external systems? Will they be held confidentially and not shared with third parties, such as government agencies? Employees have a right to ask these questions, and to be given thorough answers.

Brian Taylor was disappointed when the 28-year veteran of Stelpipe, a steel pipe manufacturer in Ontario, found out that his company was considering the use of biometric handprint scanners throughout its facilities. "They wanted to know where everybody was at any time in the plant," said Taylor, who found out about the plan indirectly through a departmental safety meeting. Taylor didn't completely reject the idea of a biometric security system at Stelpipe. He didn't even feel that the company's 460 employees had a right to veto such a plan. But he told us he was disappointed by the lack of consultation with staff. "They should tell us what they're planning, ask us what our objections are and what ideas we have. I don't think this should be unilaterally imposed on us. I do think I have the right to have substantial input on what's happening." Taylor's concerns are echoed throughout workplaces across North America. As it turns out, Stelpipe put the plan on hold.

Other technologies allow companies to monitor employees everywhere they go inside the workplace and, in some cases, even outside the workplace. Electronic badges or tags, based on the same radio-frequency identification technology used in commercial electronic toll systems, can identify and track employees throughout an office building or facility. Companies that use this technology can minimize the threat to the privacy of their employees by justifying the number of checkpoints needed. Also, there is concern that wireless tracking applications, which some companies already use for fleet management and vehicle detection, may soon be introduced to sales forces and other mobile workers. As handset-tracking services become common, GPS or wireless triangulation technologies will make it possible for companies to pinpoint the precise whereabouts of sales staff, delivery personnel and telecommuters, with or without their knowledge. We strongly recommend that companies advise their employees if this technology is being used, especially if it goes beyond the security and employee-management needs of the business. If at any point your company considers such a plan, seek full employee consultation in developing a policy. Failure to do so may be grounds for legal action, considering the potential of monitoring people during non-occupational or off-hours activities. In due course, legislation will most likely specifically address the potential abuses of this technology, both inside and outside the workplace.

Staff Testing: Drugs, Health and Genetics

Not everything is electronic — not yet, that is. The expectation of physical (biological) privacy at the workplace is another murky area, perhaps the most controversial area of all. Should employers be permitted to demand bodily fluids from their employees for testing, or to obtain the results of medical tests for such conditions as HIV status or the presence of a cancer gene — that is, tests not conducted directly for employment purposes? Some say that with the consent of the employee, such testing and access to test results should be an acceptable practice in the workplace. Yet in today's world, the word "consent" in the context of the workplace is characterized by an imbalance of power between employer and employee and, as a result, is virtually stripped of any meaning. Many would argue that few employees are in a position to deny consent when they know that doing so could jeopardize their prospects for advancement. Job applicants would certainly view saying no to such testing as a barrier to getting the job. In such cases, consent would be viewed as neither informed nor freely obtained. Indeed, the Australian Privacy Charter states that "consent is meaningless where people have no option but to consent in order to obtain a benefit or a service."

A trend among employers is the practice of subjecting employees and job candidates to drug testing, whereby a urine specimen is obtained and analyzed for the presence of illicit drugs. To prevent the employee from tampering or making substitutions, the sample is sometimes taken while others observe. Aside from being considered intrusive, such tests tend to have high error rates. Furthermore, they detect not only illicit drugs but legitimate ones too — prescription drugs, over-the-counter remedies and alcohol that has been consumed within the previous few days. It would seem to be of little value to an employer to know that an employee had earlier consumed some legitimate substances, including medications or alcohol, that do not affect performance or reflect on one's ability to fulfill job responsibilities. Is this truly useful in assessing on-the-job performance or inferring, as one bank once hinted, an employee's trustworthiness? "The paramount issue here is the substantial and needless invasion of employee privacy," said one civil rights lawyer. "A urine test tells you a lot about a person's lifecycle and tells you virtually nothing about the person's ability to do the job." Obviously, certain jobs related to public safety — say, a school bus driver or police officer — may require closer scrutiny, but the onus is on the employer to prove its case.

In the workplace, standard drug tests can detect whether a woman has stopped taking birth control pills, a piece of information that could easily lead to her dismissal in advance of maternity leave. Then there are those blood tests, like the ones performed on 36 employees at Burlington Northern Santa Fe Railroad, as mentioned in **Chapter 3**, used to perform genetic tests that could determine a predisposition to carpal tunnel syndrome. In a lawsuit against the company, it was claimed that a worker who did not want to provide a blood sample was threatened with dismissal. Again, the balance of power is generally tilted toward the employer. Employees, meanwhile, have a strong reason for being concerned: getting a job or life insurance in the future could become much more difficult if a genetic predisposition that "may" lead to a future illness raises a red flag for decision makers. In the summer of 2000, the University of California at Berkeley paid more than $2 million to settle a case in which it allegedly tested 9,000 employees for genetic flaws, sexually transmitted diseases and pregnancy, with neither their knowledge nor consent. Basing workplace decisions today on the mere *possibility* of future medical conditions arising (that may never develop) is not only unfair but, in some circumstances, highly unethical.

The former privacy commissioner of Canada, Bruce Phillips, has identified the conditions under which random mandatory drug testing of a group, "on the basis of behavioral patterns of the group as a whole," may be justifiable:

- There are reasonable grounds to believe there is a significant prevalence of drug use or impairment within the group.
- The drug use or impairment poses a substantial threat to the safety of the public or other members of the group.
- The behavior of individuals in the group cannot otherwise be adequately supervised.
- There are reasonable grounds to believe that drug testing can significantly reduce the risk to safety.
- No practical, less intrusive alternative such as regular medicals, education, counseling, or some combination of these would significantly reduce the risk to safety.[16]

As technology becomes more advanced, and as it becomes cheaper and easier to monitor the health and genetic vulnerabilities of employees, companies need to be more respectful of and sensitive to the privacy interests of their staff. One software developer in Canada has developed a system that can provide a snapshot of a company workforce's overall efficiency and health based on employee data such as blood pressure, cholesterol levels, blood sugar counts and body mass. "The enterprise can then institute programs to combat such problems as absenteeism, sickness and even job burn-out, and monitor

---

[16] Privacy Commissioner of Canada, *Drug Testing and Privacy* (Ottawa: Privacy Commissioner of Canada, 1990), p. 45.

the effectiveness of the programs over the years to see how the bottom line improves," wrote one media report.[17] Another software developer is working on a system that can monitor employee "biosigns," such as blood pressure, body temperature and heart rate, to produce on-demand health reports and stress alerts as workers sit at their computer terminals.

In both cases, the companies say employees won't be required to use or participate in the system. But again, if your company respects privacy, you should ensure that an employee with a mortgage and two kids feels that she can say no without jeopardizing her employment. "As science and technology advances, we must be vigilant and ensure that these new developments are not used in a manner that violates workers' rights," said Ida L. Castro, chair of the U.S. Equal Opportunity Commission, commenting on the Burlington Northern Santa Fe case.[18]

Technology will continue to allow companies to do many things, but before such monitoring systems are blindly installed, ask yourself: Is it truly necessary? Are there less intrusive alternatives? What do employees think about the system? Is it against the law or any human rights codes?

Finally, we urge you to resist treating all employees as potential suspects in the hopes of catching a few. The impact on employee morale will be substantial.

Employee Records

Whatever a company learns about its employees through electronic surveillance, testing or other methods of information gathering is typically stored in an employee file or record. We encourage companies to open up these records to their employees, allowing them to make sure that the information they contain is accurate and relevant to their work. Doing so will help your company in the

---

[17] Jack Kapica, "Wellness Software Can Make Bottom Line Healthier: Consultant," Globetechnology.com [online], May 1, 2001.
[18] Joe Ruff, "Burlington Northern Employees Want Genetic Test Ban," Associated Press, April 10, 2001.

long run by assuring that the information on file is accurate enough for any decision-making purposes. It will also demonstrate to your employees that you are serious about accuracy and correcting any errors, in addition to keeping their information confidential.

A study of Fortune 500 companies found that half of those surveyed had used employee medical records in making employment decisions. Of those companies, 20 per cent had not informed the employee.[19] A 1991 study by the Office of Technology Assessment of the U.S. Congress found that "almost a third of employers that maintained employee medical records let their personnel departments read those records without notifying the employee." We have found no evidence today to indicate this figure has substantially changed. Yet it is clearer than ever that notification is a key principle that should be upheld in any internal privacy policy. With the growth of company-sponsored employee assistance programs, an enormous amount of sensitive personal information may be collected by an organization. When introducing such a program, make sure you tell your employees what information will be kept on file and in which situations the information will be accessed, either by you as the employer or by some other party. Such openness and transparency will build employee morale by increasing trust between employer and employees.

What Is the Law?

In the United States, the federal statute that is most relevant to many workplace surveillance issues is the 1986 Electronic Communications Privacy Act (ECPA), which makes it illegal to intentionally intercept the oral, wire or electronic communications of another person. It also prohibits people from disclosing the contents of such communications, which can be anything from an e-mail message or a chat room discussion to a telephone conversation. But there are three exceptions to the ECPA that may be interpreted to give employers a way

[19] Ann Cavoukian and Don Tapscott, *Who Knows: Safeguarding Your Privacy in a Networked World* (New York: McGraw-Hill, 1997), p. 142.

to monitor the electronic communications of their employees, according to Eric Sinrod, a technology lawyer. "If *one* of these exceptions is satisfied, monitoring can take place under appropriate circumstances."[20]

The first exception is the "business extension exception," which can allow employers to monitor any business-related phone calls made on equipment that resides in the workplace. "But once an employer ascertains that a particular call is personal in nature, the monitoring must cease immediately," explains Sinrod. Another exception is the "consent exception," which allows for workplace monitoring as long as the employer has informed employees that such actions will — not *may* — take place. The "may" is emphasized because some courts have ruled that employee knowledge of the *capability* of monitoring should not be interpreted as implied consent. Sinrod suggests that companies get written consent to be safe. Such consent could be a policy statement, signed by employees, that explains the scope of employer monitoring and assures that personal communications will not be intercepted except in brief moments to determine whether such communications are business in nature. Sinrod warns that even with implied or actual consent, the personal communications of employees are still protected by the ECPA.

Finally, there is the "service provider exception," which could apply to companies that run their own e-mail and phone systems. This exception, which again is open to broad interpretation, allows a company to access an employee's stored e-mail messages and other communications without consent, as long as the employer does so during the normal course of the individual's employment and while the employee is engaged in work-related activity. This monitoring can be initiated only to protect a service provider's (the employer's) property rights. However, this exception may apply only to internal e-mail. Less clear is how incoming e-mail, whether through a common carrier or a Web-based service, can be lawfully monitored.

---

[20] Eric J. Sinrod, "E-Legal: Electronic Monitoring of Employees by Employers," Law.com [online], April 10, 2001.

In general, companies should be cautious when interpreting such rules. There is no guarantee that a judge will interpret them the same way, mainly because the spirit of the ECPA is to bolster privacy rights, not to erode them. When in doubt, seek the advice of a lawyer, since violation of the ECPA could include court injunctions or the awarding of actual, statutory or punitive damages, criminal penalties and costs associated with legal challenges filed by employees.

Employers must also be aware of state laws that may limit different methods of workplace surveillance, as well as common laws that have been established through the years. You might also want to consider the National Labor Relations Act and possible applications to monitoring in the workplace, as well as other laws that protect the right to privacy or prohibit discrimination and defamation. California came close to passing a workplace privacy law for e-mail in 2001, but Governor Gray Davis eventually vetoed the bill. Introduced by California Senator Debra Bowen, the bill would have complemented existing state legislation that covers telephone communications by requiring companies to notify employees of monitoring practices. "If you want to stop workers from conducting personal business on company time, you're going to be much more likely to succeed if you tell your employees about the company monitoring policies in advance," Senator Bowen said in a statement after the bill was vetoed. "The best way to do that isn't by slapping a monitoring notice on a poster in the company break room; it's to put it in an employee handbook, a memo, an e-mail message, or something else that you know will get into the hands of every employee."[21] Attempts to pass similar legislation at the federal level have so far led nowhere, but the issue continues to re-emerge year after year. It may be that federal legislation aimed specifically at workplace privacy will someday require employers to, at the very least, follow the principle of notification. In the meantime, it is always a good idea to get into the habit of notifying employees if you are using any intrusive monitoring.

---

[21] Robert MacMillan, "California Gov Vetoes E-mail Privacy Measure," Newsbytes [online], October 9, 2001.

In Canada, no legislation is targeted specifically at setting rules or requiring notification of employee monitoring activities, but Canada's federal privacy commissioner interprets the new Personal Information Protection and Electronic Documents Act, or PIPEDA, as applicable to workplace privacy for federal employees and institutions covered by the statute. "Exactly the same rules apply to the collection, use or disclosure of information about your organization's clients — and about your employees," Commissioner George Radwanski said. He emphasized that surveillance is allowable only for purposes that "a reasonable person would consider appropriate" in the circumstances.

> The standard for justification, the "reasonable person" standard, is going to give us all some interesting challenges as we interpret it. But, to my mind, it's the key to the Act. It's what makes it more than just a data protection statute. It's what establishes, not just fair information practices, but a right to privacy in the workplace.[22]

Meanwhile, amendments to the Federal Privacy Act in Australia extended privacy protection to workers in the private sector. The amendments restrict an employer's right to monitor the electronic activities of its workforce by requiring it to establish formal policies on e-mail use and Web surfing, and to make these rules clear to all staff. Employers must give 14 days notice before monitoring employee e-mail, or they must obtain a warrant from the country's Industrial Relations Commission to engage in covert surveillance. Before these amendments, businesses were allowed to go through their employees' e-mail indiscriminately. Companies must now have a justifiable reason for monitoring, such as targeting the excessive use of e-mail, weeding out offensive content or combating workplace fraud.

[22] George Radwanski, "A New Act, A New Era" (speech given at "New Developments in Workplace Privacy" conference, University of Toronto and Lancaster House, Toronto, April 6, 2001).

Taking the Right (and Smart) Approach

Even in the absence of legislative guidance and oversight with respect to workplace privacy, we recommend that companies take a fair approach to workplace surveillance and balance their needs with those of their employees. This approach will be more likely to improve staff morale, lower employee stress, and create a more trusting environment. Here are some tips to consider if your company has plans to monitor — or is already monitoring — its employees.

1. Define your purpose for collecting employee information. Is all the information collected related to protecting the company and its staff, evaluating employee performance or determining whether the individual can do the job? If not, then limit what you collect to what you truly need.
2. Define how the information will be used. Will it be shared with any third parties? How long will it be stored? Make sure your use of the information is limited to the purpose that has been defined. If necessary, do a privacy impact assessment to make sure you don't cross the line or open yourself up to employee invasion-of-privacy claims.
3. Develop a clearly written, comprehensive workplace privacy policy. The policy should explain to employees when and under what circumstances monitoring will be conducted, the types of monitoring that will take place (e.g., Web site blocking, e-mail filtering) and why the program exists. It should also define appropriate uses of internal e-mail, phones and Internet connections in the workplace, and the extent to which personal communications are permissible. (What types of Web sites should be avoided? What can and cannot be downloaded or sent through e-mail?)
4. Explain the disciplinary consequences of inappropriate use of electronic communications. Make it perfectly clear.
5. Document consent of this policy annually and as part of the hiring process by having employees read and sign off on the policy. Include the policy in an employee handbook, and complement notification efforts by posting the policy on staff bulletin boards or in areas where offline surveillance is likely to take place.

248

6. Education and training is key. Meet directly with staff, explain the policy and answer their questions. Consult with employees whenever a major change is expected to occur in the policy.

7. Measure monitoring activities against any legislation or human rights codes that might restrict or set rules for certain types of surveillance in the workplace.

8. Develop a complaints process that will treat employee concerns fairly and respectfully.

When monitoring policies are carefully explained and employees are properly notified, employers are likely to find greater acceptance than resistance to their surveillance efforts. We urge you to give it a try.

The Bottom Line

There is no question that privacy in the workplace is not the same as consumer privacy, since employers have the right to exert a certain amount of control over the communications systems and properties they own and maintain. On the other hand, blanket surveillance and full-scale intrusions on employee privacy are ethically questionable and legally challengeable. They're also unlikely to enhance your bottom line. We agree that privacy is not absolute in the workplace, but it does exist, particularly in the context of non-occupational activities. Balance is needed, as in other areas. We believe the proper balance can be achieved to meet the needs of *both* employers and employees. By following the tips suggested in this chapter, you will be well on your way to reaching workplace harmony — one more example of privacy paying off.

Chapter 11

Privacy Through Technology

"Privacy is about not being surprised. People can't
control what happens with data, but what's
important is that they know what's happening
with it, so they can choose the businesses
that treat them well and not choose
companies that don't treat them well."

Daniel Weitzner, domain leader, World
Wide Web Consortium's P3P Project

Keeping Tech in Check

We have discussed the numerous technologies that are able — and in many cases
have been specifically designed — to collect detailed information about the
personal lives of consumers, both with and without their permission. Cookies,
Web bugs, spyware, data-mining tools and other intrusive technologies have
become commonplace on the Internet, and increasingly are beyond the sight and
control of consumers. But in the same way that technology has made it easier to
be intrusive, new technologies are also making it easier to be protective. This
chapter will survey the landscape of technologies that can control and minimize
the collection of personal information as well as manage how that information
is gathered, used, shared and secured. Some of these technologies make it
possible for consumers to prevent the collection of personal data, whereas others
strive for a balance between consumer choice and the information requirements

of business. For the purposes of this book, we will call all of these technologies PETs.[1] As you will find, the use of PETs can contribute to an organization's strategy of building trust with its customers. At the same time, consumers may decide to arm themselves with PETs if they feel that an organization's data-collection practices are too intrusive for their liking.

What Are PETs?

PETs, also known as privacy-enhancing or privacy-enabling technologies, can be broadly defined as any type of technology that is designed to guard or promote the privacy interests of individuals.[2] Such technology can range from a Web site that lets people surf the Internet anonymously to a sophisticated piece of proprietary software that allows an organization to better map, manage and secure the flow of its customers' information. The Canadian government has defined PETs as technologies that "eliminate the use of personal data, or give direct control to the user over the revelation of personal information." John Borking, vice-president of the Dutch Data Protection Authority, has a more detailed definition, calling PETs "a coherent system of [technology] measures that protect privacy by eliminating or reducing the personal data or by preventing unnecessary and/or undesired processing of personal data; all without losing the functionality of the data system."[3] Consumers can use PETs to protect the privacy of their identity and at the same time continue to surf the Internet and engage in electronic commerce. Businesses can build PETs directly into information systems and other technologies to give customers more

[1] PETs commonly refer to technologies that can mask the identity of a person, but we use the term in its broadest sense, applying to technologies that minimize the use of personally identifiable data and make it easier to protect consumer privacy.
[2] The first major use of the term "privacy-enhancing technologies," or PETs, appeared in "Privacy-Enhancing Technologies: The Path to Anonymity," a 1995 joint report by the Ontario Information and Privacy Commissioner and the Dutch Data Protection Authority.
[3] John J. Borking and Charles D. Raab, "Laws, PETs and Other Technologies for Privacy Protection," *Journal of Information Law and Technology*, February 28, 2001.

control over their personal identities and profiles, and to prevent unauthorized parties from accessing, altering or taking that information.

PETs for Business

Some PETs are proprietary, created from scratch to suit an organization's particular data-protection requirements. But increasingly, companies are finding cheaper, off-the-shelf, customizable PETs that perform the same function and easily integrate with other enterprise software products. "As the science of privacy management matures, we're likely to see integrated suites of tools that address the breadth of issues that companies need to manage," wrote Karyl Scott of *Information Week*. "We're also likely to see the integration of privacy and security products."[4]

Below we have compiled a list of PETs that organizations may wish to consider as they reinforce their privacy practices with technology. Again, our definition of PETs is quite broad. Many of these technologies focus exclusively on data and network security, while others address information management, authentication and identity protection.

Encryption (Cryptography)

Encryption, or encoding of information, is a mathematical process that disguises the content of information — e-mail messages, documents, data files — using computations known as algorithms. Software or hardware or both are used to conceal (encode, encrypt or lock) the information, where it can later be revealed (decoded, decrypted or unlocked) to the authorized recipient. If anyone was to intercept the encrypted information, all that would be found is garbled, unreadable text, known as ciphertext.

The two main types of encryption are symmetric and public key, or asymmetric. In symmetric systems, both the sender and recipient use the same key (an

---

[4] Karyl Scott, "Privacy Tools and Services Debut," *InformationWeek*, August 20, 2001.

extremely large number) to lock and unlock a message. In order for this to work, the sender must also tell the recipient what the key is, leaving the key temporarily open to interception. Asymmetric or public key systems, on the other hand, are more secure because two different keys are involved: one is a public or widely distributed key for use by the sender, the other is a private key that is known only to the recipient. Users of a public key system must make their key public, either by publishing their public key in a directory or by sending it to someone for use, as in the PGP model (see later in this chapter). Someone wishing to securely transmit information to you would find your public key from the directory, for example, encrypt the message and send it to you. You would use your private key — available to no one else but yourself — to decrypt the message. Because a public key system partially eliminates the problem of leaving a key briefly vulnerable and allows individuals to encrypt communications and sign documents even without prior contact, it is more difficult to breach than a symmetric system.

Keys can vary in strength, from 40-bit to 128-bit or higher. A 128-bit key is composed of a combination of 3.4 trillion billion billion billion zeros and ones. The only way to break the key, by brute force, is to try all possible combinations, requiring an enormous amount of computing power. "A hacker is more likely to win the lottery than to crack that level of encryption using the brute-force method," reported PCWorld.[5] However, hackers are more likely to find keys by exploiting flaws in bad implementations of the security system. As computers grow more powerful and as new hacking techniques become available, the keys become easier to break. Therefore, key sizes are increasing to stay ahead of increased computing power. For example, computer security experts can now break 40-bit encryption, a long-time industry standard, in a matter of hours.

The public key system of encryption "Enables people to communicate in complete secrecy with people they've never met," wrote *Hackers* author Steven Levy in an article for *Wired* magazine. "Even more remarkable, it makes possible

---

[5] Andrew Brandt and Alexandra Krasne, "How It Works: Encryption," PCWorld [online], February 14, 2000.

a 'digital signature' assuring that an electronic message was generated by the person who claims responsibility for it. Together, these features allow us to create new forms of digital commerce with an unprecedented level of privacy."[6] A digital signature is created when public and private keys reverse roles: a private key is used to encrypt a message and a public key is used to decrypt it. If a message is encrypted with a private key that is uniquely associated with the author, the recipient is able to verify the identity of the sender and make sure the message has not been tampered with. Thus, a digital signature works much the same way as a handwritten signature on a letter or contract.

There are many applications for encryption. Most major e-mail applications have encryption settings — some based on the asymmetric Secure Multipurpose Internet Mail Extensions (S/MIME) protocol — that can help keep employee communications secure and private. Virtual Private Network (VPN) software lets employees remotely connect to an organization's internal network through what is essentially an encrypted passageway through the Internet. An organization's Web site can be designed to trigger a browser-based encryption technology called Secure Sockets Layer (SSL), a popular type of symmetric encryption developed by Netscape. SSL makes sure that credit card numbers and other personal information is encoded during e-commerce transactions and online transfers of sensitive data, such as financial information during an online banking session. SSL-enabled security products can encrypt data during HTTP, Telnet and FTP transfers. Similar encryption can be extended to wireless transactions over mobile devices. A new encryption standard, called Transport Layer Security, or TLS, has been formed through the merger of SSL and other protocols under the guidance of the Internet Engineering Task Force. TLS is expected to supersede SSL but has been designed to be compatible with the older protocol.

Companies are increasingly using encryption software to scramble sensitive information stored in corporate PCs, laptops, customer databases and other data-storage systems to comply with their corporate privacy policy. With

[6] Steven Levy, "Prophets of Privacy," *Wired* magazine, November 1994, p. 128.

information protected both during transmission and while in storage, unauthorized access can be prevented at all times and consumer and employee privacy can be better assured.

Blind Signatures

The one shortcoming of digital signatures is that the parties engaged in electronic correspondence or online transactions are identifiable, so they could ultimately be linked to the transfer. However, one's identity can be made anonymous, rendering the signature "blind." Cryptographer David Chaum, former head of the Center for Mathematics and Computer Science in Amsterdam, patented a blind signature system in 1988 that formed the basis of a company he founded called DigiCash — short for digital cash. DigiCash pioneered the anonymous electronic payment system, which has been called the cryptographic equivalent of an envelope with carbon paper. Essentially, blind signatures allow a transaction or communication to be authenticated without revealing the identity of the person behind it, making the source of the transfer untraceable. During an electronic transaction, a Web retailer does not need to know who is making the transaction; it needs to know only that the digital money being transferred is legitimate. Similarly, blind signatures could be used for electronic voting — officials need to know only that the vote is authentic, not who is voting. DigiCash filed for bankruptcy in November 1998 and its assets — and encryption patents — were sold to a company called eCash Technologies, which, along with several of its industry peers, continues to promote the concept of digital cash. Chaum has since founded an electronic voting company called SureVote, inspired by the problems surrounding the November 2000 U.S. election. Chaum plans to pursue the idea of anonymous online voting systems, which a number of countries are currently studying.

Biometrics

As we discussed in **Chapter 8**, biometric systems can be used to intrude upon a person's life. But when biometrics are used as a person's private encryption key, the technology can be a valuable tool in protecting the privacy of consumers and employees by securing and managing access to personal information that is in

256

electronic or physical storage. Organizations can use biometrics in conjunction with other privacy and security measures to control access to and manage the flow of personal information.

Network Firewalls

Security software called firewalls can keep a network secure from intruders by blocking out unwanted IP addresses, e-mail addresses, Web sites and other applications. Firewalls are commonly used to separate a company's public Web server from internal networks, creating a wall that is difficult for hackers or snoopers to bypass. A firewall can also be used within the enterprise to keep a departmental network — such as human resources or accounting — protected from internal threats. Several security companies sell firewall technology, along with anti-virus, intrusion-detection and virtual private network software. Firewalls have long been considered a must-have technology for protecting data networks and the personal information flowing through them.

Privacy-Management Technology

This broad class of software helps organizations collect, store, access and use information in ways that are compliant with regulations, policies and the personal preferences of customers. Often built into this software are audit features that electronically track the movement of personal data throughout an organization, recording where and how the information is collected, how it is being used, whether it has been accessed while in storage, who accessed it and when it was accessed. In essence, all rules, regulations, policies and practices are "codified" or "digitized," after which they can be automatically measured against an organization's data flow. The company can be alerted if a noncompliant action is detected.

Pseudonymous and Anonymous Systems

One of the best examples of PETs are technologies that disguise or remove the identities of individuals as they navigate the Internet or when organizations collect their personal data. Some systems will allow a person to create a number of pseudonyms, or fictional identities, that can be used in various circumstances. A person might have one pseudonym for visiting health sites, another for conducting financial transactions and still another when visiting online gambling or adult sites — the *choice* belongs to the individual. The pseudonym masks a person's identity but at the same time allows an organization to verify that this person is indeed a customer. It is like being invited to a masquerade ball — you have your ticket, which authorizes your invitation, but the mask you wear prevents others at the party from knowing your identity. "A merchant doesn't need to know your name," wrote security expert Bruce Schneier. "But it does need to know that you legitimately bought the merchandise you are now trying to return."[7] Anonymous systems go one step further by excluding both true and fictional identities — the equivalent of sending a letter in the mail with no return address.

Web Scanning and Assessment Software

As corporate Web sites continue to get larger, it becomes more difficult for companies to keep track of how customer information is collected and stored. When and where does a site use cookies and Web bugs? What kind of information is being collected? Can the information be inadvertently shared with third parties? On a day-to-day basis, is a Web site compliant with an organization's privacy policy, as well as local, state, federal and international regulations? Scanning and assessment software acknowledges that Web sites are a constantly changing part of any business. For this reason, they are in need of regular monitoring to make sure that stated privacy objectives are being met. Such software accomplishes this task automatically, 24 hours a day.

Smart Cards

Typically the size of credit cards, smart cards are plastic cards that contain one or more microchips. The microchip is what makes the card "smart," transforming

---

[7] Bruce Schneier, *Secrets & Lies* (New York: John Wiley & Sons, 2000), p. 64.

it into a miniature computer, enabling it to collect, store and in some cases process data. Smart cards, like biometric technologies, can be used either as a technology of privacy or as a technology of surveillance, depending on whether the collected information resides only on the card itself (privacy-protective) or is transmitted to a central database (more likely to facilitate the tracking and monitoring of your activities). Generally, smart cards can strengthen access controls that allow you to enter an office building or a computer system by providing a means of identification and authentication. The security of smart cards is even greater when they are used along with pass-words or biometric technologies.

P3P Tackles the Web

In 1997, the World Wide Web Consortium — W3C — embarked on a mission to build privacy directly into the Web through the Platform for Privacy Preferences Project — P3P. The consortium's objective was simple: create an automated way for users to gain greater control over the collection and use of their personal information on Web sites. A second objective was to have P3P become a standard feature for all Web sites. So far, the W3C project is off to a strong start. For more detailed information about the W3C and P3P, visit **www.w3.org**.

Essentially, P3P embodies a set of standardized multiple-choice questions that cover various aspects of a Web site's privacy policy. What information is desired? How will it be collected? How will it be used? Will it be shared with any third parties? A Web site operator's answers to these questions provides a clear snapshot of how the site handles the personal information of those who visit. P3P converts these answers into a standard, machine-readable format (based on the XML programming language), making it possible for P3P-enabled browsers to automatically "read" a Web site's privacy policy. The browser then compares the policy to the user's own privacy preferences, which have previously been selected and saved. If the user's preferences match the Web site's policy, then the browser proceeds to the site, and any agreed-upon information — which could include name, phone number, address, credit card numbers, bank account numbers and surfing data, depending on the user's choices — may be transferred from the user to the Web operator. If the user's preferences and the Web site policy conflict — for example, the Web operator wants to share the data with a third party and the user is opposed to this — then there can be an attempt to negotiate different terms. "P3P enhances user control by putting privacy policies where users can find them, in a form users can understand, and, most importantly, enables users to act on what they see," states the W3C.

P3P makes surfing the Web easier for online consumers, who are no longer required to comb through what are often complex privacy policies buried within Web sites. If a site does not meet the user's privacy requirements, then the site can be avoided altogether. If a user is prepared to hand over all or part of their personal information, then P3P-enabled browsers can automatically conduct the transfer without the need to retype the information on the site. Another feature of P3P-enabled browsers is that users can create pseudonyms for use at different Web sites. Each pseudonym represents a unique relationship with a Web site, and therefore represents a unique P3P agreement that stipulates what data can and cannot be transferred or used. The browser's job is to match the pseudonym with the Web site whenever the site is revisited.[8]

Hundreds of Web sites have been designed as P3P-compliant, including travel site Expedia.com, Web portal MSN.com, information site About.com and the U.S. Department of Commerce's Web site, and the number continues to grow. Microsoft gave an encouraging boost to P3P when it announced in 2000 that part of the technology would be built directly into its Windows XP operating system and its Internet Explorer 6.0 browser, which now boasts tens of millions of users. Unlike previous generations of Internet Explorer, Microsoft designed the browser to, by default, reject third-party cookies and limit the uses of first-party cookies

---

[8] For versions of Internet Explorer that are not P3P-enabled (versions 5.01 and 5.5), AT&T has come out with free software called AT&T Privacy Bird that searches for P3P-compliant privacy policies and matches them with user preferences. Users can tailor warning messages to meet their privacy concerns. The software can be downloaded from **www.privacybird.com/**.

when it confronts a Web site that is not P3P-compliant. It is expected that many more Web sites will choose to become P3P-compliant as a way to overcome IE 6.0's default setting. Failure to do so has its consequences: Web site shopping-cart applications won't work properly and banner ads will have difficulties loading. "Firms must pay attention," warned Forrester Research analyst Paul Hagen. "Firms without acceptable [P3P] policies run the risk of having a small 'privacy unsafe' icon appear at the bottom of the browser — or a pop-up warning if the site is the first one visited by the new browser — spooking customers and alerting press to cookie-dropping practices."[9] Companies need to get a clear handle on their cookie usage and should stop dropping unnecessary cookies, said Hagen. As well, companies that use cross-site cookies to collect data and deliver content should think seriously about designing a P3P-compliant policy — if they haven't done so already. In the section that follows, we list some companies that can help your organization build P3P into its Web properties. You can also find links to free P3P policy generators (IBM P3P Policy Editor, PrivacyBot.com, and YouPowered's SmartSense Consumer Trust) at **www.w3.org**, or go to the Privacy Council's Web site at **www.privacycouncil.com** for its Free P3P Solution.

The W3C does not promote P3P as a one-stop shop for privacy compliance, but the technology does go far in addressing many privacy concerns, fostering an environment of openness and transparency — and, ultimately, trust — on the Internet. P3P gives online consumers more awareness of and control over how their information is collected and used, and it alerts consumers to sites whose privacy policies may be inconsistent with the user's own preferences. It should be pointed out, however, that P3P does not assure that a company's privacy practices are legally compliant, or that the information the Web site collects is kept accurate, secure and accessible to the user. P3P — as with most PETs — also lacks mechanisms for accountability and enforcement, though it is expected that the U.S. Federal Trade Commission will enforce existing laws that prohibit unfair or deceptive practices if an organization does not follow through on its P3P promises.

---

[9] Paul R. Hagen, "P3P: More Privacy Confusion" (Forrester Research, October 29, 2001).

Critics of P3P suggest that the technology may oversimplify privacy policies, making it difficult for organizations to express important nuances in their policies and even more difficult for consumers to get a true picture of an organization's privacy practices. "In some ways, [companies] are going to have to fit the square peg into the round hole," said Ruth Hill Bro, senior associate for e-commerce law at Chicago law firm Baker & McKenzie. "They will have to narrow their specific policy to match more standard criteria."[10] Is the collected information personally or non-personally identifiable? Will it be shared with affiliates, third parties or both? How much of the information collected is actually shared? Is the Web site governed by any privacy laws? Under what exceptions will information be shared (e.g., an FBI request for data after a terrorist attack)? In other words, P3P cannot adequately express *all* limitations on collection, use, disclosure and retention of personal information.

Despite these challenges, we believe that P3P is a crucial step in the right direction, promoting greater openness and transparency in Web practices. It is a step that Web sites will increasingly feel pressured to take. While P3P is not expected to silence the privacy debate, Web operators that embrace P3P today will have a key advantage over competitors that do not: they will be able to negotiate past the default "cookie-crunching" feature that is becoming popular with new Web browsers. They will also give consumers that use P3P-enabled browsers a basic snapshot of a Web site's privacy policy. Let's face it, while survey after survey suggests that consumers are highly concerned about their online privacy, survey after survey also indicates that a majority of consumers do not take action — likely because they do not know how. P3P meets them halfway, giving Internet users an easy and efficient way to gauge a Web site's respect for consumer privacy. It also gives organizations a simple, privacy-friendly way to interact and build relationships with their online customers, and in the process, obtain the personal information they need to operate.

---

[10] "P3P's Arrival Raises Concerns that Tool May Create Liability, Drive Away Site Traffic," *Electronic Commerce and Law Report*, vol. 6, no. 38, October 31, 2001.

We conclude this section with one word of caution: P3P is where you want to begin, but it is not where you end. As a technological standard, it is one of many PETs that are available to fulfill your privacy objectives. Customers may choose to enter a Web site based on its P3P promises, but they should still be encouraged to read the Web site's full privacy policy, which itself should comply with fair information practices and any relevant legislation. P3P does not replace a privacy policy. It was designed as a tool to reassure consumers and to foster an environment of trust in the digital economy, by alerting consumers to inconsistencies between their privacy preferences and a Web site's stated privacy policy. It is also a work in progress. The W3C, which has officially endorsed P3P, continues to improve the standard as privacy needs evolve. Over time, we believe that P3P will come to play a major part in every company's privacy strategy.

Self-Help for Consumers

When organizations fail to take measures that are designed to win the trust of their customers, they face the risk of backlash. Some customers will either stop doing business with the organization or begin using consumer-based PETs to disguise their identity and withhold personal information. Teenagers are a case in point. A study from Forrester Research found that 55 per cent of North American Internet users between the ages of 13 and 22 intentionally avoided Web sites that asked for their personal information. Furthermore, 43 per cent removed cookies from their hard drive and 27 per cent disabled their Web browser's cookie feature. Worse still for online businesses, 53 per cent said they gave false information to Web sites, an action that can seriously harm a company's marketing efforts.[11] These figures should concern you. Not only do these young consumers represent a demographic with spending power, they are a techno-savvy bunch that will mature into

---

[11] Michael Antecol, with Becky Bermount, "Wired Teens Aren't Naïve About Online Privacy" (Forrester Research, July 24, 2001).

adults with significant purchasing power. They are your customers of the future, and they cherish their privacy. For this reason, companies should be aiming to disarm this privacy-aware crowd by proactively incorporating PETs into their privacy strategies. If consumers — young or old — trust you, then they are less likely to use PETs themselves or resort to falsifying personal information that may well be the lifeblood of your business.

Here are some of the more popular consumer-based PETs, many of which can be downloaded for free off the Internet.

Anonymizer Services/Software/Sites

Several companies offer people a way to disguise or block their identities when they send e-mail messages, surf Web sites, participate in chat groups or use instant messaging services. Most of these companies use some form of encryption, such as SSL, to scramble HTTP data, URLs and IP addresses. At some Web sites — such as Anonymizer.com, Subdimension.com and IDzap.com — users can enter their online destination in a special URL line and be sent to that destination in stealth mode. Essentially, these Web sites act as proxies, leaving no trace of your identity on the remote site you are visiting.

IDsecure, part of IDzap.com, charges about $50(U.S.) a year for encrypting all data traffic coming and going from your computer. Anonymizer.com offers a similar fee-based service; for about $120 a year it encrypts the link between your computer and Anonymizer.com servers so that all e-mail, Web browsing and newsgroup messages cannot be intercepted and read by your Internet service provider or anybody else. Even URLs in your browser history list are kept encrypted. Two of the most popular free services were SafeWeb (SafeWeb Inc.) and Freedom (Zero-Knowledge Systems), which both provided a high degree of browser security and anonymous computing and communications over the Internet. Unfortunately, financial circumstances forced both companies to shut down their respective services in late 2001 — though SafeWeb, whose technology is used by the U.S. Central Intelligence Agency, has indicated it may resurrect its service in response to "overwhelming" outside interest.

Cookie Crunchers

Software products that monitor, block or filter cookies when you visit a Web site are called cookie crunchers or cookie managers. As we discussed in **Chapter 8**, cookies are those little software files that are increasingly being placed in your computer's hard drive when you visit Web sites. In a single day of Web surfing, you might easily be hit with hundreds of cookies, many of which are trying to study your consumer preferences. These files help Web operators track who you are and what you're doing on their sites. How do you think Amazon.com "remembers" the books you like to read every time you visit the site? For many people, the added level of customer service and convenience that cookies make possible is appreciated, but some online consumers would rather keep their browsing habits to themselves.

Zero-Knowledge Systems, Network Associates (McAfee) and Symantec (Norton) all sell personal Internet security products that include a cookie-crusher feature. The software allows a person to reject all or only specific types of cookies. For example, third-party cookies from an online advertising network like DoubleClick might be rejected, while first-party cookies, which on some sites are necessary for using shopping carts and conducting e-commerce transactions, might be accepted. As well, the software can keep track of which sites are using cookies, what type of cookies they are using and the likely purpose for these cookies, allowing users to make educated decisions about which to accept or reject. Free software designed to crush or filter cookies includes Internet Junkbuster (**www.junkbusters.com**), WebWasher (**www.webwasher.com**) and IDcide's Privacy Companion (**www.idcide.com**). The Limit Software's Cookie Crusher (**www.thelimitsoft.com**) costs $15(U.S.).

Encryption-Enabled Browsers

Netscape's Communicator and Microsoft's Internet Explorer have a built-in encryption feature called Secure Sockets Layer, or SSL. This symmetric encryption is used to encode credit card numbers and other information during e-commerce transactions. Consumers know they are in an SSL session in two ways: If a locked padlock can be viewed in the bottom corner of the browser, and if the URL line in the browser reads "https://" instead of "http://." SSL also authenticates Web sites: simply click on the padlock and you will be presented with a digital certificate that is signed by a trusted third party.

Pretty Good Privacy

An example of an excellent system of public key encryption is PGP (Pretty Good Privacy). Cryptographer Phil Zimmermann created a program that makes computer files, network connections and electronic mail almost "spy-proof." Free versions for personal use can be downloaded from a number of Web sites, including the International PGP Home Page at **www.pgpi.org**. Zimmermann, chairman of the OpenPGP Alliance, is also chief cryptographer at HushMail Communications (**www.hushmail.com**), which uses the OpenPGP standard to provide "the world's premier secure Web-based e-mail system" — also free. The high level of encryption in PGP was initially enough to fuel concern from the U.S. government, which during the mid-1990s had sought to use export control laws to prevent the export of encryption technology. On PGP's tenth anniversary, in 2001, Zimmermann posted a letter on the Web in which he remarked on how successful the technology had become. "It was shortly after PGP 2.0's release that U.S. Customs took an interest in the case. Little did they realize that they would help propel PGP's popularity, helping to ignite controversy that would eventually lead to the demise of U.S. export restrictions," he wrote.

Personal Firewalls

Just as companies can install firewalls to protect their corporate networks, home users can install personal firewalls to prevent hackers, Trojan horses and spyware from peeking into, or transmitting information from, their hard drives. As more consumers subscribe to high-speed Internet services — for example, through cable modem, digital subscriber line (DSL) or satellite services — they face a greater risk of being hacked or exposed to data-gathering programs on the Internet. The reason is simple: high-speed access is typically always on, giving hackers and their probing programs more time to seek out vulnerabilities and back doors that can be exploited.

Personal firewalls essentially act as a guard dog for your PC, allowing you to barricade your hard drive against unauthorized intrusions but also giving you the option of selecting which software applications can connect to the Internet. Some personal firewalls can even block unwanted banner and pop-up advertisements, and most allow the user to keep a running time-stamped log of authorized and unauthorized attempts to enter and leave your computer. Personal firewall products include Symantec's Norton Personal Firewall, ZoneLabs' Zone-Alarm Pro, Network Associates' McAfee Internet Security, Zero-Knowledge Systems' Freedom Personal Firewall and BlackICE Defender from Network ICE (now owned by Internet Security Systems). Most, if not all, of these programs contain additional content-filtering, anti-virus and cookie/Web bug detection features.

One-Time Credit Cards

The story is all too familiar: a high-profile e-commerce site becomes the victim of a security breach, and a hacker walks away with hundreds or thousands of valid credit card numbers. In response to such breaches, American Express introduced a special Internet card in 2000 that creates a unique, one-time credit card number for each purchase conducted over the Web. After each purchase the number is thrown away, making it useless. Some banks have also introduced credit cards that work the same way, making it more difficult than ever for a cyber thief to steal your customers' card numbers. One-time or "disposable" credit cards help prevent consumers from being victims of identity theft, which is a fast-growing problem in North America and one of the most serious intrusions into our personal privacy. They also help to minimize the amount of personal information that Web sites can collect. "The use of one-time credit cards has a direct privacy benefit, making it harder for merchants to track customer shopping behavior," states security software firm ZoneLabs.

There is also a low-tech way to minimize your customers' concerns when they shop online: encourage them to get a separate credit card with the lowest credit limit possible (usually $500 to $1,000) and tell them to dedicate this card for exclusive use when purchasing goods from online companies that don't have brick-and-mortar outlets, such as Amazon.com. This way, if a credit card number is stolen or compromised, the hacker can do little damage.

How to Codify FIPs, and Where to Get Help

We have discussed some of the PETs that businesses might consider as they reinforce their privacy strategy, including technologies that encrypt, block, filter, anonymize, authenticate, codify, scan, assess and manage personal information. But there are also products that can assist in building fair information practices into customer information systems. In this section we highlight a handful of companies that are devoting substantial resources to the development of privacy-enhancing/enabling technologies for businesses and government.[12] In addition to these companies, we expect over time that many — if not most — makers of database and enterprise software will begin incorporating some privacy features into their core product offerings.

IBM (www.ibm.com)

In November 2001, IBM created two groups dedicated to nurturing the development of privacy-enabling technologies. The first group, the IBM Privacy Management Council, is composed of customers that have agreed to test and provide feedback on privacy technologies being developed by IBM and its systems-management software unit, Tivoli Systems. The second group, the IBM Privacy Institute, is the industry's first formal research effort dedicated to developing privacy-enabling and data-protection technologies for businesses. These technologies cross many areas, including e-commerce, pervasive and mobile computing, data mining, knowledge management and network security. "We are responding to the marketplace," IBM chief privacy officer Harriet Pearson said on

---

[12] This section discusses companies that sell PETs. Pure consulting companies and the Big Five accounting firms are excluded from this list; also excluded are the many security-focused vendors that sell firewall, intrusive-detection, anti-virus or authentication software, including firms such as Entrust, RSA, Check Point and BorderWare. While security is a component of privacy, our intention here is to highlight the emerging market for privacy-management and -assessment products.

the day the two groups were announced. "We have had customers ask 'What should we do about the issue of privacy and how do we manage information?' "[13]

At the core of IBM's efforts is its Enterprise Privacy Architecture, or EPA, a blueprint for the design of privacy-enabling technologies and comprehensive privacy programs for large e-businesses; beginning with the identification of privacy objectives, the development of a strategy, the mapping of customer data flows and business processes, and ending with the design and implementation of appropriate privacy-enabling applications. The entire program was designed with OECD principles of fair information practices in mind, in addition to major regulatory developments in the United States (GLBA, HIPAA, COPPA), the European Union (Directive on Data Protection) and Canada (PIPEDA). "A unique aspect of EPA is that it provides an analysis of privacy in the context of real business processes by stripping privacy down to its most essential form of actors, rules and data," IBM's Web site states. The company has invited the rest of the vendor community to help evolve EPA into an industry-wide standard.

Tivoli Systems (www.tivoli.com)

IBM's EPA lies at the heart of Tivoli's SecureWay Privacy Manager product, which can take an organization's privacy policy and integrate it with all relevant business processes and applications.[14] Bob Kalka, senior security "evangelist" at Tivoli, says Privacy Manager applies a common set of rules against a given set of data for multiple business applications. For example, if an organization has a mixture of 50 legacy and Web-based applications and 32 of those applications (e.g., customer relationship management or mail-merge applications) come into contact with personal information kept in customer databases, then Privacy Manager consistently applies an organization's privacy rules — based on an established policy — to all 32 applications. If the policy changes, either

---

[13] Mark Evans, "IBM Groups Will Target Privacy Protection," *National Post*, November 12, 2001.

[14] SecureWay Privacy Manager was announced in 2001 as an extension of SecureWay Policy Director. The product was initially promoted as a way to help financial institutions deal with new privacy regulations in the Financial Services Modernization Act (also known as GLBA).

because of new legal rules or modifications to internal policies, Privacy Manager can make the changes centrally. Today, most companies must go through the costly, grueling and inefficient effort of programming these rules directly into each application.

The Bank of Ireland is using Privacy Manager to control how employees and business partners can access the personally identifiable information it collects from customers, based on the role of the person trying to access the data and taking into account customers' opt-out requests. When applications try to access the bank's customer database, a "rules engine" in Privacy Manager will check to see whether the customer has previously opted out. If so, the engine refuses the access request. Privacy Manager also provides the bank with a running audit of who has accessed customer data, the type of data accessed, the software application through which it was accessed, when it was accessed and the purpose for which the data was accessed.

Kalka says a challenge arises when dealing with off-the-shelf applications, as it is difficult to get inside these applications to enforce privacy rules. Some organizations, in trying to overcome this problem, have taken the impractical route of physically separating opt-out customer data from other data so that an application such as mail-merge software can't access it. This all-or-nothing approach is ultimately crippling to a company's data-collection and marketing efforts. Kalka asks, "If one customer says don't use my phone number for anything, and another says don't use my zip code for anything, how can you manage that for several off-the-shelf applications without having to partition data to another place where it can't be accessed by any application?"

A new generation of Privacy Manager aims to solve this dilemma by intercepting and removing opt-out data before it reaches an off-the-shelf application. Here is the scenario: A customer enters your company's Web site. During online registration she puts "opt-out" checkmarks in fields representing the information she does not want used for marketing purposes. That opt-out information is codified and then stored in a directory that is essentially a metadata directory of user preferences. "Then what we build is a set of interceptors for a set of databases," explains Kalka. "When that off-the-shelf mail-merge application comes in and wants information, our interceptors will actually filter the information as it goes back, based on the metadata preferences. It's sharp. It's automating a process that's very difficult to automate." This new version of Privacy Manager takes privacy- and permissions-management software to a new level, says Kalka. "When you can apply something like this without any changes to applications, that's when you can begin enforcing your privacy policies without having to do physical work."

The cost of Tivoli's privacy-management software and IBM's EPA both vary depending on the size of the company, degree of customization and required features.[15]

IDcide (www.idcide.com)

One reason the Roman Empire fell is that it grew too large too quickly — to the point where it became bureaucratically rigid and cracks began to form. Its defenses slowly weakened, allowing enemies to slip in and out without detection. One could argue that the empire didn't have enough troops to guard its ever-expanding borders, nor did it have anybody to make sure the troops were doing their jobs. The same thing can happen to Web sites: the more information, Web pages, third-party links, cookies and Web bugs that are created, the more difficult it is to keep track of them, meaning the greater your risk of an empire-crumbling data leak. It is not an exaggeration to say that some organizations have lost track of how many Web bugs, or beacons, they have planted on their own Web sites, or which pages on their sites drop first- or third-party cookies. This is a serious issue that companies will increasingly find necessary to address.

When IDcide launched its PrivacyWall line of products in 2001, the company knew that organizations needed a piece of software that could automatically

---

[15] In 2002, Tivoli released its IBM Tivoli Privacy Wizard, a free software download that translates company privacy policies into an electronic language that various applications can understand and apply. The policies can also be exported to P3P format. Go to **www.tivoli.com** and type "privacy wizard" into the search window.

scan their Web sites to identify privacy risks and privacy compliance hot-spots. That is exactly what PrivacyWall Site Monitor does: the software allows privacy and security officers to scan their organization's Web properties, 24 hours a day, to make sure that all cookies, Web bugs, banner ads, HTML forms, third-party links and other data-sensitive components are compliant with privacy policies and, ultimately, the law. The software can also identify what needs to be done to a Web site for it to become P3P-compliant.

Procter & Gamble, one of the first customers of PrivacyWall Site Monitor, has more than 100 Web sites and must keep track of more than 50,000 pages on those sites. Not an easy job when done manually. Automating the process has made continuous monitoring possible without the need for a large staff to routinely perform manual searches. Further, all kinds of Web pages can be analyzed, including password-protected pages, pages that appear after a trans-action is completed and pages that can be found only through search tools.

PrivacyWall Site Analyzer performs similar functions but is designed for privacy consultants and auditors. Site Analyzer can scan Web sites — either in-house or remotely — at a rate of 36,000 pages an hour. When a scan is complete, the consultant or auditor can generate a detailed report so the client will know how to modify their data-collection practices, plug up security holes and reinforce potential leak zones. Professional services firm Ernst & Young and privacy consultancy Privacy Council have both incorporated IDcide's Site Analyzer into their privacy diagnostic services.

Privacy Council (www.privacycouncil.com)

Though the Privacy Council was created primarily as a consulting business, it has slowly been adding privacy software to its offerings. In 2001, the company released PrivacyScan, powered by IDcide's PrivacyWall, which performs a remote diagnostic — similar to PrivacyWall Site Analyzer — of an organization's Web site. After Privacy Council completes the diagnostic, it issues a confidential report to its client that lists, among other things, where the Web site collects personal information, where security leaks have been found, where hidden domains are located, where privacy policy links are lacking and where there are any P3P-compliance gaps. Dr. Larry Ponemon, chief executive of Privacy Council, says PrivacyScan gives businesses a report card on how their online privacy initiatives are working and how they can be improved. As well, companies can download a free P3P policy generator, called Free P3P Solution, from Privacy Council's Web site.

PrivacyRight (www.privacyright.com)

PrivacyRight's TrustFilter system is designed to help health-care institutions, financial services companies and e-businesses better manage the customer information they collect and use. TrustFilter is middleware that can integrate with an organization's legacy and Web-based information-management systems, making sure the sensitive customer information flowing through these systems complies with privacy regulations, internal policies and customer opt-in/opt-out preferences.

The first component of TrustFilter is the Permissions Engine. When a request comes in for customer information, the Permissions Engine analyzes the request (and the target data), after which it will be measured against established privacy rules and customer preferences. If the request is deemed to violate a rule or preference, access to the customer record is denied. The same safeguards can be applied to employee records. The Permissions Engine can even determine when one privacy rule takes precedence over a conflicting rule — for example, when a particular request falls under both state and federal law. PrivacyRight calls its Permissions Engine "non-invasive" because existing applications do not need to be reprogrammed.

The second component of TrustFilter is the Audit Server, which records all functions of the Permissions Engine, including authentication details for disclosure requests and whether requests were permitted or denied. An audit report can then be created to help systems administrators keep on top of corporate compliance initiatives.

Privacy Council sells and supports TrustFilter as part of its own privacy consulting practices, giving the TrustFilter product greater exposure in the business community. PricewaterhouseCoopers is another PrivacyRight partner.

Watchfire (www.watchfire.com)

Watchfire Corp. designed WebCPO to scan an organization's Internet, intranet and extranet Web sites in search of privacy risks, security vulnerabilities and privacy compliance issues. WebCPO analyzes the code on all the pages in a Web site, no matter how large. If a company has a million pages on its site, WebCPO will find out which ones gather data and where exactly on those pages personally identifiable data is collected. Does the page comply with a privacy policy? Does it link to a privacy policy? Is there a technical glitch on the page that allows a customer's personal information to inadvertently be shared with a third party? These are the types of questions that WebCPO will answer. The software also tracks Web bugs, cookies and other information-gathering programs and determines whether they are violating a stated privacy policy. And, like PrivacyWall, WebCPO will scan a site to determine whether it is compliant with P3P-enabled browsers, such as Internet Explorer 6.0, and suggest modifications necessary to achieve compliance. "In most cases, what companies think they are doing on their Web site doesn't necessarily correspond with what they're actually doing," Michael Weider, CEO of Watchfire, told us. He adds that the people who write privacy policies and those who design Web sites often work in separate worlds. "WebCPO is trying to bridge the gap."

Weider says companies have traditionally taken one of three approaches to managing privacy on their Web sites — none of which are very effective. The first approach, and the least advisable, is to do nothing. The second approach is to assess and audit a Web site only at the time of launch, a task that is usually assigned to the legal department. In such cases, a Web site is incorrectly viewed as a static brochure-like document. "But it's a changing document, and it changes the day you launch it," says Weider. The third approach is to perform periodic, manual spot checks of a Web site, a task that grows increasingly difficult and labor-intensive the larger the Web site becomes. Weider says spot checking is like taking an eyedropper to the ocean as a way to measure pollution. "It's not going to accomplish much." Alternatively, by automating the process with a product like WebCPO, companies can constantly monitor and assess their Web sites. The software also alerts key privacy officials via wireless devices and e-mail as soon as it detects changes on privacy-sensitive areas of the Web site.

WebCPO, developed with PricewaterhouseCoopers and launched in 2001, is aimed at large enterprises in the financial services, health-care, government and retail sectors. PricewaterhouseCoopers has licensed WebCPO as part of its privacy and security risk management services. Both companies are jointly marketing and selling the product.

Zero-Knowledge Systems (www.zero-knowledge.com)

Like many companies in the privacy industry, Zero-Knowledge began as a provider of privacy technology for consumers. Its Freedom software allowed people to surf the Web and send e-mail messages anonymously or under several different pseudonyms. Freedom still exists, but has largely been transformed into a home security package that includes cookie-cruncher, firewall and anti-virus features — anonymous surfing is no longer included. Zero-Knowledge has instead dedicated more of its resources toward developing privacy-management software for enterprises, what the company terms "privacy rights management" — similar in purpose to products offered by Tivoli and PrivacyRight. "Systems really weren't built for privacy from the get-go," says Mark Weidick, general manager of Zero-Knowledge's enterprise unit. "We recognized an opportunity to combine our knowledge of privacy, our knowledge of technology, our knowledge of policy and our understanding of the business problem into a product that we call Enterprise Privacy Manager."

EPM helps companies "optimize" the use of their customer data while helping them comply with policy, legislation and customer opt-out/opt-in preferences. According to Zero-Knowledge, EPM "provides CPOs with an automated tool to effectively identify, analyze, manage and report on the location and handling of customer information through the enterprise." Austin Hill, chief strategy officer and co-founder of Zero-Knowledge, says EPM should be considered just as necessary to a CPO as enterprise resource planning (ERP) software is to a chief financial officer. Automated tools have become a standard requirement for monitoring and managing company resources. The argument is that the same tools should be available to assist with privacy management.

The first phase of EPM consists of a "privacy console," which includes a discovery and inventory module, a modeling module and a reporting module. The first module identifies the personal information a company holds. It then classifies the data in a central inventory from which all information can be managed. "It's about accumulating the inventory of data and understanding where it is, what it is, who has it, where it is housed," says Weidick. "It's able to glean what personally identifiable information is housed in your customer relationship management (CRM) applications and salesforce automation applications." The second module creates a model of how information flows and is handled across the enterprise. The idea is that all privacy practices, policies and rules will be converted into a machine-readable language. This allows the handling-practices model to be automatically measured against these codified privacy policies and rules, including regulations and fair information practices. The final module generates reports to assist with management and audits.

EPM is being designed for use with legacy systems, capable of supporting applications ranging from traditional client-server applications delivered over corporate intranets to customer-facing Web services. At the heart of the application is Privacy Rights Markup Language, or PRML, which Zero-Knowledge is attempting to establish as an open-industry standard for formalizing privacy policies and procedures. The language, based on OECD fair information practices, captures complex relationships between business operations and personal information. Using PRML, the company plans to build automated enforcement of privacy rules into its next phases of EPM. The product was still in development at the time of writing. The initial target markets are large online retailers and financial institutions.

Build It In – Whenever Possible

From a business perspective, the importance of "building it in" when dealing with PETs cannot be understated. Imagine going through the effort of constructing a brand-new house, only to realize as you turn on the bathroom faucet for the first time that the plumbing was not installed. Sure, you have electricity, a furnace and even a natural gas line, but without plumbing, you will have to go back and rip apart most of the house to install running water — an unnecessarily messy, time-consuming and costly exercise. You might be able to function without water, but will your guests feel comfortable enough to visit? Will municipal lawmakers consider the structure a violation of fire-safety codes? At some point, in order for your house to become a properly functioning home, the plumbing will be necessary.

The same situation applies when we speak of privacy: building PETs into your information systems, processes, procedures and projects from the very beginning will virtually always mean a more efficient, cost-effective and flexible design, one that can more easily meet the requirements of both consumers and lawmakers. This proactive approach to privacy contrasts with a reactionary approach, whereby organizations often find themselves in a costly, last-minute scramble to comply with new regulations or try desperately to manage public relations disasters. Middleware or "plug-ins" may be available — and as we have discussed, there are many interesting products on the market that aim to make a CPO's job much easier — but if good privacy processes and procedures have not been built into a company's information infrastructure, significant work will still be required to make it all function properly.

It is important that the "build it in" approach involves those doing the building — that is, the engineers and programmers who draw up the project designs and weave them all together. Privacy has never been top-of-mind for most in-house professionals, yet as the issue continues to gain a higher profile, the high-tech architects of our information economy may need to incorporate privacy and security concerns into their work ethic. Peter Hope-Tindall, chief privacy architect for dataPrivacy Partners, told us "For years we have been teaching our programmers and systems analysts and database designers to collect all the information they can, to provide as much flexibility to users as possible, to plan and design ahead for future functionality and rarely, if ever, to destroy data. Privacy changes all that — with its prescribed collection, retention, use and destruction of data. It may be that, to ensure adequate privacy protection in the future, we have to rethink how we educate our next generation of programmers. Quite possibly, the message may have to change from 'maximum capability and flexibility of design' to 'prescribed capabilities and privacy-effective design.' " In the long run, we believe this strategy will increase both the effectiveness and the efficiency of your customer information systems.

It's a message that Jules Polonetsky, CPO of online ad-serving firm DoubleClick, has been trying to emphasize with his company's programmers. He points to a service from DoubleClick that clients can use to deliver advertisements to their mobile phone customers. When Polonetsky analyzed the service, it became clear to him that DoubleClick could receive more information than it needed in the process of serving the advertisements. "There were a number of carriers, for instance, that were previously sending the user's phone number as the ID along with the message [needed to serve the ad]," he said in an interview with us. "Well, we don't want to get that. So we built what we call a wireless privacy barrier, so that any unwanted information that is sent to our wireless ad server gets caught, scrubbed and deleted, and the only information that hits us is what we're supposed to be getting — that is, instructions to deliver this or that particular ad to this or that wireless gateway."

When Polonetsky asked the programmers to create and add the wireless privacy barrier to the mobile ad-delivery technology, they agreed, but said it would take a little more time. In Polonetsky's view, the little bit of extra time at the beginning of the process prevented lengthier interventions later on. "It would have been a much harder thing to tack on afterwards," he says. "After I did that once or twice, most of the folks got quite wise, and they will now bring in new ideas early. If there is no plan to use certain kinds of information, it is often much easier to plan not to have it from the outset." In other words, if you don't need it, don't collect it — data minimization is an important design feature.

Michael Weider, CEO of Watchfire, says new technologies like P3P are increasingly bridging the gap between corporate technologists and policy experts. Traditionally, Web site designers have been responsible for posting privacy statements on Web sites and providing the links to privacy policies, but they did not appear to have intimate knowledge of the policies themselves. Almost overnight, P3P changed all of that. Now having a fully functional Web site requires compliance with P3P standards. Privacy has become part of the design process. Technologists must know a company's privacy policy and all privacy risks associated with the site. They must also codify the policy and constantly monitor the risks if a site is to work properly with P3P-enabled browsers. "P3P helped enormously in raising privacy from a 'nice to have' to a 'need to have' — it put privacy on the radar screen of technologists," says Weider.

One "STEP" Forward

Shortly after the September 11 terrorist attacks on the United States — not to mention the subsequent anthrax scare — the natural tension between privacy and security was considerably amplified. Whereas there had always been a fine balance between security and privacy, law-enforcement agencies and legislators suddenly found themselves in a position to tilt the scales heavily in favor of security. And with images of passenger jets flying into the World Trade Center still fresh in their minds, the public was firmly behind any initiatives that would help protect the world from suicide bombers and unimaginable tragedies. In the corporate world, attention also shifted to security, often, and unnecessarily, at the expense of privacy.

We should make it clear that, except in circumstances where law-enforcement authorities request access to customer databases as part of an investigation, the September 11 attacks should have little bearing on the privacy strategies of most organizations. In interviews with dozens of privacy officers, consultants, advocates and technologists for this book, the general consensus was that maintaining customer trust and consumer confidence is still a top priority, and this means having privacy policies that comply with fair information practices and information-management systems that support privacy objectives. Terrorists or no terrorists, consumer privacy as a business issue is not going away. Privacy has a direct impact on the growth of our online economy, and laws still protect consumer data.

But even if security has become a focus for executives and government officials, that's not necessarily a bad thing for privacy. Security and privacy have always been viewed as polar opposites — opposing forces in a zero-sum game, where the more you have of one, the less you have of the other. There is no reason why this win-lose paradigm can't be changed through the use of technology. In January 2002, the Information and Privacy Commissioner of Ontario launched an initiative called STEPs, short for Security Technologies Enabling Privacy.[16] STEPs are essentially security technologies that protect privacy rather than invade it. We have already discussed a number of them in this chapter, such as biometrics and smart cards, but STEPs could also include technologies of electronic surveillance — designed to provide security against terrorism and sabotage, without giving away privacy in the process.

Shifting to a new paradigm in the security-privacy context is not as far-reaching as some may think, but it will clearly involve creative, innovative thinking. Technologies such as facial-recognition software and smart cards might appear to be privacy-invasive, yet when designed with adequate safeguards and implemented under sound policies and rules, they can accomplish their goal of providing stronger security while minimizing the impact on personal privacy. It is a new mindset that, we believe, businesses, governments and privacy advocates alike should work toward.

Technology Can't Do It All

Technology isn't a fix-all. PETs, including privacy-management tools, Web site analyzers, e-mail encryption programs and P3P-enabled browsers, represent only one part of a comprehensive privacy strategy that should take into account multiple elements — processes, procedures, policies, practices and people. You could call them the "Five Ps." John Borking of the Dutch Data Protection Authority and Charles Raab, professor of government at the University of

---

[16] For more information on STEPs, go to **www.ipc.on.ca**.

Edinburgh, wrote that PETs are part of a systematic approach to privacy protection, one that "accords a significant role to technological means of protection without assuming that they are a 'magic bullet' that can be aimed at the target without the accompaniment of legal, organizational, ethical and educational tools."[17] As privacy technologies improve, they will no doubt become an increasingly valuable tool for automating how organizations manage their data, how they create and apply their policies and how they ultimately enforce the rules. But PETs — whether privacy-enhancing or privacy-enabling — should not be viewed as the sole method for implementing fair information practices and protecting privacy.

The Bottom Line

There are technologies that ensure that data is kept secure, either during transmission or in storage. There are technologies that give consumers greater control over how their information is collected, used and shared. There are technologies that can probe and assess Web sites, looking for potential data leaks, improper collections of personal information and other violations of privacy rules. And there are technologies for designing, implementing and managing privacy and information strategies, as well as automatically enforcing the rules on which those strategies are based. We refer to all these broadly as PETs. We encourage you to seriously consider the use of PETs as your company embarks on its privacy initiatives. Although the market for these technologies may be small now, over time, we expect it to grow considerably. There will also be a greater selection of more affordable PETs to serve the needs of your business — and the privacy needs of your customers. But we urge you to

[17] Borking and Raab, *supra*, note 3.

do your research: make sure the PET you choose is the best fit for your organization. Most important, enlist the support of technology in your efforts to follow fair information practices. Embedding fair information practices into the design of your systems will make the task that much easier.

Chapter 12

Where to Begin:
An Action Plan for Business

"For most businesses, good privacy practice
doesn't mean never gathering information,
using it, or sharing it. The companies that
succeed will be those that figure out just how
much privacy — and personalized attention —
their customers really want ... Now is a good
time for businesses to figure out whether
they've found the proper privacy balance."

Jeff Sweat, *InformationWeek*, August 2001

Taking the First Step

In this chapter, we bring together some of the key messages that have appeared throughout the book and present them as part of a quick-reference "tips" list — a checklist of privacy points that will help guide you in the right direction. We have covered much ground so far, and we hope you have found this book a useful source of information as the privacy strategy of your business unfolds and evolves. Below, we present our recommendations on how to approach implementing privacy in concrete terms: a collection of 25 points that an organization should keep in mind when developing its privacy policy, designing its systems and documenting its data flows, all ultimately culminating in best practices. Perhaps most important, a number of the points suggest the approach an organization should take in its direct dealings with customers. A detailed case study of a company's information-management practices and what that company might do to reinforce its commitment to consumer privacy can be found on page 292.

Top 25 Tips for a Privacy Payoff

A. Build Your Privacy Team

1. **Treat customers as partners.** Think of your relationship with your customers as a partnership in which you have certain responsibilities. At the top of the list is respecting personal information about customers as if it was their property. Recognize that mishandling this information will lose you their trust.

2. **Appoint a chief privacy officer (CPO).** If that is not feasible, appoint someone with dedicated responsibility for protecting privacy within your organization, with a direct reporting relationship to a senior executive. Give him or her the authority to stop a privacy-invasive collection, use or disclosure of personal information, with sign-off on IT systems development. If you lack the resources to appoint a separate CPO, then designate an existing manager with the additional responsibility for protecting privacy. But make sure that person has a true understanding of privacy as the application of fair information practices.

3. **Build a strong, cross-departmental privacy team.** Bring together members of your various departments — such as information technology, marketing, policy development, legal, business development, accounting, human resources and customer service — under the direction of your lead privacy officer. This officer could be a CPO or some other designate responsible for taking the organization's privacy message to its various departments. The privacy team should identify privacy issues as they arise throughout the business. This way, accountability for privacy will permeate through the entire organization, creating a culture of privacy that will, in time, provide

you with competitive advantages and decreased risks of negative exposures (e.g., bad publicity, legal liabilities).

B. Develop Your Privacy Policy

4. **Keep it simple; drop the jargon.** Develop an accessible, easy-to-read privacy policy based on fair information practices (described in **Chapter 3**). Post this policy prominently on your Web site, with links on the homepage and any other page where customer information may be collected. Make sure this policy is widely available in print form as well, such as in product brochures and service applications.

5. **Keep it short.** If you need to have a lengthy, detailed policy to satisfy your lawyers, reserve this as a link from your main, easy-to-understand, plain English policy. Remember: the purpose of communicating your privacy policy is to tell your customers how you intend to use and safeguard their information. The objective is to gain your customers' trust. Give them something they will be willing to read and can understand; keep it short and easy to grasp. Your customers are busy people — they don't have the time or patience to read through a lengthy policy.

6. **Lead with the primary purpose.** Begin your stated privacy policy with the reason you are collecting the information. Why do you want the information you are seeking from your customers? What is the primary purpose of the collection? How do you intend to use the information? Then ask only for what you need.

7. **Don't stray — no secondary uses without consent.** As part of your privacy policy, restrict your use of customer information to the primary purpose that was stated and for which it was collected. Don't use it for other, secondary purposes without obtaining additional consent from your customers. In other words, go out and ask them. Let your mantra be, "No consent, no secondary use."

8. **Go directly to the source.** Where possible, try to obtain your information *directly* from your consenting customers. They are in the best possible position to give you the most accurate, up-to-date information. If you have to get this

information indirectly, again — try to obtain consent. This may not be easy and may entail additional costs, but if you plan ahead, you can incorporate this step as a design feature of your program. When in doubt, think "informed consent." This means consent that is both meaningful and voluntary. How do you get consent? If using an opt-out check-box, either on a Web page or on paper, make it clear and specific and, if possible, offer a range of options beyond yes or no. You'll be more likely to get positive responses if more choice is given. But remember that positive consent is preferable from a privacy perspective. For more sensitive data, offer your customers the opportunity to opt in. Those who understand the difference will appreciate it.

C. Implement Your Policy via Solid Practices and Procedures

9. **Align practice with policy.** Design and implement your information systems so that they parallel your organization's privacy policy. In order for this to work, your policy staff will have to talk to and work closely with your IT staff. This step may seem obvious, but it is certainly not the norm, especially with larger businesses, which have many departments with separate mandates. And don't forget to include your Web designers in this process — some companies have literally thousands of Web pages, which often serve as the points of entry to the data-collection process involving customers. Remember to include your entire privacy team.

10. **Map your data flows.** Working with your privacy team, document how your customers' personal information moves through your company's information systems: Where does data sit in storage? How many points of access to the data are there for employees? How many instances of use, retention and reuse of data are there? If you've never mapped this out, start with a free tool like the Privacy Diagnostic Tool (PDT), discussed in **Chapter 5**, to gauge the overall privacy temperature of your operations. The PDT will provide you with an assessment of your information-handling policies and practices, alerting you to weaknesses and areas in need of improvement. Track customer preferences and build rules into the architecture of your

information-management systems to control the flow of data and to make sure you know who is accessing data, when and for what purpose.

11. **Develop a culture of privacy.** Cultivate an atmosphere of privacy awareness in your company. Your company's privacy policy should be clearly communicated to all staff members. A thorough knowledge of the policy should permeate down to the front lines — to those actually dealing with your customers. Have all employees who have access to customer information sign a privacy agreement containing a confidentiality clause. It should state that the employee understands and agrees to comply with your company's privacy policy. Only then can a sense of confidence in your policy be passed on to your customers.

12. **Train, educate and retrain.** Remember to regularly repeat the message — a one-time exposure to your privacy policy will not be enough. Periodic reminders and reviews of the policy will enhance the likelihood that it will be understood and actually followed. Occasional spot checks will also help. Try to think and act like a customer and test your policy.

13. **Keep it human.** Provide a live body for customers who have privacy concerns or complaints. Web sites that provide only a generic corporate e-mail address or, worse, a mailing address do not send a positive message to customers who are worried about their privacy. Your Web site should provide the name and contact information (e-mail and/or phone number) of your company's privacy point person. Providing quick and easy contact to such a person can often neutralize potentially larger privacy problems. If the problem has already taken place, the damage is done — privacy lost is seldom regained. At that point, your main line of defense may be to accept responsibility, offer a sincere apology and, most important, tell customers how you will remedy the situation to prevent future occurrences.

14. **Think smart — don't erect barriers.** Don't threaten to withdraw your services if a customer doesn't agree to let you use their information for secondary purposes. In these times of fierce competition, you may end up the loser — customers will take their business elsewhere. Some Web sites prevent visitors

from entering if they don't provide their personal information. A better approach is to give these people basic access first and full access if they agree to receive more personalized service in exchange for their personal information. But let them know why you want the information, how you intend to use it and what they will get in exchange. Encourage them to familiarize themselves with your privacy policy. Let them take the next step on their own terms. By doing so, you will gain their trust.

D. Handle Data in an Atmosphere of Privacy

15. **Keep it open and transparent.** Your customers will appreciate being advised of your information-handling practices. In addition, allow your customers to access their personal information upon request. Correct any mistakes quickly, and notify customers that such corrections have been made. If you think of privacy as an information-management tool, this will greatly assist in maintaining the accuracy of your company's information holdings. Remember: incorrect information is useless information. No one is in a better position to know if their information is accurate than the customers involved. It helps you, it helps them — everyone wins. Openness and transparency are key.

16. **It's got to be accurate.** In the absence of your customers' assistance, take reasonable steps to make sure that the information you use is accurate and up-to-date. It is not only in your customers' best interests — it is in your best interests. A direct-marketing campaign based on inaccurate or outdated information is a waste of time and resources.

E. Keep It Safe – Keep It Secure

17. **Ensure the necessary level of security.** Adopt a reasonable standard of security, appropriate to the degree of sensitivity associated with the information. Extremely sensitive information such as medical or financial data may require much stronger safeguards, such as encryption and firewalls. Procedural controls may suffice for less sensitive information. Regardless, ensure that proper audit trails are in place to detect possible infractions.

And include a review of your systems-penetration testing capabilities. A clearly written policy and set of procedures for accessing customer data are a must.

18. **Make sure it's in the contract.** If your company enters into contracts with third parties, add a carefully worded nondisclosure clause to ensure that they will honor your privacy practices. Make it clear what uses of your customers' information are permitted and that no other uses are permissible. Also, add contractual language relating to computer security — you want your partners to safeguard the information as carefully as you do.

19. **Use it — then lose it.** Store personal information only for as long as required to achieve the purpose for which it was initially collected (or as required by law). Develop appropriate retention schedules to guide how long you keep various types of information.

20. **Destruction of data should be irreversible.** Not much thought is usually given to how you dispose of information that is no longer wanted. Secure disposal practices keep information confidential at all times. This could save you much embarrassment; it could also save you from lawsuits and unwanted scrutiny from the media. "Dumpster divers" are notorious for rummaging through outside garbage bins in search of the personal details of individuals' lives. Your garbage could serve as the raw material for identity theft, the fastest-growing form of consumer fraud. Think about investing in paper shredders or a shredder service. For electronic data, be aware that simply pressing the delete button is not enough. Use permanent forms of disk-erasing software for digital data, so that rogue employees or hackers haven't a chance of recovering it. This is particularly important if you're disposing of or recycling computer equipment. You may think you've deleted the hard drive, but there are too many documented cases of information in resold laptops and PCs ending up in the wrong hands (such as when Washington Mutual, a Seattle-based savings and loan company, found out in 1997 that it had sold dozens of company computers containing the financial data of customers, including job histories and loan applications. The company had not properly erased the hard drives).

F. Tackle New Initiatives

21. **Conduct a privacy impact assessment (PIA).** For any new programs, systems or technologies you plan to introduce, conduct a PIA to identify potential risks to privacy. The effect of any new product, service or computer system should be assessed before its development and implementation — know what you're getting into, from a privacy perspective. A privacy risk assessment should become an integral part of the design stage of any initiative. Once the risk to privacy is identified, then the necessary protections can be built in to minimize or eliminate them.

22. **Make privacy a design goal.** Build privacy into the architecture of your systems — embed privacy into the design. Add privacy to the checklist of features you address in the development of applications or initiatives. Hold someone accountable for ensuring that this happens, with meaningful consequences for its omission. Remember, the fault does not simply lie with the software programmer if privacy isn't built into the system. Although programmers should care about privacy and security, you have to make it crystal clear. It is the manager requesting the program who must identify privacy, up front, as one of the deliverables.

23. **If necessary, consult the experts.** If a problem arises for which you feel you lack the necessary in-house expertise, hire a privacy consultant or architect. A number of highly reputable consulting firms and organizations offer privacy expertise, as well as data-protection and privacy-management technologies (PETs and STEPs). Address problems early for the most cost-effective results.

G. Ensure Employee Compliance and Privacy

24. **Conduct an annual review and privacy audit.** Once a year, review your privacy policy and practices with your staff to ensure that actual practices conform to the policy and that employees continue to be mindful of privacy-related issues. An annual privacy audit can be the best vehicle to ensure that the company's practices are in compliance with the company's stated privacy policy. It is vital that actual behavior matches the intent of

the policy. An annual audit can note any deviations and recommend steps to prevent them from happening again. A third-party audit, such as a WebTrust audit from a certified public accountant, can add more credibility to your efforts.

25. **Develop a workplace privacy policy.** Start by respecting your employees' rights to some degree of privacy at the workplace. If technologies of surveillance are to be used for quality control or security purposes, then take the least intrusive route. Rather than blanket monitoring, perform occasional spot checks and put in place filtering and blocking technologies that prevent certain undesirable activities from taking place. Most important, communicate any new workplace privacy policy to employees. Listen to any concerns or feedback they might have and try to work toward a mutually agreeable solution that will minimize the impact on morale and productivity. When employees are given a seat at the table, they are more likely to understand why certain measures are needed.

PRIVACY PRACTICES CASE STUDY

Prepared by Dr. Larry Ponemon, CEO, Privacy Council

This study is based on an actual privacy audit conducted by a Big 5 firm for a large U.S.-based retail banking organization with operations in Europe and Asia. The organization had attempted to implement a privacy initiative over the past three years. The failure of this initiative is described according to seven key elements outlined below. We also outline what is necessary to bring this company to a best practices scenario.

Governance

The privacy initiative of the organization had no clear or visible leader. Several groups within the organization claimed to "own" privacy and data-protection compliance, but these groups had no formal way of communicating with each other and none of these groups had the authority or budget to implement effective compliance solutions. This problem was compounded by the fact no one individual directly reported to executive management.

As a result, there was no consistency in administrative practice or procedure for privacy, data protection or information security across the company. In some cases, privacy practices actually conflicted with each other — for example, privacy policies posted on the Web site were not supported by actual back-office practices. As a result, the company violated fair information practices and the law.

Individuals from key groups met as an informal body for information-sharing purposes only. Meetings tended to be superficial (and sometimes confrontational) rather than constructive. People with a legal or regulatory focus seemed to have significant differences of opinion with those in the information technology and marketing areas on privacy philosophy and strategy.

At the insistence of the Audit Committee, the chief financial officer engaged an outside auditor to provide a roadmap to comply with all applicable laws and regulations. The auditor did not have specific background or training in the privacy or data-protection field. As a result, audit findings did not match actual requirements for regulatory compliance.

Turning Worst Practices into Best Practices

- The company implements a privacy and data-protection strategy.
- Senior management supports the privacy compliance program.
- Privacy compliance ranks in the top 50th percentile of company issues.
- The company advertises and promotes privacy compliance with customers.
- Privacy becomes part of the company's branding or marketing program.
- A central control is named over the publication and maintenance of privacy policies.
- A high-level officer is dedicated to the privacy compliance program.
- This high-level officer reports directly to senior management.
- This high-level officer presents the results of the privacy compliance program to the board.

Privacy Policy

The organization's privacy policy had too much legalese and was difficult to read. It was inconsistent in certain places. For example, it suggested that consumers have a choice to "opt out" of data sharing with non-affiliated third parties. But the policy also suggested that the company does not share information with non-affiliated third parties.

The company did not maintain version control over its privacy policy. As a result, there were multiple outdated versions of the privacy policy seemingly in existence in various business units.

The company had different privacy policies for different subsidiaries. For example, it had a marketing subsidiary that was in the business of collecting data from multiple internal business units, and then selling this information to other financial service organizations (non-affiliated third parties) for a fee. The company had no plans to sell or spin off this marketing subsidiary even though it directly violated the company's own "do not share" statements in the privacy policy.

The policy did not provide any information on how to contact responsible parties within the organization if a consumer or customer had a concern or complaint about privacy. Also, there was no formal way to express choice or "opt out" of secondary data-sharing practices.

The privacy policy posted to the Web site had been edited by the marketing department to read like a brochure rather than a statement of fact. The Web site privacy policy is not accessible from the home page and is not linked to every Web page.

The privacy policy pertained to consumer data usage in the United States. There was no mention of employee, agent or contractor data usage. There was no mention of data collection, usage, sharing or storage outside the United States (which represents a material part of the organization's business operations).

The privacy policy did not explain how customer and non-customer information collection, sharing, usage and storage differ. In places, the policy confused non-customer with customer data-protection practices.

The company had not provided notice of its privacy practices in a consistent manner. Some units provided written notice, others posted a notice on their company Web site, and a few did not provide notice (even though this is required by U.S. federal law).

The privacy notice, when issued, was typically attached to another mailing, usually in smaller print on a standard document such as the monthly statement, rather than a stand-alone mailing.

Turning Worst Practices into Best Practices

- Create a clean, concise privacy policy.
- Circulate and explain the privacy policy to all employees.
- Make the privacy policy available to customers.

- Disclose the privacy program in company reports to stakeholders.
- Require business partners to comply with the privacy policy.
- Have version control of the privacy policy.
- Police all policies for internal consistency.
- Post the privacy policy to the Web site.
- Link each page of the Web site to the privacy policy.
- Create all necessary P3P-compliant (XML) policies.

Awareness and Education

Most employees were completely unaware of the organization's privacy practices and requirements, including personnel in high-risk privacy areas such as customer support, telemarketing and call centers.

Moreover, the company's training programs for sales and marketing as well as marketing practices directly conflicted with its own privacy policy, as well as legal requirements. Even with this knowledge, the company's marketing leader tacitly approved.

The company incorporated a review of privacy practices in the new employee handbook, but the section on privacy and data protection had an outdated and incomplete version of the company's privacy policy.

Turning Worst Practices into Best Practices

- Have a privacy-awareness activity for new employees.
- Provide the privacy policy to new customers.
- Provide the privacy policy to contractors, vendors and agents.
- Institute a program for training employees on privacy.
- Provide privacy training to all relevant contractors, agents and vendors.

Controls

The company did not have internal controls to prevent or even lessen the risk of sharing personal information internally or outside the company. Lower level supervisors had the authority to share personal information about customers with all affiliated companies and many business partners (without determining how this information would be used or protected). The company used information collected during one campaign for other completely unrelated marketing campaigns. The company did not provide customers with access to the personal information collected and used.

The company did not have a centralized procedure or process for collecting customer permissions or "opt outs." As a result, there was no way to determine whether individual choice was honored. The information collected for marketing purposes was not well managed. As a result, data was usually inaccurate or incomplete.

Printed information about customers was easily accessible. The information was typically unorganized in large box files. There was no document-retention policy for personal information. Unknown to the employees, even data about them was incorporated into the marketing database.

The organization's Web site used persistent first- and third-party cookies and Web beacons to capture information about visitors. An outside Web-design company placed these devices on the Web site without the express permission of company officials.

The company's management (including its internal legal counsel) overlooked privacy abuses, even when it had knowledge that privacy had been violated.

Turning Worst Practices into Best Practices

- Institute formal controls over maintaining and changing the privacy policy.
- Change the privacy policy only after authorization by senior executives or the board of directors.
- Communicate to employees and customers in a timely way any changes to the privacy policy.
- Clear your privacy policy with outside legal counsel before publication.
- Monitor contractor or vendor compliance with your privacy policy.
- Make sure your company's legal contracts make reference to the privacy policy.

- Maintain central control over the publication and maintenance of privacy policies.
- Maintain control over all domains linked to the company's Web site.
- Review Web site updates for privacy before executing production.
- Review new software applications for privacy issues before putting them into production.
- Provide customers and employees access to their personal information.
- Allow customers and employees to correct or change personal information used by the company.
- Share information with non-affiliated third parties only as stated in the privacy policy.
- Allow persistent third-party cookies, Web beacons, and personalization technology on the Web site only as stated in the privacy policy.
- Use data-integration services only as stated in the privacy policy.
- Gain employee agreement before sharing their data with affiliates.
- Share employee data with non-affiliated third parties only with employee consent.
- Share customer information with direct marketers only when expressly revealed in the privacy policy.
- Control the use of customer information used by direct marketers.

Information Security

The organization did not place sufficient firewall technology around CRM applications or data-marts. As a result, personal data, such as name, address, social security numbers and credit card numbers were relatively easy to hack or attack. There was no information security policy for protecting, storing or retaining personal data on consumers, customers or employees.

The company used a wireless (Wi-Fi or 802.11b) network to regularly send to ATMs sensitive personal information such as customer passwords, social security numbers, credit card information and other items, without sufficient control over the network.

The company did not assess intrusion activity to personal data, even though control logs were kept in the IT department.

Customer passwords (four-digit alpha-numeric field) to individual accounts were not randomized or rotated. Passwords were not hidden, and were part of the customer file that could be obtained by internal employees or hackers.

The organization regularly maintained surveillance of employees and customers without providing disclosure of these practices. Security personnel routinely reviewed e-mail and Internet activities of employees, even though they did not have adequate understanding of the organization's privacy practices.

Turning Worst Practices into Best Practices

- Integrate information security with privacy compliance.
- Use Secure Socket Layer (SSL).
- Authenticate visitors to your Web site.
- Use encryption in the exchange of sensitive customer and employee information.
- Use network firewalls to guard customer and employee data.
- Employ an intrusion-detection system (IDS) to monitor unauthorized attempts to access data.

Monitoring

The company did not have a formal monitoring or internal audit program to determine the adequacy of privacy, data protection or information security practices.

The internal audit department sent a compliance survey to all business unit leaders on their privacy compliance activities. Survey responses were low (less than 20 per cent) and there was no follow-up survey, analysis or investigation.

The company did not have a due diligence procedure to determine the adequacy and consistency of privacy practices when it acquired another business or established a business partnership.

Turning Worst Practices into Best Practices

- Monitor internal compliance with the privacy policy.
- Monitor privacy issues on a regular basis.
- Share the results of compliance monitoring with senior executives and board members.
- Monitor contractor and vendor compliance with the privacy policy.
- Conduct a privacy audit on a quarterly (or more frequent) basis.

Redress

The organization did not have a formal redress program for privacy. As a result, customers that had questions or concerns about privacy initiatives at the company were directed to customer-service personnel who had little knowledge of the privacy policy or information-sharing practices.

The organization did not have a formal "crisis management" process for dealing with significant privacy breaches. As a consequence, the organization was extremely vulnerable to reputation damage (and loss of customer loyalty) if an incident were to occur and be reported in the nation's press.

Turning Worst Practices into Best Practices

- Provide customers and employees with a redress mechanism for resolving privacy concerns.
- Clearly label the redress process in the privacy notice or policy.
- Make the redress process easily accessible.
- Provide a time and execution commitment with the redress process.

Epilogue: The Road Ahead

*"Companies looking for the enthusiastic
participation of consumers will
have to not only clearly communicate
their data handling practices but will
need to prove that they in
fact follow them."*

Kristin Valente, partner, Ernst & Young

At the time this book went to press, there was no lack of evidence that privacy issues continue to profoundly impact the business community and public policy. The Mobile Marketing Association, or MMA, issued a series of self-regulatory guidelines to its members as a "first call-to-action" for privacy standards in North America, with a particular emphasis on location-based wireless technology and its proper use for mobile marketing purposes. The MMA's goal was to spur debate and raise awareness of privacy, with an eye to protecting consumers and furthering the growth of mobile marketing. Meanwhile, the Swedish government tabled draft legislation on the "protection of personal integrity in working life," which would create rules for collecting employee information — including data on personal health and drug use. These rules would describe the extent to which employers could electronically monitor and keep logs of employee activity, perhaps paving the way for similar legislation throughout Europe and other parts of the globe. A similar draft Code of Practice was issued in Hong Kong. The Australian Competition and Consumer Commission announced that it would conduct a broad sweep of Australian

Web sites to make sure they complied with the country's new private-sector privacy legislation. In Japan, Hong Kong and the United States, governments began aggressive crackdowns on junk e-mail, while the U.S. Direct Marketing Association urged its members to use only permission-based electronic mail lists for marketing campaigns or face possible expulsion. A tsunami of privacy-protection initiatives is sweeping the globe, and the wave continues to build momentum.

Are you ready?

In grappling with privacy, businesses have a crucial decision to make. Is privacy simply a legal matter — a cost of doing business where the main objective is compliance with the law? Or is the protection of consumer data and adherence to accepted privacy principles viewed as a way of creating long-term customer relationships that ultimately translate into revenues and profits? There are three certainties as we look to the future of electronic commerce. First, the world's digital and mobile networks will continue to multiply and swell with personal information as it becomes increasingly desirable for businesses to know their customers better. We can only imagine how technology will influence our lives in 10, 15 or 25 years, but there is little doubt that the lifeblood of most businesses will continue to be customer information — more detailed and more revealing than ever. This brings us to the second certainty: as more personal information is sought from consumers, there will be a corresponding increase in concern for how that information is collected and ultimately used. Consumers will want more control over the fate of their personal information and will turn to corporate brands that deserve their trust by respecting their privacy. Third, as governments around the world weigh the interests of consumers and businesses, lawmakers will continue to impose baseline consumer-protection standards on all businesses, while leaving enough headroom for those organizations that wish to achieve competitive advantages over their rivals by distinguishing themselves through best practices.

Many organizations are taking a wait-and-see approach, choosing to focus only on regulatory compliance rather than to proactively evaluate the ways in which good privacy practices can win customers and better prepare their business operations for the future. Privacy policies and statements, often buried in the legalese of service agreements, are being used primarily as legal disclaimers when they could be used as relationship builders. This approach may be shortsighted — over the long run, it does little to build a corporate brand that stands above the competition. David Holtzman, former chief technology officer with Network Solutions, says many businesses are missing out on a valuable opportunity. "Relationships are based upon trust and trust is created based upon how expectations are met or not met over time. Consumer expectations are defined by the marketing message, not by the fine print in the service agreements or privacy policies," says Holtzman, who describes many privacy statements as "parking-garage disclaimers" or "hot coffee can burn" signs that are no more than legal Muzak for the masses. Holtzman continues:

> Lawyers achieve consensus through formal contracts and refine it through judicial interpretation. Business, of course, doesn't actually work this way. Good business is ultimately about good relationships. A business deal that is based on less than sound principles is doomed to fail, contract or not. Written contracts are mandatory just as some privacy legislation is needed because they provide an objective mechanism for resolving ambiguity in case of a dispute. However, they are not a substitute for the stated or implied promises that constitute the actual business deal.[1]

The good news is that more businesses are getting that message, particularly when it applies to their online operations. The Progress and Freedom Foundation, a Washington, D.C.-based think-tank that studies the impact of the digital revolution on public policy, concluded in a 2002 report that the most popular e-commerce and information sites on the Internet are reducing the amount of personal information they collect from online visitors.[2] Specifically,

---

[1] David Holtzman, "The Privacy Imbroglio," CNET News.com [online], March 21, 2002.
[2] William F. Adkinson Jr., Jeffrey A. Eisenach and Thomas M. Lenard, "Privacy Online: A Report on the Information Practices and Policies of Commercial Web Sites" (special report from the Progress and Freedom Foundation, March 2002).

of the 85 busiest sites on the Web, 84 per cent said they collected personally identifying information from visitors (in addition to e-mail addresses). This figure was down from 96 per cent two years earlier, when the U.S. Federal Trade Commission conducted a similar survey of Web sites. "By every relevant measure, the extent of online information collection has declined since May 2000," the more recent report concluded. It also found that substantially fewer sites — from a poll of major sites and a random sample of smaller sites — are using third-party cookies, and that consumers are being given greater choice over how their personally identifiable information is used. Of the popular Web sites, 32 per cent are seeking opt-in consent from consumers before personal information is shared with third parties, compared with 15 per cent two years prior. "The privacy practices and policies of commercial Web sites are continuing to evolve, and, by at least some criteria, to improve," the report states. "Some of the most significant changes are in the areas that have been identified as raising the greatest concerns for consumers — such as the placement of third-party cookies and third-party sharing of information."[3]

The trend is encouraging, but it is only beginning. A long-term commitment will be required. As consumers become more privacy-aware, they will increasingly judge organizations by their privacy promises and practices. Those businesses that, over time, can consistently meet customers' expectations in a predictable way will be rewarded with their patronage.

It is a win-win approach. Not only are customers happier, but companies mitigate their exposure to lawsuits, bad publicity and government investigations while easily complying with the baseline standards set by the law and regulation. It just makes sense — good business sense. And if done properly, you will find, indeed, that privacy pays off.

---

[3] The Progress and Freedom Foundation has financial supporters that include AOL Time Warner, IBM, Intel, Oracle and Sun Microsystems. The organization is generally opposed to new privacy laws, believing that industry is responding to consumer privacy concerns in its own "evolutionary" way.

Bibliography

Adkinson, William F., Jr., Jeffrey A. Eisenach and Thomas M. Lenard, "Privacy Online: A Report on the Information Practices and Policies of Commercial Web Sites" (special report from the Progress and Freedom Foundation, March 2002).

Administrative Office of U.S. Courts, "Judicial Conference Approves Recommendations on Electronic Case File Availability and Internet Use" (press release, September 19, 2001).

Alderman, Ellen, and Caroline Kennedy. *The Right to Privacy* (New York: Alfred A. Knopf, 1995).

Allen, Anita quoted in Sheri Alpert, "Smart Cards, Smarter Policy: Medical Records, Privacy and Health Care Reform," *Hastings Center Report*, vol. 23, no. 6 (1993).

American Management Association, "2001 Electronic Monitoring and Surveillance" (annual survey, April 18, 2001).

American Management Association, "Beware Workplace E-mail, a New Survey Says" (press release citing results from 2001 Electronic Policies and Practices Survey, August 10, 2001).

Analysis Research, "Mobile Location Services to Generate US$18.5bn Global Revenues by 2006" (press release, February 14, 2001).

Angus Reid Group, "Security and Privacy Issues Keeping Millions from Shopping Online" (survey, April 27, 2000).

Antecol, Michael, with Becky Bermount, "Wired Teens Aren't Naïve About Online Privacy" (Forrester Research, July 24, 2001).

ARC Group, "Privacy Is Not a Barrier to the Success of Mobile Advertising" (press release, October 15, 2001).

"Bank Identity Thefts Doubled in 2000," Associated Press, June 19, 2001.

Benner, Jeffrey. "Nailing the Company Spies," *Wired News*, March 1, 2001.

Benner, Jeffrey. "Privacy at Work? Be Serious," *Wired News*, March 1, 2001.

Bennett, Colin J. "Computers, Personal Data, and Theories of Technology: Comparative Approaches to Privacy Protection in the 1990s," *Science, Technology, and Human Values*, vol. 16, no. 1, Winter 1991.

Bennett, Colin J. *Regulating Privacy: Data Protection and Public Policy in Europe and the United States* (New York: Cornell University Press, 1992).

Berger, Matt. "Judges Take on Digital Snooping Tuesday," *InfoWorld*, September 11, 2001.

Better Business Bureau, "New Online Privacy Tool to Transcend Borders" (press release, May 18, 2000).

"Beware of the Threat from Within" (*InformationWeek* survey of 2,375 U.S companies, October 16, 2000).

Borking , John J., and Charles D. Raab. "Laws, PETs and Other Technologies for Privacy Protection," *Journal of Information Law and Technology*, February 28, 2001.

Brandt, Andrew, and Alexandra Krasne, "How It Works: Encryption," PCWorld [online], February 14, 2000.

Branscomb, Anne Wells. *Who Owns Information? From Privacy to Public Access* (New York: Basic Books, 1994).

Cannon, Carl M. "The Real Computer Virus (Misinformation on the Internet)," *American Journalism Review*, vol. 23, no. 3 (April 2001).

Cavoukian, Ann. "Balancing Access and Privacy: How Publicly Available Personal Information is Handled in Ontario, Canada" (conference proceeding highlights presented at Symposium on the Protection of Information in Local Governments, Tokyo, Japan, October 2000).

Cavoukian, Ann. "Biometrics and Policing: Comments from a Privacy Perspective" in *Polizei und Datenschutz – Neupositionierung im Zeichen der Informationsgesellschaft* (Data Protection Authority of Schleswig-Holstein, 1999).

Cavoukian, Ann. "Commissioner Issues Challenge to Technologists: Take the Next STEP" *Kitchener-Waterloo Record,* January 10, 2002.

Cavoukian, Ann. "Genetic Privacy: The Right 'Not to Know,'" (paper presented at the Tenth World Congress on Medical Law, Jerusalem, Israel, August 28 – September 1, 1994).

Cavoukian, Ann. "Genetic Testing and Data Protection," (paper presented at the Thirteenth Annual Data Protection Commissioners Conference, Paris, France, October 2-4, 1991).

Cavoukian, Ann. "Law and the Human Genome Review," (conference proceeding highlights presented at BBV Foundation, Provincial Government of Biscay, Spain, June 1995).

Cavoukian, Ann. "Public Safety is Paramount – But Balanced Against Privacy" (**www.CBC.ca**, September 2001).

Cavoukian, Ann. "The Promise of Privacy-Enhancing Technologies: Applications in Health Information Networks" in Bennett, Colin J., and Rebecca Grant, eds., *Visions of Privacy: Policy Choices for the Digital Age* (Toronto: University of Toronto Press: 1999).

Cavoukian, Ann. "The State of Privacy and Data Protection in Canada, Australia and Japan" (conference proceeding highlights at Third Annual Institute on Privacy Law: New Developments and Issues in a Security-Conscious World, June 24, 2002).

Cavoukian, Ann and Don Tapscott. *Who Knows: Safeguarding Your Privacy in a Networked World* (New York: McGraw-Hill, 1997).

Cavoukian, Ann, and Mike Gurski. "Privacy in a Wireless World" *Business Briefing* (World Markets Research Centre, January 2002).

CDMA, "Direct Marketers Call for National Privacy Legislation" (press release, October 3, 1995).

Challis, William S., and Ann Cavoukian. "The Case for a U.S. Privacy Commissioner: A Canadian Commissioner's Perspective" *The John Marshall Journal of Computer and Information Law*, vol. xix, no. 1, Fall 2000.

Chaum, David. "Achieving Electronic Privacy," *Scientific American*, August 1992.

CIO KnowPulse (*CIO* magazine press release reporting poll of 200 chief information officers, April 25, 2001).

Clement, Andrew. "Considering Privacy in the Development of Multi-Media Communications." *Computer Supported Cooperative Work*, vol. 2, 1994.

Clement, Andrew. "Electronic Workplace Surveillance: Sweatshops and Fishbowls." *Canadian Journal of Information Science*, vol. 17, no. 4, December 1992.

Computer Security Institute, "Financial Losses Due to Internet Intrusions, Trade Secret Theft and Other Cyber Crimes Soar" (press release, March 12, 2001; **www.gocsi.com**).

Consumer Bankers Association, "New Survey Findings Reveal Shift Toward 'Privacy Pragmatism,'" *CBA Reports*, February 1, 2001.

Council of Europe, Convention for the Protection of Individuals with Regard to Automatic Processing of Personal Data, no. 108, January 28, 1981.

Delio, Michelle. "Rent-a-Car Motto: Speed Bills." Wired News [online], July 12, 2001.

Direct Marketing Association, "New DMA Survey Shows Privacy Issues Get CEO Attention" (press release, September 5, 2001).

Dixon, Pam. "A Report on the Privacy Practices of Monster.com" (report for the Privacy Foundation, September 5, 2001).

Dixon, Tim. "Public Attitudes to Privacy: A Global Overview" (presentation at Computers, Freedom and Privacy, Sydney, March 8-9, 2001).

Doherty, Sean. "Monitoring and Privacy: Is Your Head Still in the Sand?" *Network Computing*, June 25, 2001.

"Drug Makers Unprepared for HIPAA, Survey Finds," **www.drugstorenews.com**, January 17, 2002.

EKOS Research Associates, "Business Usage of Consumer Information for Direct Marketing: What the Public Thinks" (study commissioned by the Public Interest Advocacy Centre, August 2001).

Evans, Mark. "IBM Groups Will Target Privacy Protection," *National Post*, November 12, 2001.

Flaherty, David H. "Privacy Impact Assessments: An Essential Tool for Data Protection," (presentation at "New Technologies, Security and Freedom," 22nd Annual Meeting of Privacy and Data Protection Officials, Venice, September 27-30, 2000).

Flaherty, David H. "The Need for an American Privacy Protection Commission," *Government Information Quarterly*, no. 1, 1984.

Flaherty, David H. *Protecting Privacy in Surveillance Societies: The Federal Republic of Germany, Sweden, France, Canada, and the United States* (Chapel Hill: University of North Carolina Press, 1989).

Forrester Research, "Worldwide eCommerce Growth," 2000-2004, **www.forrester.com**.

Fox, Susannah. "Trust and Privacy Online: Why Americans Want to Rewrite the Rules" The Pew Internet and American Life Project, August 20, 2000).

Francoeur, Jacques. "Online Trust: The Five Principles" (executive white paper, NetFront Communications. Sunnyvale, California, March 1, 2000).

FTC Identity Theft Data Clearinghouse, "Identity Theft Complaint Data: Figures and Trends on Identity Theft, January 2000 through to December 2000," **www.consumer.gov/idtheft/reports.htm**.

Garfinkel, Simson. *Database Nation: The Death of Privacy in the 21st Century* (Sebastopol, California: O'Reilly & Associates, 2000).

Gartner Group, "Gartner Survey Shows Consumers Largely Disinterested in Microsoft Passport, But They Sign Up Anyway," (media release, August 23, 2001; **www.gartner.com**).

Gartner Inc., "Firewalls Bypassed in Wireless LANs" (press release, August 9, 2001).

Gates, Bill. "Privacy: Who Should Know What About Whom," *New York Times*, September 15, 1995.

Gavison, Ruth quoted in Ferdinand D. Schoeman, ed. *Philosophical Dimensions of Privacy: An Anthology* (Cambridge: Cambridge University Press, 1984).

Gaw, Jonathan. "Online Personalization in an Era of Privacy Enforcement" (report for International Data Corp., October 2000).

Geist, Michael. "A Troubling Snapshot of E-Privacy in Canada" *Globe and Mail*, December 7, 2000.

Gellman, Robert. "Privacy, Consumers, and Costs" (March 2002, **www.epic.org/reports/dmfprivacy.html**).

Ghosh, Anup K. *Security and Privacy for E-Business* (New York: John Wiley & Sons, 2001).

Gilder, George. *Telecosm: How Infinite Bandwidth Will Revolutionize Our World* (New York: The Free Press, 2000).

Graham Scott, Gina. *Mind Your Own Business: The Battle for Personal Privacy* (New York: Insight Books, 1995).

Guidelines Governing the Protection of Privacy and Transborder Flows of Personal Data, 1981, I.L.M. 422, OECD Doc. No. C(80)58 final; **www.oecd.org/EN/document/o,EN-document-43-1-NO-24=10255-43,00.html**.

Gustavson, John. "New Privacy Law a Win-Win for Consumers, Business," *Globe and Mail*, December 14, 2000.

Hagen, Paul R. "P3P: More Privacy Confusion" (Forrester Research, October 29, 2001).

Hahn, Robert W. "An Assessment of the Costs of Proposed Online Privacy Legislation" (May 7, 2001; **www.actonline.com**).

Hamilton, Tyler. "Big Brother Goes Digital," *Toronto Star*, November 5, 2000.

Hamilton, Tyler. "Experts Debate Importance of Chief Privacy Officer" *Toronto Star*, March 13, 2001.

Hamilton, Tyler. "Privacy Mishaps Can Sink Firms" *Toronto Star*, January 8, 2001.

Hamilton, Tyler. "Privacy Policies Are a Joke," *Globe and Mail*, September 23, 1999.

Hawkins, Dana. "Gospel of Privacy Guru: Be Wary; Assume the Worst," U.S. News & World Report, June 25, 2001.

Holtzman, David. "The Privacy Imbroglio," CNET News.com [online], March 21, 2002.

Horrigan, John B. "New Internet Users: What They Do Online, What They Don't, and Implications for the 'Net's Future" (Pew Internet and American Life Project, 2000).

Hunter, Lawrence, and James B. Rule. "Toward Property Rights in Personal Information," (paper presented to the Information and Privacy Commission/Ontario, December 17, 1993).

"Identity Theft Runs Rampant on Net, Inspector General Says," USA Today, May 23, 2001.

Ipsos-Reid, "Email Marketing: What the Future Holds" (special supplement to Canadian Interactive Reid Report, March 2002).

Joyce, Andee. "Egghead's Hacking Nightmare" RetailTech, April 2001.

Kapica, Jack. "Wellness Software Can Make Bottom Line Healthier: Consultant," Globetechnology.com [online], May 1, 2001.

Kirby, Carrie. "Identity-Theft Victims Struggle Against Rising Tide of Abuse," San Francisco Chronicle, February 10, 2001.

Krebs, Brian. "DoubleClick Joins US-EU Safe Harbor Program" Newsbytes [online], August 22, 2001.

Krebs, Brian. "Online Privacy Policies Apply to Offline Data Practices — FTC" Newsbytes [online], December 10, 2001.

Krever, Justice Horace. Report of the Commission of Inquiry into the Confidentiality of Health Information (Toronto: J.C. Thatcher, 1980).

Larson, Erik. The Naked Consumer: How Our Private Lives Become Public Commodities (New York: Henry Holt, 1992).

Laudon, Kenneth C. The Dossier Society: Value Choices in the Design of National Information Systems (New York: Columbia University Press, 1986).

Laudon, Kenneth C. "Markets and Privacy," (paper presented at the Annual Conference on Privacy and Business, Washington, D.C., October 5, 1994).

Left, Sarah. "Complaints Over Data Privacy Soar" Guardian Unlimited [online], July 12, 2001, **www.guardian.co.uk**.

Levy, Steven. "Prophets of Privacy," Wired magazine, November 1994.

Lewis, Neil A. "Rebels in Black Robes Recoil at Surveillance of Computers," New York Times, August 8, 2001.

Lohr, Steve. "Privacy Group Is Taking Issue with Microsoft," *New York Times*, July 25, 2001.

MacMillan, Robert. "California Gov Vetoes E-mail Privacy Measure," Newsbytes [online], October 9, 2001.

Manjoo, Farhad. "Another Thing to Fear: ID Theft," Wired News [online], October 1, 2001.

Marron, Kevin. "Ads That Track You Down," *Globe and Mail*, June 8, 2001.

Martin, David. "TiVo's Data Collection and Privacy Practices" (investigative report for the Privacy Foundation, March 26, 2001).

McCarthy, Mary Pat, and Stuart Campbell, with Rob Brownstein, *Security Transformation: Digital Defense Strategies to Protect Your Company's Reputation and Market Share* (New York: McGraw-Hill, 2001).

McNealy, Scott. "The Case Against Absolute Privacy," Washington *Post*, May 29, 2001.

Melymuka, Kathleen. "Premier 100: Data Privacy Key to Global Business, Panel Says," **www.computerworld.com**, May 21, 2001.

Meta Group, "Privacy Requires Standards," special commentary for CNET News.com [online], March 5, 2001.

Montague, Claudia. "Privacy: Getting the Information You Need Without Offending the Customers You Serve," *Marketing Tools*, November/December 1994.

Mosquera, Mary. "Global Web Privacy Presents Cultural Challenges," TechWeb News [online], September 13, 2000.

Neumann, Peter G. "Computer Insecurity," *Issues in Science and Technology*, Fall 1994.

Neumann, Peter G. *Computer Related Risks* (New York: ACM Press, 1995).

Noam, Eli. "Privacy in Telecommunications: Markets, Rights, and Regulations," in *Ethics in Telecommunications* (Cleveland: Office of the United Church of Christ, 1994).

Nunes, Paul F. and Ajit Kambil. "Internet Privacy: A Look Under the Covers" (Accenture Institute for Strategic Change, no date; **www.accenture.com**).

Nussbaum, Karen. "Workers Under Surveillance," *Computerworld*, vol. 36, no. 1 (January 6, 1992).

OECD, *Guidelines Governing the Protection of Privacy and Transborder Flows of Personal Data* (Paris: OECD, 1981).

Office of the Information and Privacy Commissioner/Ontario and the Advanced Card Technology Association of Canada. "Multi-Application Smart Cards: How to Do a Privacy Assessment," August 2000.

Office of the Information and Privacy Commissioner/Ontario and the Advanced Card Technology Association of Canada. "Smart, Optical and Other Advanced Cards: How to Do a Privacy Assessment," September 1997.

Office of the Information and Privacy Commissioner/Ontario and the Centre for Democracy and Technology. "P3P and Privacy: An Update for the Privacy Community," March 2000.

Office of the Information and Privacy Commissioner/Ontario and Microsoft Canada. "An Internet Privacy Primer: Assume Nothing," August 2001.

Office of the Information and Privacy Commission/Ontario and the Registratierkamer, The Netherlands. "Intelligent Software Agents: Turning a Privacy Threat into a Privacy Protector," April 1999.

Office of the Information and Privacy Commissioner/Ontario and the Registratierkamer, The Netherlands. "Privacy-Enhancing Technologies: The Path to Anonymity (Vols. I and II)," August 1995.

Olsen, Stefanie. "Privacy Group Shines Light on Web Bugs," CNET News.com [online], June 7, 2001.

"P3P's Arrival Raises Concerns that Tool May Create Liability, Drive Away Site Traffic," *Electronic Commerce and Law Report*, vol. 6, no. 38, October 31, 2001.

PeopleFirst.com, "PeopleFirst.com Launches First Annual Privacy Week" (press release, April 4, 2001).

Perrin, Stephanie, Heather Black, David Flaherty and T. Murray Rankin, *The Personal Information Protection and Electronic Documents Act* (Toronto: Irwin Law, 2001).

Personalization Consortium, "Survey Finds Few Consumers Unwilling to Provide Personal Information to Web Marketers in Exchange for Better Services" (press release, April 5, 2000).

Phillips, Heather Fleming. "Wireless Industry Treads Carefully on Privacy," San Jose *Mercury News*, February 7, 2001.

Power, Richard. *Tangled Web* (Indianapolis: Que. Corp., 2000).

Privacy and American Business and the Association of Corporate Privacy Officers, "New Survey Shows Privacy Officers Take Hold in Key Consumer Industries and

Report to Top Management" (press release, December 6, 2001).

Privacy Commissioner of Canada, *Drug Testing and Privacy* (Ottawa: Privacy Commissioner of Canada, 1990).

Radwanski, George. "A New Act, A New Era" (speech given at "New Developments in Workplace Privacy" conference, University of Toronto and Lancaster House, Toronto, April 6, 2001).

Rabb, Charles D., and Colin J. Bennett. "Protecting Across Borders: European Policies and Prospects" *Public Administration*, vol. 72, no. 1, Spring 1994.

Regan, Priscilla M. *Legislating Privacy: Technology, Social Values, and Public Policy* (Chapel Hill: University of North Carolina Press, 1995).

Reidenberg, Joel R. "Privacy in the Information Economy: A Fortress or Frontier for Individual Rights?" *Federal Communications Law Journal*, vol. 44, no. 2 (1993).

Reidenberg, Joel R. "U.S. Business Practice in the Absence of a General Data Protection Law" (paper presented at Privacy Laws and Business Seventh Annual Conference, Cambridge, England, July 11, 1994).

Rosen, Jeffrey. "The Eroded Self" *New York Times Magazine*, April 30, 2000.

Rosen, Jeffrey. *The Unwanted Gaze* (New York: Vintage, 2001).

Rosenberg, Jerry M. *The Death of Privacy*. (New York: Random House, 1969).

Ross, Rachel. "Web Site Exposes Data on 44,000" *Toronto Star*, January 23, 2001.

Rotenberg, Marc. "Communication Privacy: Implications for Network Design" *Communications of the ACM*, vol. 36, no. 8, August 1993.

Rothfedder, Jeffrey. *Privacy for Sale: How Computerization Has Made Everyone's Private Life an Open Secret* (New York: Simon & Schuster, 1992).

Ruff, Joe. "Burlington Northern Employees Want Genetic Test Ban," Associated Press, April 10, 2001.

Rule, James B. *Private Lives and Public Surveillance: Social Control in the Computer Age* (New York: Schocken Books, 1974).

Schneier, Bruce. *Secrets & Lies* (New York: John Wiley and Sons, 2000).

Schulman, Andrew. "The Extent of Systematic Monitoring of Employee E-mail and Internet Use" (report for the Privacy Foundation Workplace Surveillance Project, July 9, 2001).

Schwartz, John. "Giving Web a Memory Costs its Users Privacy," *New York Times*, September, 4, 2001.

Scott, Karyl. "Privacy Tools and Services Debut," *InformationWeek*, August 20, 2001.

Seben, Larry. "Survey: Privacy Plus Personalization Equals Sales," CRM Daily.com [online], May 10, 2001.

Simitis, Spiros quoted by David H. Flaherty, *Protecting Privacy in Surveillance Societies* (Chapel Hill: University of North Carolina Press, 1989).

Sinrod, Eric J. "E-Legal: Electronic Monitoring of Employees by Employers," Law.com [online], April 10, 2001.

Sinrod, Eric J. "To Make Legal Terms Stick, Make Web Users Click," USA Today.com (Law.com [online]).

Slack, Michele, Alison Day and Evan Neufeld. "Proactive Online Privacy: Scripting an Informed Dialogue to Allay Consumers' Fears" (Jupiter Communications, June 1999).

Slane, Bruce. "Data Mining and Fair Information Practices: Good Business Sense" (June 1998; **www. privacy.org.nz**).

Smith, H. Jeff. *Managing Privacy: Information Technology and Corporate America* (Chapel Hill: University of North Carolina Press, 1994).

Stanley, Jay, John C. McCarthy, Michael J. Tavilla and Jeremy Sharrad. "Surviving the Privacy Revolution" (Forrester Research, February 2001).

Statistical Research, "How People Use the Internet 2001" (study, June 2001).

Stevenson, Betsey and Alanna Denton. "Privacy Worries Cost Online Travel $2.8 Billion" (Forrester Research, December 3, 2001).

Stoughton, Stephanie. "Turning to Technology to Stanch Privacy Leaks" Boston *Globe*, August 27, 2001.

Surtees, Lawrence. "Nowhere to Hide: Privacy Implications of Wireless Location Technology" (IDC Canada, August 2000).

"Survey Suggests Consumers Don't Want Businesses Using Private Information," Canadian Press, September 6, 2001.

Swire, Peter and Robert Litan. *None of Your Business*, (Washington, D.C.: Brookings Institution, 1998).

Tapscott, Don, and Art Caston. *Paradigm Shift: The New Promise of Information Technology* (New York: McGraw-Hill, 1993).

Tapscott, Don. *The Digital Economy: Promise and Peril in the Age of Networked Intelligence* (New York: McGraw-Hill, 1995).

Taylor, William C. "Permission Marketing," *Fast Company*, April 1998.

Tristam, Claire. "Innovation: Behind BlueEyes," MIT *Technology Review*, May 2001.

U.S. Department of Health, Education, and Welfare *Records, Computers and the Rights of Citizens, Report of the Secretary's Advisory Committee on Automated Personal Data Systems* (Washington, D.C., 1973).

U.S. Information Infrastructure Task Force, Privacy Working Group, *Privacy and the National Information Infrastructure: Principles for Providing and Using Personal Information*, June 6, 1995.

"U.S. Multinationals Slow to Implement Emerging Global Privacy Practices, Andersen Study Shows" (Andersen press release, August, 16, 2001).

"Up for Sale: Privacy on the Net," Knowledge@Wharton, CNET News.com. [online] March 25, 2001.

Warren, Samuel, and Louis Brandeis. "The Rights to Privacy," *Harvard Law Review*, vol. 4, 1890.

"Web Bugs: A study of the presence and growth rate of Web bugs on the Internet," prepared by Brian H. Murray and James J. Cowart of Cyveillance Inc., released August 2001.

Wegert, Tessa. "E-mail Marketing and the Fight Against Spam," *Globe and Mail*, October 10, 2001.

Westin, Alan. *Privacy and Freedom* (New York: Antheneum, 1967).

Westin, Alan F., and Michael A. Baker. *Databanks in a Free Society: Computers, Record-Keeping, and Privacy* (New York: Quadrangle Books, 1972).

Winkler, Connie. "Privacy Protector" Network World [online], March 26, 2001.

Web Resources

Practices Support

American Institute of Certified Public Accountants (WebTrust) — **www.aicpa.org**

Canadian Institute of Chartered Accountants (WebTrust) — **www.cica.ca**

Council of Better Business Bureaus (BBB*Online* Privacy Seal) —
www.bbbonline.com

TRUSTe (Privacy Seal) — **www.truste.org**

WebTrust (Privacy Seal) — **www.webtrust.org**

Technology Firms

Entrust — **www.entrust.com**

Guardent — **www.guardent.com**

IBM — **www.ibm.com**

IDcide — **www.idcide.com**

Privacy Council — **www.privacycouncil.com**

PrivacyRight — **www.privacyright.com**

Tivoli Systems — **www.tivoli.com**

Watchfire — **www.watchfire.com**

Zero-Knowledge Systems — **www.zero-knowledge.com**

Consultants

Arthur Andersen — **www.arthurandersen.com**

dataPrivacy Partners — **www.dataprivacy.com**

Deloitte & Touche — **www.deloitte.com**

EPrivacy Group — **www.eprivacygroup.com**

Ernst & Young — **www.ey.com**

IBM — **www.ibm.com**

KPMG — **www.kpmg.com**

PricewaterhouseCoopers — **www.pwcglobal.com**

Privacy Council — **www.privacycouncil.com**

Business Resources/News

The Center for Social and Legal Research — **www.privacyexchange.org**

The Online Privacy Alliance — **www.privacyalliance.com**

Privacy and American Business — **www.pandab.org**

Consumer PETs

Anonymizer.com — **www.anonymizer.com**

Hushmail Communications — **www.hushmail.com**

IDcide's Privacy Companion — **www.idcide.com**

IDsecure — **www.idzap.com**

Internet Security Systems/Network ICE (BlackICE Defender) —
www.networkice.com

Junkbusters — **www.junkbusters.com**

The Limit Software (cookie cruncher) — **www.thelimitsoft.com**

Network Associates (McAfee Internet Security) — **www.mcafee-at-home.com**

Pretty Good Privacy (PGP e-mail encryption) — **www.pgpi.org**

Subdimension.com — **www.subdimension.com**

Symantec (Norton Personal Firewall) — **www.symantec.com**

World Wide Web Consortium (P3P) — **www.w3.org/P3P/**

Zero-Knowledge (Freedom Personal Firewall) — **www.zero-knowledge.com**

ZoneLabs (Zone Alarm firewall) — **www.zonealarm.com**

General/Consumer Resources

American Civil Liberties Union — **www.aclu.org**

Center for Democracy and Technology — **www.cdt.org/privacy**

Consumer.net — **www.privacy.net**

Electronic Frontier Foundation — **www.eff.org**

Electronic Privacy Information Center — **www.epic.org**

Junkbusters — **www.junkbusters.com**

Privacy Foundation — **www.privacyfoundation.com**

Privacy International — **www.privacy.org/pi**

Privacy Rights Clearinghouse — **www.privacyrights.org**

Industry Organizations/Associations

American Management Association — **www.amanet.org**

Canadian Marketing Association — **www.the-cma.org**

Cellular Telecommunications and Internet Association — **www.ctia.org**

Direct Marketing Association (United States) — **www.the-dma.org**

Identrus — **www.identrus.com**

International Biometrics Group — **www.biometricgroup.com**

Internet Advertising Bureau — **www.iab.net/privacy**

The Liberty Alliance Project — **www.projectliberty.org**

Mobile Marketing Association (merger of Wireless Advertising Association and the Wireless Marketing Association) — **www.waaglobal.org**

Network Advertising Initiative — **www.networkadvertising.org**

Wireless Location Industry Association — **www.wliaonline.com**

Government Watchdogs/Legislation

EU Directive on Data Protection — **aspe.os.dhhs.gov/datacncl/eudirect.htm**

Gramm-Leach-Bliley Act — **www.ftc.gov/privacy/glbact/index.html**

Health Insurance Portability and Accountability Act — **aspe.os.dhhs.gov/admnsimp/**

Media Talent Network (unofficial COPPA site) — **www.coppa.org**

New Zealand Privacy Commissioner — **www.privacy.org.nz**

OECD Policy Statement Generator — **www.ftc.gov/privacy/index.html**

Office of the Federal Privacy Commissioner (Australia) — **www.privacy.gov.au**

Ontario Information and Privacy Commissioner — **www.ipc.on.ca**

PIPEDA and CSA Model Code — **www.privcom.gc.ca/legislation/index_e.asp**

Privacy Commissioner of Canada — **www.privcom.gc.ca**

U.S.-EU Safe Harbor overview —
www.export.gov/safeharbor/sh_overview.html

U.S. Federal Trade Commission — **www.ftc.gov**

Virtual Privacy Office — **www.privacyservice.org**

Index